MOTHERS OF THE NATION:
WOMEN, FAMILIES, AND NATIONALISM
IN TWENTIETH-CENTURY EUROPE

Studies in Comparative Political Economy and Public Policy

Editors: MICHAEL HOWLETT, DAVID LAYCOCK, STEPHEN MCBRIDE, Simon Fraser University

Studies in Comparative Political Economy and Public Policy is designed to showcase innovative approaches to political economy and public policy from a comparative perspective. While originating in Canada, the series will provide attractive offerings to a wide international audience, featuring studies with local, subnational, cross-national, and international empirical bases and theoretical frameworks.

Editorial Advisory Board

For a list of books published in the series, see p. 227.

PATRIZIA ALBANESE

Mothers of the Nation

Women, Families, and Nationalism
in Twentieth-Century Europe

UNIVERSITY OF TORONTO PRESS
Toronto Buffalo London

© University of Toronto Press Incorporated 2006
Toronto Buffalo London
Printed in Canada

ISBN-13: 978-0-8020-9015-7
ISBN-10: 0-8020-9015-X

Printed on acid-free paper

Library and Archives Canada Cataloguing in Publication

Albanese, Patrizia
    Mothers of the nation : women, families, and nationalism in
twentieth-century Europe / Patrizia Albanese.

    Includes bibliographical references and index.
    ISBN 0-8020-9015-X

    1. Women's rights – Europe – History – 20th century.   2. Women –
Government policy – Europe – History – 20th century.   3. Family –
Government policy – Europe – History – 20th century.   4. Nationalism –
Social aspects – Europe.   I. Title.

    HQ1236.5.E85A42 2006   305.42'094'0904   C2005-905391-7

University of Toronto Press acknowledges the financial assistance to
its publishing program of the Canada Council for the Arts and the
Ontario Arts Council.

University of Toronto Press acknowledges the financial support for its
publishing activities of the Government of Canada through the Book
Publishing Industry Development Program (BPIDP).

Contents

Acknowledgments

This work has been supported in part by a grant from Ryerson University and the dean, Faculty of Arts.

I am indebted to Margrit Eichler, Nancy Howell, Metta Spencer, Aysan Sev'er, Susan McDaniel and Bonnie Erickson. To Sara Giovannetti and Frank Albanese, thanks for trying to do something creative and different.

Extra special thanks to Slobodan Drakulic for being there time and again.

MOTHERS OF THE NATION:
WOMEN, FAMILIES, AND NATIONALISM IN
TWENTIETH-CENTURY EUROPE

Introduction

Just over ten years ago newspapers and magazines contained headlines like 'New Testimony from the Rape/Death Camps Reveals *Sexual Atrocities* Being Used as Pornography' (*Ms.* July/Aug. 1993; original emphasis). Many, like Catharine MacKinnon, wrote about war rape as a form of ethnic cleansing and a 'tool of genocide' in the wars following the break-up of Yugoslavia. When she exclaimed that 'xenophobia and misogyny merge here' and that 'ethnic hatred is sexualized,' the world listened (MacKinnon, 1993, 27). But it was not long before international attention moved to other stories, other crimes, and other atrocities. For as long as nationalist abuses were sensationalized and sexualized and took the form of 'mass rape' by a brutal ethnic 'other,' they made the front pages. On the other hand, the everyday regulation of women's sexuality and reproductive lives by nationalist leaders and states was and remains virtually ignored. We watched, we listened, we cared when women were sexually abused by their ethnic nemesis neighbours, but we lost interest when women returned to their 'normal' lives under repressive nationalist regimes. This book examines the virtually unpublicized side of nationalist traditionalism, xenophobia, and misogyny: what nationalist regimes do to and for their *own* women when the rest of the world is looking, but not seeing.

Many of us are much more familiar with the fictional take on this same theme, for example, as it appears in Margaret Atwood's *The Handmaid's Tale* (1985), a dystopian futuristic novel about the rise to power of a totalitarian theocracy. After a revolution of sorts, all women's bank accounts were frozen; they were removed from the paid labour force and expected to live as dependants on their husbands. A group of fertile women was specially selected to produce babies for a barren elite. These women went through rigorous training to prepare to live their lives as walking wombs – 'reproducers of the nation.'

What an imagination! Surely, these things could never come to pass, we tell ourselves as we read such stories. Or could they? Atwood admits that her novel is based on facts and real events – tales from around the world that she clipped from newspapers. We have seen examples. Iranian women, who fought for their rights in the 1940s, 1950s, and 1960s succeeded in achieving major gains, only to lose them following the Iranian revolution. They won the right to vote in 1963 and rapidly made inroads into the public sphere by the middle of the 1970s. They succeeded in changing family laws to curb polygamy and challenge men's unilateral right to divorce, and a husband's right to decide his wife's occupation was tempered by an increase in her power to make decisions on the matter (Afshar, 1989). Successes were short lived, however, some lasting only a couple of years, as the Iranian Revolution not only overturned many of these gains, but also set out to return women to the home and renew 'moral standards,' thus controlling women's sexuality and reproduction. This was not a fictional storyline in a dystopian futuristic novel. It was real life for many women who lived through the period.

Not two decades later, similar headlines appeared; this time about Afghanistan. During the rise of the Taliban Afghan women went from being prominent figures in public life to being shoved out of politics, paid employment, and education. Headlines in North American newspapers, especially after that fateful day in September 2001, focused on the brutal treatment of Afghan women by their fundamentalist leaders. That revolution left women powerless at the hands of the new regime.

Scanning through those headlines, I also could not help but sense the omnipresent 'otherness' projected by the stories: *those* archaic leaders *there*, re-patriarchalizing previously 'modernizing' societies. But are we in the west safe from re-patriarchalizing 'revolutionaries' to whom *they* seem so vulnerable?

Eventually, it became clear to me that nationalism, ethnic unrest, and religious zeal can and do have serious consequences for women, and that this situation is not unique to *those* backward-looking leaders over *there*. This book shows that nationalism has played and continues to play a key role in shaping and reshaping modern Europe. The question then remains: could nationalist movements in Europe seek to alter and constrain women's rights and roles in the way that some of the Islamic movements were doing? This book shows there have been European cases throughout the twentieth century where they do so.

In recent years countless books and articles in a number of academic disciplines have been written on the topic of nationalism, particularly in a European context. Older texts have been revised and republished (Anderson, 1983/1991; Kedourie, 1963/1993), and new publications have been plentiful. It appears that, with the collapse of the Soviet Union and the break-up of Yugoslavia, nationalism has once again come to the fore (Smith, 1991; Kedourie, 1963/1993; Hobsbawm, 1995). One exemplary text among the many on nationalism opens with the statement: 'Nationalism is back' (Kupchan, 1995, 1).

Scholars appear to be scrambling to understand where this new wave of nationalism has come from and how best to react to it (Kupchan, 1995). In this scramble, a new nomenclature has emerged. Eric Hobsbawm (1995), for example, has come to identify it as the 'new separatist nationalism of the Crisis Decade' (426) or *fin de siècle* ethnic nationalism. There are others who would not be alarmed by what is transpiring, as they claim that we are living in an age of nationalism (Kohn, 1962; Gellner, 1983) and are simply seeing one of many nationalist outbursts of this century. Despite the volumes written on the subject, relatively little ink is devoted to identifying and explaining the impact of nationalism on the lives of women. Most authors have little or nothing to say about women, despite the fact that there appear to be attitudinal and policy shifts on gender issues that emerge when nationalists rise to power.

I also noticed that when feminist authors focused on the position of women in selected countries touched by nationalism, their work was virtually ignored by other authors and academics. There seemed to be a sense that these were 'women's issues,' to be situated in 'women's studies,' and were not of general importance; the 'real' studies of nationalism were for men, by men, and about men, and they remained typically 'ungendered.' Women's issues and the impact of nationalism on women seem to come to the fore only if and when they serve a broader political agenda and often as a justification for international action. Rarely has the gender dimension of nationalism been treated as 'mainstream' in the area.

This book provides accounts of what happens to women's roles, rights, and obligations when nationalist regimes form governments in selected European nations. Four cases are analysed at two points in the twentieth century, in the interwar period and again in the post-1989 period, to control for the impact of political change and the passage of time. In the first chapter, I review definitions of nationalism and present a theoretical debate that has surfaced in recent studies of nationalism. As I see it, the theoretical debate is resolved by assessing the impact of the rise to power of nationalists on gender relations and family policies. In chapters 2 to 9 I outline the position of women and family policies in the four European cases. In chapters 2, 3, 4, and 5 I do so for Germany, Italy, Russia, and Yugoslavia, respectively, during the interwar period. The same approach is used in chapters 6, 7, 8, and 9, in the same four polities post 1989. Not all four cases, in both periods, were ruled by nationalist leaders: only two of the four cases in the first period and two in the second period were seriously touched by nationalism. The two remaining cases in both periods act as control groups; they were selected because the two cases of nationalism in the first period became non-nationalists in the second period and vice versa. Each of these chapters opens with a brief presentation of ecomonic, demographic, and political circumstances before the nationalist rise to power. An account of circumstances surrounding the rise of nationalism in each of the cases is followed by an exposition of policy shifts geared at altering gender roles and family relations while nationalist leaders held power. In the last part of each chapter and chapter 10 the impact of the policy changes is assessed. Where nationalists ruled, how 'successful' were they in achieving their desired goals? Chapter 11 echoes the central focus of the entire book: to show that policies under nationalist regimes in Europe differed from policies of non-nationalists. My aim in this book is therefore to expose and explain shifts in family policies that were the result of the nationalist rise to power, not in distant lands, with alien customs and patriarchal prophets/dictators, but rather, closer to home, not so long ago, and not so far away.

When nationalists use the terms 'national fraternity' and 'brothers in harmony,' they accurately denote the absence of women from the benefits of nationalism. This book illustrates that under nationalist regimes in Europe there have been attempts to re-traditionalize and re-patriarchalize gender and family relations. Whether these attempts result in an actual deterioration in the status of women in societies ruled by nationalist governments is explored in the body of this work. This re-patriarchalization, as I have come to understand it, is often accompanied by a glorification of the past and renewal of religious traditions and includes the reinforcement and/or (attempted) renewal of traditional roles within the family. Such a process of patriarchal renewal has often sought to erase advances made under previous political regimes – even in Europe. In this work I assess how it occurs, what it involves, and its success in selected European cases.

In brief, I test the validity of competing general perspectives on nationalism by examining how nationalism and nationalist regimes treat half of their populations, especially those commonly associated with traditional social forms such as family, neighbourhood, and religious community: women. I do so by outlining and assessing nationalist government attitudes, policies, and practices that apply to women and families. I hope to move one step closer to settling this issue by asking: do policies of selected nationalist governments in twentieth-century Europe, on the whole, modernize gender relations, or do they represent an outright traditionalist renouncing of gender equality that aims to preserve or re-establish traditional or pre-modern gender relations – in effect, archaizing them?

1

Nationalism: Definitions and Debate – A Brotherhood of Nationals?

Authors of different intellectual and political persuasions have argued that ethnicity and nationalism emerge from traditional forms of social organization. Some early observers, such as Emile Durkheim (1893) and Ferdinand Tönnies (1940), have argued that a historical evolutionary movement takes human society away from traditional affiliations based on irrational, kinship bonds (blood ties) and into affiliations founded upon contractual, rational obligations grounded in mutual interest and need (Bonacich, 1980/1991, 60). Along the same lines, Karl Marx wrote: 'National differences and antagonisms between peoples are daily more and more vanishing, owing to the development of the bourgeoisie, to freedom of commerce, to the world market, to uniformity in the mode of production and in the conditions of life corresponding thereto' (1848/1933, 225). Towards the end of the nineteenth century it appeared that class had prevailed, both as an explanatory and mobilizing principle, while the dynamics of ethnicity and nation seemed to be a waning force. This process and line of thinking were first halted, then reversed, after 1914, when the ruling classes of much of the world led their nations into armed conflict in the First World War. The international proletariat and its organizations were put to the test: they would either remain true to their promise of responding to an international war with a class war or follow the orders of their national bourgeoisies and kill their class comrades on the battlefield. They chose the latter.

Nationalism triumphed as workers flocked to their respective national causes. Reflecting on the time, Magnus Hirschfeld wrote that 'in those days there were only a few who were immune to the mass psychosis and practically everyone was enthusiastic for war' (1946, 26).

The 'war to end all wars' marked a turning point in national and nationalist politics.

The map of Europe was twice significantly altered in the twentieth century. National borders within Europe were redrawn after the partitioning of the Habsburg (Austro-Hungarian) and Ottoman (Turkish) empires following the First World War (at the Paris Peace Conference of 1919) and again after the collapse of communism in the Soviet Union and other parts of eastern Europe after 1989. At both historical points, one of the instruments used in the carving-up of Europe was nationalism.

Benedict Anderson (1991) noted that nation, nationality, and nationalism 'all have proved notoriously difficult to define' (3). Part of the difficulty is that nationalism has been defined as an ideology (Anderson, 1991), a theory of political legitimacy (Gellner, 1983), a mass-sentiment (Kohn, 1962), faith (Hayes, 1960), and a political principle (Gellner, 1983), among other things. According to Anthony Smith (1991), the term has been used to signify many things, including the whole *process* of forming and maintaining nations; a *consciousness* of belonging to the nation; an *ideology*, including a cultural doctrine of nations and the *national will* and prescriptions for the realization of national aspirations; and a *social and political movement* to achieve the goals of the nation and realize its national will. He argued that nationalism is an ideological movement for attaining and maintaining autonomy, unity, and identity on behalf of a population deemed by some of its members to constitute an actual or 'potential' nation (Smith, 1991).

Similarly, Gellner's (1983) classic definition describes nationalism as a political ideology that maintains that the political and national unit should be congruent. In both cases, the definition of nationalism identifies the central role played by ethnic or cultural identity. Kedourie (1963/1993), for example, noted that in nationalist doctrine, language, race, culture, and sometimes even religion constitute different aspects of the same primordial entity – the nation. Nationalism celebrates the imagined political/ethnic community (Anderson, 1991) known as nation. In short, nationalism is the embracing of, among other things, the idea that nations are and should be institutionally, and especially politically, complete cultures (Buchanan, 1998).

Much of the current literature on nationalism defines nation as a group of people who share objective (language, religion, etc.) and subjective (identity, myths, common beliefs, a sense of historical continuity) characteristics (Nootens, 1998). Yet, a nation is not simply a collection of individuals – a people; it is a conglomeration of a land and a people (Dahbour, 1998). Kupchan (1995) explains that by drawing on existing common attributes and generating shared historical experiences and myths, nationalism elevates the nation state to a place of primacy, 'one that transcends class, kinship or regional affiliations in commanding popular loyalty' (2). Many have noted that, despite the actual inequality that exists within an ethnic group, nationalism delineates the nation as a deep, horizontal comradeship or family. In other words, through nationalism, traditionally fragmented, dissimilar, and stratified social groups within a polity come to see themselves as united by real or imagined 'blood ties' or ethnicity. As a result, the nation has commonly been described as a 'brotherhood of all nationals' (Smith, 1991, 76). The question remains, does this brotherhood include sisters, and, if so, in what capacity?

This book explores the implications of this principle, especially as it applies to women. It focuses on the impact of nationalism on women and families as it appears in some of its more extreme forms, including fascism – one variant of nationalism (Brooker, 1995). According to Breuilly (1994), fascism cannot be understood outside a nationalist frame of reference. It has been defined as an extreme right-wing totalitarian ideology developed in Italy by Benito Mussolini. Its name is derived from the *fasces*, or bundle of rods, which represented unity and authority, carried by magistrates of the Roman republic. This ideology included ideas from a number of thinkers; for example, from Hegel it derived the belief that the state is more than a collection of citizens: it has an organic life of its own, which transcends individual mortality, and individuals, families, and organizations become subordinate to the state (Townson, 1995). According to Kedourie (1963/1993), the individual cannot then be considered on his/her own, but rather 'forms part of, and derives meaning from the whole' (31). It is a totalitarian system that seeks to control all aspects of a citizen's life (Linz, 1978). The main difference between fascism and nationalism is that nationalism in its less extreme forms is shared by many political movements.

Fascism, like intensified forms of nationalism, has either an implicit anti-international component or a pan-nationalist element, which tends to challenge existing states with aggressive, expansionist, foreign policy (Linz, 1978). At the same time, the nation is almost constantly perceived as being in danger; threatened by external enemies or enemies from within (Durham, 1998). In effect, this doctrine constructs a unified, national 'self' and pits it against a real or mythic, inimical 'other.'

A Debate in the Literature

My introduction to this area began when I got caught up in what seemed to be a dull, academic, theoretical debate. Within traditional studies of nationalism there are a number of ongoing debates, which seem to have been rekindled as a result of events surrounding the break-up of the Soviet Union and of Yugoslavia. One of the debates that caught my attention when I started working in this area concerned whether nationalism is a 'modern or modernizing' phenomenon or whether it is 'anti-modern' in nature. There are those, like Ernest Gellner (1983), who argue that nationalism is a powerful and necessary force that assists in liberating ethnic groups from the tyranny of oppressive monarchs or, more recently, from that of imperialist colonizers (Anderson, 1983/1991).

According to Gellner (1983), in the past the ruling classes in agrarian societies formed a small minority of the population, rigidly separated from the great majority of agricultural producers, or peasants. This social arrangement (feudalism) amplified the inequality of classes: favouring, inventing, and reinforcing cultural cleavages, so that the minority at the top lived in 'another world' (10). Gellner believed that, with the coming of 'the age of nationalism,' this situation changed. He argued that nationalism is the external manifestation of a deep adjustment in the relationship between polity and culture – unavoidably triggered by industrialization – and explained that nationalism is not an awakening of the past, but on the contrary, 'the crystallization of new units, suitable for the conditions now prevailing' (49). As nationalism emerged, the role of national culture and education was to turn out 'worthy, loyal, and competent members of the total society whose occupancy of posts within it will not be hampered by factional loyalties to sub-groups within the total community' (64). In other words, nationalism, in promising universal education, homogenization, unity, and some form of basic equality, made subgroups and factions virtually indistinguishable. Nationalism was said to have liberated 'the people' from the grip of autocratic rule, thus paving the way to 'modernity.'

Similarly, Hans Kohn (1962) noted that, in its origins, western nationalism was connected to the concepts of individual liberty and rational cosmopolitan currents that were characteristic of the eighteenth century. In other words, nationalism was a move away from traditional forms of political organization that were unequal, irrational, and provincial.

According to William McNeill (1985), in its earliest forms the nationalist ideal of unity was effective in transforming 'outcasts of society into obedient soldiers' (48). Modern drills, regular pay, food, housing, and uniforms made recruits obedient, efficient soldiers 'no matter where they came from or what their political and social ideas may have been before they found themselves in the ranks' (50). It served to homogenize otherwise very diverse groups in society and promised greatness to those who could act 'together as brothers in harmony with one another and with their government' (51). In other words, nationalism bridged linguistic, political, religious, and class differences that existed within a nation, using rhetoric like 'national fraternity.'

Nationalism helped otherwise disunited individuals to feel part of a unified whole, because the nationalist ideal signified cohesion and the brotherhood of all nationals (Smith 1991). Anthony Smith argued that the family metaphor underlying the concept of nation appears in a political guise: 'as the union of fraternal citizens' (1991, 76). Nationalism did so effectively by locating the source of individual identity within a 'people,' which is seen as the bearer of sovereignty, the central object of loyalty, and the basis of a 'collective solidarity' (Greenfeld, 1992, 3). According to Liah Greenfeld (1992), when the word 'nation' was made synonymous with the word 'people,' it lost its derogatory connotation and began to denote a positive entity, acquiring the meaning of 'bearer of sovereignty, the basis of political solidarity, and the supreme object of loyalty' (7). Greenfeld added that this made it possible for *any* member of 'the people' to partake in 'its elite quality'; consequently, a stratified national population is perceived as essentially homogeneous, and the lines of status and class are seen as superficial. Without a redistribution of wealth, nationalism in this way is a relatively economical way to achieve class peace.

These theorists have argued that nationalism originally developed as a kind of democracy, which implies the symbolic elevation of the populace, wherein 'the people' are able to act as a political elite, actually exercising sovereignty (Greenfeld, 1992). According to Anthony Smith (1991), nationalism operates at the social level by 'prescribing the mobilization of "the people," their legal equality as citizens and their participation in public life for the "national good"' (91). Smith and others have claimed that not only has nationalism penetrated every corner of the globe but 'national identity everywhere underpins the recurrent drive for popular sovereignty and democracy' (143).

Nationalism thus helped to liberate and empower individuals. It is also said to have helped to emancipate polities around the globe from empires and from colonialism. Writing on 'the dependent world' of the first half of the twentieth century, especially about colonized regions, Eric Hobsbawm (1995) noted that 'movements for national liberation and independence were the main agents for political emancipation of most of the globe' (169). Similarly, writing on nationalism at the end of the century, Charles Kupchan (1995) wrote that nationalism is central to the process of transforming desperate and politically weak ethnic and cultural groups into modern states. He noted that 'stable state structures and the transference of political loyalties from the local to the national level in turn provide fertile ground for mass political participation and the growth of liberal democracy' (3). Along the same lines, Anthony Smith (1991) stated that nationalism may not be responsible for the many instances of reform and democratization of tyrannical regimes, but it is frequently a source of pride for downtrodden peoples 'and the recognized mode for joining or rejoining democracy and civilization' (76).

In summary, these contemporary theories of nationalism suggest that nationalism is a new political ideology unique to the modern world (Gellner, 1983; Greenfeld, 1992), which promises 'the people' education, literacy, homogeneity, autonomy, identity, unity, fraternity, and democracy – in brief, a modernizing and liberating force. Nationalism brings together otherwise heterogeneous groups – divided, in most cases, along class and other lines – into a unified 'brotherhood' of nationals. In this case, nationalism whitewashes existing divisions within a society and unites a group into a unified national whole, usually against an ethnic other. For proponents of this body of theories, nationalism, industrialization, and 'development' go hand in hand (Gellner, 1983). Some other theorists would not agree. In fact, others have argued that nationalism is a conservative reaction to modernization and social change.

According to Elie Kedourie (1963/1993), the ideological currents in modern western political thought are a response to 'the *predicament* of modern man' (xv; my emphasis). He noted that, in response to this predicament, there were two different ideologies that became influential in Europe and later in the wider world in the twentieth century. One was nationalism; the other was socialism. Nationalism, like socialism, he argued, provided a remedy for human alienation and unhappiness. Kedourie explained: 'nationalism looks inwardly, away from and beyond the imperfect world' (82). In this case, nationalism is seen not as liberalizing and modernizing, but rather as an escape from the modern world – clearly a different view of what nationalism is and does.

Kedourie (1963/1993) stated further that, in societies suddenly exposed to new philosophies of the Enlightenment, orthodox ways began to seem ridiculous and useless, amounting to a rift between fathers and sons, 'a species of civil strife between generations' (96). Nationalism, therefore, was seen as a movement that satisfied a need to belong within a coherent and stable community and that perceived itself to be under threat by modernity. According to Kedourie, such a need was normally satisfied by the family, the neighbourhood, or the religious community. All three, he added, bore the brunt of violent social and intellectual change. In other words, such institutions were perceived to have been threatened by modernization.

Allen Buchanan (1998) argued that nationalism promotes *illiberal* tenets, since nationalist ideology grants the nation a unique moral status above all other cultures, subcultures, and communities. Furthermore, he stated, nationalist ideology generally asserts that individual autonomy ought to be subordinated to the nation. If so, nationalism cannot be characterized as a liberal ideology.

Similarly, Andrew Levine (1998) claimed that nationalism represents an illusory solution to an increasingly pressing modern problem – 'the need for real community' (355). He added that nationalism is a response to historical exigencies that have recently developed. Therefore, a nation is an expression of a wish for a community that extends throughout time (an attempt at preservation, tied to the fear of becoming extinct), uniting generations, across space, and incorporating strangers. Moving in a nationalist direction is part of a deep historical process that has shaped the modern world. Owing to modernity and modernization, there is a material cause and a psychological need to forge new solidarities. Nationalisms are therefore deliberately contrived and promoted by 'political entrepreneurs who mold popular longings for communal forms in nationalist directions' (Levine, 1998, 361).

Thus, in sharp contrast to the first group of authors, there are those who have argued that political crises and the rise of nationalist dictators were part of a broader conservative reaction to modernization, namely, a reaction to urbanization and industrialization (Overy, 1994). Historian R.J. Overy (1994) noted that nationalist dictators were reacting to the powerful and often popular hostility towards 'the imperious march of the modern age' (24). Overy added that for those in smaller communities, modernization undermined their world – 'the structure of family and kin, the world of established status, economic well-being, complex systems of belief and social behavior' (24). To some, including Hitler, modernization was seen as a destructive force: 'Nothing is anchored any more, nothing is rooted in our spiritual life any more. Everything is superficial, flees past us. Restlessness and haste mark the thinking of our people. The whole of life is being torn completely apart' (Hitler, cited in Nolte, 1969, 510). Seymour Martin Lipset (1959/1983) also noted that Fascist parties found their support from segments of the middle class who felt oppressed 'by developments fundamental to modern society' (489). He added that the rise of Fascism represented, in part, a 'revolt against modernity': 'These movements generally looked back nostalgically to an idealized image of a highly cohesive and stable preindustrial society characterized by an alliance of throne and altar, state and church, in which status was defined by an interrelated complex of roles and in which the state, church, and aristocracy fulfilled the values of *noblesse oblige* and took responsibility for the welfare of the average person' (489).

For proponents of this explanation, nationalism was a conservative reaction to endless attempts to upset the balance of power, traditional ways of life, and familiar forms of social organization, which were ushered in by industrialization and modernization (Lipset, 1983; Kedourie, 1993). It could be said that for them nationalism was an attempt to return to traditional social arrangements. It was believed to provide a remedy for human alienation, which so often accompanied economic modernization (Kedourie, 1993). It was seen as a conservative response, a move away from and beyond the imperfect modern world. Nationalism was a promise or an attempt to return to community – a national community or 'superfamily' – reconnecting individuals through rhetoric about real or imagined blood ties.

Both theoretical camps provide interesting insights, but the questions remain: Is nationalism a liberating, modernizing, and democratizing force, or is it a conservative response to a fear of loss of community, an attempt to return to a lost 'golden age'? Is nationalism a move forward, or a move backward?

Towards Empirical Verification – The Impact of Nationalism on Gender Relations

Writing on women, Karl Marx noted that, from the relationship of man to woman, 'one can ... judge man's whole level of development. From the character of this relationship follows how much *man* as a *species-being*, as *man*, has come to be himself and to comprehend himself; the relation of man to woman is the *most natural* relation of human being to human being. It therefore reveals the extent to which man's *natural* behaviour has become *human*' (Marx and Engels, 1844/1974, 296; original emphasis). In other words, according to Marx, one can measure a society's level of (human/social) development by assessing its treatment of women. One should be able to look at how a society treats its citizens, including women, to determine whether a society is 'developing' or 'developed,' modern or anti-modern (archaic in nature). A number of feminist thinkers both in the past and today have come to similar conclusions.

Mary Wollstonecraft (1792/1988), a child of the Enlightenment, was keenly aware of the fact that the early 'moderns' saw themselves as members of a free and equal confraternity and that this 'brotherhood' excluded women: 'the civilization which has hitherto taken place in the world has been very partial' (7). She added: 'To render mankind more virtuous, and happier of course, both sexes must act from the same principle; but how can that be expected when only one is allowed to see the reasonableness of it? To render also the social compact truly equitable, and in order to spread those enlightened principles, which alone can meliorate the fate of man, women must be allowed to found their virtue on knowledge, which is scarcely possible unless they be educated by the same pursuits as men' (173). Clearly, to Wollstonecraft, modernity meant women's access to the public realm, namely, to public education: 'It is plain from the history of all nations, that women cannot be confined to merely domestic pursuits, for they will not fulfil family duties, unless their minds take a wider range' (174). She continued, 'Make them free, and they will quickly become wise and virtuous, as men become more so; for the improvement must be mutual, or the injustice which one half of the human race are obliged to submit to, retorting on their oppressors, the virtue of men will be worm-eaten by the insect whom he keeps under his feet' (175).

Along the same lines, and 160 years later, Simone de Beauvoir (1952) wrote that the 'modern' woman 'accepts masculine values: she prides herself on thinking, taking action, working, creating, on the same terms as men; instead of seeking to disparage them, she declares herself an equal' (676). It can be said that one of the general changes that seems to have accompanied modernization has been in the nature of women's activities in society and changing expectations surrounding their public roles (Hobsbawm, 1995). Has nationalist ideology in 'modern' Europe facilitated women's transition into the public sphere or has it attempted to impede it?

A number of feminist thinkers have noted that literature in the studies of nationalism has left ethnic identity ungendered (Enloe, 1993). Ethnicity has been discussed and researched as if it is gender neutral. But is it? In cases where nationalists come to power, are female members of an ethnic group treated in the same way that male members are? Are they presented with the same opportunities, expectations and roles? That is, when nationalists govern, are men and women allowed to share equally in the 'benefits' of national belonging? Is the position of women changed or 'improved' compared with its status when non-nationalists were in power before them?

It has been noted that nationalism, as a political ideology, often includes prescriptions for gender-appropriate behaviour and uses women as potent symbols of cultural identity (Charles and Hintjens, 1998; Yuval-Davis and Anthias, 1989). Charles and Hintjens (1998) wrote that we must recognize that 'defining and controlling women is central to demarcating ethnic and national boundaries' (2). Consequently, the study of ethnic nationalism must involve the recognition of women's importance to the maintenance of collectivities and the problems they encounter with gendered and ethnically based notions of citizenship and democracy.

Nation-states create symbols to represent the nation. Often, the nation is represented as a family to which citizens should owe their primary emotional allegiance. Donald Horowitz (1985), for example, has likened ethnic groups to 'super-families' of fictive descent – one huge family linked by mythical ties of filiation and ancestry (Smith, 1991). It follows that if nationalism is ethnically based and defines ethnicity as something that runs in the blood of nationals, then it necessarily involves a tight control over women's sexuality in order to define and maintain the boundaries of the ethnic community (Charles and Hintjens, 1998). Many feminists have noted that images of women as chaste, modest mothers and preservers of tradition were central to the ideology of nationalism. Enloe (1993) explained that it is precisely because 'sexuality, reproduction, and child-rearing acquire such strategic importance with the rise of nationalism that many nationalist men become newly aware of their need to exert control over women' (239). Controlling women becomes a way of protecting or reviving the nation.

Yuval-Davis and Anthias (1989) remind us that there is no unitary category of women that can be unproblematically conceived as the focus of ethnic, national, or state policies and discourses: women are divided along class, ethnic, and life-cycle lines. However, they point out that, in a nationalist context, there appear to be at least five major ways in which women have tended to participate in ethnic and national processes and state practices. Women are used as biological reproducers of ethnic groups; as reproducers of boundaries for these groups; as transmitters of culture; as signifiers of ethnic differences; and as participants in national, economic, political, and military struggles. Using a selected number of cases of nationalism in Europe this century, I intend to determine if and to what degree this occurs, and to what consequence. If nationalism is an attempt to protect or revive traditional social forms, let us begin our enquiry by looking at how nationalists treat traditional social institutions such as the family. If nationalism is indeed a conservative reaction to social change and modernization, one would expect to find attempts to strengthen, revive, or reinforce traditional forms of social organization like traditional nuclear families. If nationalism is a modernizing or emancipatory force (Hobsbawm, 1995), traditional forms of organization would be ignored or would not matter to the nationalist agenda at the very least, and, at best, we should see nationalism's emancipatory forces at work within families. By understanding how nationalist regimes view and 'treat' gender and family relations, one can begin to get a better understanding of whether nationalism is modernizing or anti-modern in nature.

My aim in this book is to identify the impact of political changes on the lives of women that lived through them. Did their membership in an ethnic and national body amount to inclusion in the political forum? Did inclusion, equality, and political autonomy characterize their place in the nationalist agenda? I attempt to answer such questions by focusing on how women experience nationalist politics in selected European countries. The goal is to identify any changes in the experiences, social status, and prescribed social roles of women that accompany a nationalist rise to power. Also, where nationalists attempted to affect change in women and families, to what extent were they successful? Should nationalist treatment of women appear emancipatory, we will have some indication of its modernizing character. Should nationalist treatment of women include attempts to return women to traditional social roles in order to 'strengthen' the traditional family, there is some indication of its anti-modern character.

Comparative case-oriented research has been commonly used in the studies of nationalism. Respected scholars have used this approach for the past thirty-plus years. For example, Barrington Moore's (1966) study included England, France, United States, China, Japan, and India. Charles Tilly et al. (1975) compared France, Germany, and Italy. Theda Skocpol (1979/1995) examined France, Russia, and China. Liah Greenfeld (1992) wrote about England, France, Russia, Germany, and the United States. In fact, it appears that comparative case-oriented research is a norm in the studies of nationalism.

Skocpol (1979/1995) used a comparative historical approach to develop an explanation of the causes and outcomes of the French, Russian, and Chinese Revolutions. According to Skocpol, comparative historical analysis can proceed in two main ways. She explained that, first, one can try to establish that several cases having in common the phenomenon one is trying to explain also have in common a set of causal factors, although they vary in other ways – an approach that has been called the 'Method of Agreement' (36). Second, one can contrast the cases in which the phenomenon to be explained and the hypothesized causes are present with other cases in which the phenomenon and causes are absent – also known as the 'Method of Difference' (36). Skocpol added that, taken alone, the 'Method of Agreement' is better suited for establishing valid causal associations, but combining these two comparative logics is certainly 'desirable' (37). In this book I follow her recommendation.

By comparing cases where nationalists have come to power with cases where they have not, I control for the effects of global structural trends that may have an overall effect on women in general at that time, for example, Europe-wide economic changes, such as recessions that affected women's employment rates in general. I analyse two relatively concurrent cases where nationalists came to power, and I compare them with two concurrent non-nationalist cases, in order to control for nation-specific economic and social trends. Such controls help to isolate the effect of nationalism. I focus on two historical periods in order to control for changes over time.

This analysis centres around two periods in the twentieth century that have been marked by nationalist outbursts. As stated above, the borders of European countries were twice significantly altered in the twentieth century – in both cases with the help of nationalism. National borders within Europe were redrawn after the partitioning of the Habsburg and Ottoman empires following the First World War and

TABLE 1.1
The Research Model

Period 1: Interwar period		Period 2: Post-1989	
Nationalism's highs	Nationalism's lows	Nationalism's highs	Nationalism's lows
Nazi Germany	Revolutionary Russia	Post-Soviet Russia	Post-Reunification Germany
Fascist Italy	Kingdom of Yugoslavia	Independent Croatia	Today's Italy

again after the collapse of communism after 1989. Both periods provide an abundance of cases to choose from.

The specific periods of study for each case are not identical, but rather vary in length and do not begin and end in the same years. In other words, I did not select one specific time period – for example, beginning in 1919 and ending in 1945 – for all four cases, since those specific dates may not be significant in a particular case. Also, it did not seem useful to set unflexible blocks of time – twenty-year blocks, for example – if the years are meaningless and arbitrary and have no relevance within particular contexts. Instead, I focused on periods that were generally within the parameters specified above, yet began with a government's or regime's rise to power and ended when that regime was defeated.

Upon reviewing the cases of nationalist and non-nationalist regimes found in Europe in the twentieth century, I concluded that Italy, Germany, U.S.S.R./Russia and Yugoslavia/Croatia would be used in this analysis (see table 1.1). The most important criteria for selecting these rather than other states were that all four experienced both nationalist and non-nationalist governments during the twentieth century and that the states that were non-nationalist in the early part of the century became nationalist in the last part of the century and vice versa. Italy and Germany were selected as examples of nationalist regimes in the interwar period because they were indisputably fascist/nationalist under Mussolini and Hitler, respectively (DeGrand, 2000; Nolte, 1969). They were also suitable as examples of lower-level/non-nationalist cases in the post-1989 period. The same proved to be true in the case of the U.S.S.R. and of Yugoslavia. While being low-level or non-nationalist (internationalist or multinational) in parts of the interwar period, as the Kingdom of the South Slavs and revolutionary Russia under Lenin, both proved to have higher-level nationalist regimes in the post-1989 period. Numerous authors have noted that both Yeltsin in Russia (Reynolds, 2000; Burlatsky, 1998; Zaslavsky, 1993) and Tudjman in Croatia (Ramet, 1999a; Denitch 1994; Babić, 1992) 'cultivated' nationalism in their rise to power.

This comparative two-by-two model is meant to control for the impact of overall changes in the position of women in modern society, that is, the impact of modernity itself. My view is that the role of nationalism in the modern history of gender relations is not sufficiently clear. Its clarification is not a theoretical but an empirical issue. This book therefore tests whether nationalism intends to modernize or archaize gender and family relations at both points and to what degree it suceeds in doing so.

In this work I compare the development, nature, and objectives of family policies implemented by nationalist governments, analysing the social and political context under which these policies were introduced. I answer a general question – what is the impact of nationalist rise to power on the lives of women – by identifying specific nationalist policies that pertain to women and families. My aim was to determine if a nationalist rise to power is followed by attempts to change or reinforce prescribed traditional social roles of women. The next eight chapters identify laws, policies, and practices implemented by nationalist and non-nationalist governments, paying particular attention to their attempts, if any, to modify laws and practices put in place by previous regimes. In other words, the emphasis is on policy *shifts*. Do family policies get changed? By whom? Under what circumstances? Why? And, more specifically, do nationalist regimes shift more towards re-establishing 'traditional' social roles, in effect, attempting to re-patriarchalize society?

Part I
The Interwar Period

2

Nationalism in the Interwar Period: Germany

The Political and Economic Situation following the First World War

The first half of the twentieth century was especially turbulent in Germany. Germany fought and lost the First World War, and almost simultaneously, the 'Revolution of 1918' resulted in the abdication of the Kaiser and the proclamation of the Weimar Republic on 9 November 1918. Civil war ensued as Social Democrats fought communists over control of the new republic (Abel, 1938). According to Ralf Dahrendorf (1969) 'in 1918, one of the most skilled elites of modern history, the authoritarian elite of Imperial Germany lost its political basis'; he added that 'the state, the moral ideal of which was anchored in the claim for certainty advanced by traditional leadership groups, began to float' and no counter-elite 'emerged to fasten it.' Furthermore, the Treaty of Versailles, signed in 1919, resulted in Germany's increased economic hardship and humiliation (MacMillan, 2001).

Abel (1938) noted that many Germans blamed the government of the Weimar Republic for accepting the terms of the Treaty of Versailles and for the economic hardships that resulted; they felt that the government had misled them with false hopes and had brought about too much social change. He explained that 'the majority of the people were in a holy wrath against the regime for having brought about an intolerable situation ... They longed to go back to work, to recapture the old state of stability and order' (17). The economic situation only worsened after the onset of the Great Depression in 1929. The majority of Germans at the time sought a return to prosperity and political stability and a renewal of national pride, but in the period between 1918 and 1933 they experienced little of either.

Under the terms of the Treaty of Versailles Germany was made to accept sole responsibility for causing the First World War. It had to cede large parts of its empire, pay war reparations, keep an army no larger than 100,000 men, pay for civil damages, and sell German property abroad (MacMillan, 2001; Langer, 1987). Many German assets outside Europe were confiscated. The treaty itself was thorough, outlining in detail the amount of gold, commodities (including food, livestock, and raw materials), and securities that were due (Treaty of Versailles, 1919, Articles 231–47). In April 1921 the Allies presented Germany with a bill for reparations in the sum of 132 billion gold marks or US$33 billion (Shirer, 1960). As a result, Germany was in economic ruin.

Average Germans experienced economic insecurity, political uncertainty, shock, and humiliation (Gailus, 2002). The unemployment rate in Germany hit 18 per cent in 1926, compared with the United Kingdom's 8.8 per cent, in the same year (Mitchell, 1992). Germans were especially hard hit by inflation: there were huge leaps in the Cost of Living/ Consumer Prices Indices, for example, from 661 in 1920 to 10,324 billion in 1923 (ibid., 848). The mark was valued at about 4 to the dollar before 1914, 75 to the dollar just after the war, 500 to the dollar in July 1922, and 22,400 to the dollar in January 1923 (Koonz, 1981). Economic circumstances were so grave that Germans could spend their entire life savings to buy a trolley ticket (40,000 marks). One German woman reported that, when her husband died of his war injuries, she was entitled to a sum of 100,000 gold marks from a life insurance company. She explained that 'originally 100,000 gold marks had been something like £5,000, a sum big enough to give some security to a family. With the devalued money I got, I could not even buy a rose tree for the grave' (Thomas, 1943, 22). To make matters worse, the 1929 Wall Street crash profoundly affected German society. Citizens were hard hit by tax hikes, loan recalls, wage reductions, cuts to the welfare state, and countless business bankruptcies (Quine, 1996).

The Demographic Situation

The German birth rate had been rising throughout much of the nineteenth century, but it came to a standstill in the 1880s and began to decrease after about 1900 (Mitchell, 1992; Quine, 1996). Nonetheless, owing to declining mortality rates, in the first decade of the twentieth century Germany's population grew from 56 million to 65 million (Gilbert, 1984). The birth rate peaked in 1876; it was one of the highest rates in Europe at 42.6 live births per 1,000 inhabitants. The rate dropped to

28.3 by 1912 and continued to drop thereafter (Mitchell, 1992). This decline prompted alarmists to warn of 'race suicide.' To make matters worse, German losses and casualties in the First World War were great: Germany suffered the greatest number of war dead and wounded (about 6 million) in all of western Europe (Gilbert, 1984). Not only did this fact heighten the fears that depopulation had begun, but these war losses left Germany with a sex ratio imbalance, since the war dead were predominately young men.

Fears of depopulation were rampant even before the rise to power of the National Socialists (Sachße, 1993). In fact, leaders of the Weimar Republic, which preceded the period of Nazi rule, showed a growing willingness to introduce pronatalist reforms, but the economic crisis at the time prevented much investment in the matter. At the same time, the new policies met with resistance by women's groups, who had recently gained political and social power. The Bund Deutscher Frauenvereine (BDF) was a woman's organization that promoted the importance of the family from the female and national point of view. It was critical of the 'moral laxity' of Weimar culture and demanded reform of the marriage provisions of the Civil Code, full equality for women in education and the professions, and equal pay for equal work (Evans, 1976).

Furthermore, Germany shared with its neighbours the experience of social change that was concomitant with industrialization. Industrialization was accompanied by a shift in attitude towards children: in the wake of urbanization, industrialization, and declining infant mortality rates, German families, like many other European families at the time, concentrated on having fewer children, who would not merely survive but who, it was hoped, would rise to a higher socio-economic level than that of their parents (Bridenthal, 1977). Fewer children meant that parents could invest in their prolonged skills training, education, career, and personality development. Thus, family resources went towards grooming one or two children, especially sons, rather than propagating many. Clearly, the new regime in post–First World War Germany had to combat changing social attitudes as it sought to boost birth rates. A debate opened about not only increasing the quantity of Germans, but improving the quality as well.

Women's Emancipation and 'Progress' in the Weimar Republic

The majority Socialists and their labour allies who rose to power in 1918 made social policy a primary means to realize social rights of the working class (Rimlinger, 1987). Women of all classes also benefited from this political change. The new Weimar Constitution of 1918/19 stipulated that men and women should have the same rights and duties. Women's groups in Germany waged vigorous campaigns, especially after 1902, when the Deutscher Verband für Frauenstimmrecht (German Union for Women's Suffrage) was established, to win the right to vote (Evans, 1976). Under the new Weimar Constitution, women were eligible to vote and hold public office (Article 22), and pursue careers (Article 150). In effect, the republic introduced female suffrage in late 1918, even before some other European nations. Between 70 and 90 per cent of all eligible women took advantage of this fact and voted in Weimar elections (Koonz, 1977). In the Weimar Republic, owing to the sex ratio imbalance caused by the First World War, women voters outnumbered men by more than 1 million (Evans, 1976). Furthermore, women made up between 6 and 9 per cent of elected delegates in the Reichstag. Nineteen female members of the German Social Democratic Party (SPD) and a number of Independent Social Democratic women (USPD) were elected in January 1919 (Quataert, 1979). Therefore, at least to a certain extent, women were a force to be reckoned with on implementation of social policies. Rimlinger (1987) noted that 'in a sense, policy was now being shaped by the demands "from below"' (59). Women's groups pressed parliament for progressive legislation, including the promotion of 'voluntary motherhood' and the heightening of women's sexual freedom. In 1926 the government went so far as to liberalize abortion laws by reducing the severity of sentences for women and abortion providers (Quine, 1996). Though not a fundamental change, it effectively made abortion a misdemeanour. Only one year later, in 1927 the German Supreme Court ruled that abortion for medical reasons was legal if the pregnancy posed a danger to the mother. This allowed for a wider interpretation of the law, and as a result abortion clinics were created throughout Germany. Birth control clinics were also set up to provide cheap contraceptives to the working class (ibid.). At the same time a long series of measures was introduced, culminating in Sections 35–41 of the National Child Welfare Law of 1922, to protect the rights of 'legitimate' and 'illegitimate' children (Friedlander and Myers, 1940). The entire German system of nationalized welfare was becoming one of the most advanced of its day (Quine, 1996).

In addition, women in the Weimar Republic experiencing advances in education and paid employment. Women made up about 20 per cent of all university students, and about one-third of the labour force was female. After the First World War, the number of women rose from about 6 to 35 per cent of students at all German universities (Merkl, 1975). Some felt that Weimar reforms meant personal emancipation for only well-educated and privileged women, while the average woman was merely exploited as a wage slave to the capitalist economic order (Koonz, 1977). On the other hand, women in Germany at the time were the most unionized in Europe (Bridenthal, 1977). The passing of the 1927 Maternity Protection Act established Germany as one of the first nations to endorse the International Labour Organization's rulings on the rights of women workers (Quine, 1996; Stoehr, 1991).

The October 1929 stock market crash, the ensuing economic crisis, and the rise of National Socialism after 1933 brought the republic's social experiments and advance to an end. Out of Germany's economic turmoil and political crisis emerged Adolf Hitler and the Nazi (National Socialist) Party, which had been on the political scene for about a decade but had not had the opportunity to rise to power until Germany's economic and political crises after 1930 created favourable circumstances. In a bid for support of the masses, Schleicher, the last chancellor of the republic, opened conversations with trade unions (which he had previously opposed and disregarded). Industrialists and big landowners rose up against him and his proposed programs to assist workers and unions during the economic crisis (Shirer, 1960). Schleicher overestimated his supporters and underestimated the power of his opponents. Following conspiracies, alliances, concessions, and much instability, at noon of 30 January 1933 President Hindenburg, 'acting in a perfectly constitutional manner,' entrusted the chancellorship to Adolf Hitler (ibid., 187). This move signalled the end of democracy in Germany.

National Socialist Policies on Women

The rise of National Socialism after 1933 changed the lives of average Germans. Women and the German family became a special focus of the party. It should be noted, however, that National Socialist policies on and attitudes towards women and the 'woman question' changed considerably throughout the party's years in power. These policies represented a strange synthesis of reactionary and progressive views (Evans, 1976) but were always in the interests of the nation rather than individual women. Nazi Party attitudes regarding the 'woman question'

went through at least three phases (Koonz, 1977). The first phase occurred even before 1933, when the party was struggling to gain public
recognition. At the time, women in the movement worked shoulder to
shoulder with male colleagues, raising awareness, support, and funds.
In the second phase, after the Nazis' seizure of power, Hitler ordered
employed women to relinquish their jobs and dedicate themselves to
'feminine virtues,' which involved the revival of the Kaiser's 'Kinder,
Kirche, und Küche,' part of the 'back to the home movement.' But in
preparation for war (the third phase), after 1937, the party attitude
changed again: Hitler reversed his policy and began to encourage women
to work in factories, offices, and fields (ibid). In all three phases women
were seen as essential to the cause, but at no time did they exert much
influence over policies that deeply affected their lives (except that many
voted for the Nazi Party; ibid.).

Phase 1. Early Nazi Attitudes/Policies: Women as Party Supporters

In the 1920s women made up about 20 per cent of the Nazi Party
membership. Young women were especially drawn to the movement
(Evans, 1976). They did not merely follow their husbands and fathers,
but in many cases joined the party against their families' wishes, and
some husbands lost their jobs because of their wives' pro-Nazi activities
(Koonz, 1977). Seymour Martin Lipset and Stein Rokkan (1967) noted
that in the 1920s and 1930s the more conservative or religious a party,
the higher its 'feminine support' (140). Evidence of contributions of
money and moral support for the movement from women was found in
a collection of autobiographical accounts of why individuals joined the
Nazi movement.

In 1934 Theodore Abel organized a writing contest, asking for autobiographical accounts of why individuals had joined Hitler's movement. There were 683 responses, of which forty-eight were written by
women. Abel (1938) analysed the male responses and Merkl (1975)
analysed those of women. One woman explained that in 1928, at the
age of fifty-seven, she began to care for the 'unemployed fighters of
Hitler,' to collect money to proselytize 'even among the Communists'
and to propagandize for the coming of the Third Reich (124). In his
analysis Merkl wrote that it was worth noting 'the frequency with
which Nazi women drew their offspring and other family members
into the party' (127). For example, one woman waited for the death of
her husband before she felt free to join the Nazi Party. Upon doing so,

she convinced her teenage son to join the Hitler Youth and then the *Schutzstaffel* (SS). In other words, some women in this early phase not only directly supported the party, but were active in drawing others to it.

In an interview published in the *New York Times* on 10 July 1933 Hitler proclaimed that women had always been among his staunchest supporters: 'They feel that my victory is their victory. They know I serve their cause in working to redeem German youth, to create a social order, to restore hope and health' (Baynes, 1942, 528). Hitler openly thanked female party supporters for preserving the party while he was in prison: 'When after thirteen months of imprisonment I was released, when the Party had been broken up, it was essentially the women-comrades who sustained the Movement. They did not allow themselves to be guided by any shrewd and reasonable calculations, but they acted as their hearts dictated, and through their emotions they have remained with me until to-day' (531–2). He praised women for being emotional, while men where rational – a theme echoed in other speeches he made at the time. For example, in an address delivered at the *Parteitag* in Nuremberg on 12 September 1935 he explained: 'it is not an equality of rights, it is unity. Man and Woman represent two quite different characteristics: in Man the understanding is dominant, but more stable than that is emotion which is the mark of Woman' (531). Hitler relied on 'common sense' and emotion to win support. One witness at the time wrote that Hitler himself 'was emotional, he was sentimental, he was never intellectual' (Thomas, 1943, 25).

Hitler often turned to women for support in the early period. One feminist, an opponent of Hitler, wrote: 'The only Hitler meeting I ever attended took place at the beginning of October 1932 in a well-known town in middle Germany where I had been sent in the course of my newspaper work. I had noticed the posters when I stepped out of the night train. "Come and bring your worries to Adolf Hitler – throw your burden on his shoulders." That appeal clearly was aimed at women' (Thomas, 1943, 23). Although no woman ever held a party office, women were given the opportunity to organize their own relatively independent associations, edit their own newsletters and pamphlets, and discuss their views on the 'woman question' (Koonz, 1977). Many of these Nazi women openly expressed their contempt for liberalism, individualism, and the emancipation of women, since Nazis regarded feminism as part of a Jewish conspiracy to undermine the German race (Evans, 1976). Many female party supporters saw the entry of women into the paid labour force as an unnatural double burden. Others blamed materialism and 'Americanism' for the emancipation of women. They urged women to return to the security of their traditional roles and thus worked to return them to a (mythical) past in which women had respect and security in the domestic sphere.

Frequently in speeches Hitler told the '*Frauen des einfachen Mittelstandes*' (women of the petit bourgeoisie) that women were the guardians of the family, that each mother in giving children to Germany was worthy of being called a hero 'and being waited on hand and foot by the nation' (Thomas, 1943, 26). At the time, many women not only accepted this view, but helped to promote it and other party policies. In this first phase, the Nazi party needed and used its female supporters on the front lines to spread these and similar ideas to the general public. Thus, it can be said that some women's commitment to the Nazi Party even before 1933, contributed to its rise to power.

Phase 2. Nazi Attitudes and Policies: Women as Mothers

Even though the Nazi Party held traditionalist views on women, it had little power to act upon those views until after 1933. For example, sitting in prison writing *Mein Kampf* (1925/1943), Hitler could do little to realize his view and decree: 'German boy, do not forget you are a German,' and 'Little girl, remember that you are to become a German mother' (12). After the party's rise to power in 1933, the Nazis were quick to implement changes that would polarize men's and women's roles both in the party and in Germany as a whole.

According to Hitler, Germans must fight to safeguard the nation and 'race,' and 'every thought and every idea, and every doctrine and all knowledge, must serve this purpose' (1925/1943, 214). For example, he explained that 'marriage cannot be an end in itself, but must serve the one higher goal, the increase and preservation of the species and race. This alone is its meaning and task' (252). Once the party was in power, one of its main concerns regarding women was to convince them to become bearers of the future 'master race.' To this end, after 1933 they implemented policies of eugenic selection and control with a stronger element of coercion and regimentation than had ever been seen before in Germany.

Hitler made health and welfare pivotal to his pronatalist program. In this second phase, German women were encouraged to take pride in their womanly qualities of motherliness, loyalty, and self-sacrifice for family and nation (Quine, 1996). Nazi propaganda focused on the importance of women to the party's demographic campaign: men and women must have separate but complementary roles. Hitler was careful to stress that women were not inferior but rather, in their own way, equal: 'providence has entrusted to women the cares of that world which is peculiarly her own, and only on the basis of this smaller world can the man's world be formed and built' (Baynes, 1942, 528). He added: 'these two worlds are never in conflict. They are complementary to each other, they belong together as man and woman belong together' (528), but 'neither sex should try to do that which belongs to the other's sphere' (529). He argued that women were performing the equivalent of military service by risking their lives in childbirth (Evans, 1976). In this second phase, National Socialist family and gender policies directly addressed returning women to traditional, patriarchal gender roles, with the goal of boosting marriage and birth rates; a series of measures were introduced to that end.

Pronuptialism

Throughout the 1920s and 1930s Germany was in a peculiar demographic dilemma: the losses of the First World War had resulted in a sex ratio imbalance among citizens of marriageable age. Germany was said to be facing an 'impending shortage of parents' (Kirkpatrick, 1938, 151). National Socialists were quick to respond to this crisis by implementing policies to boost marriage rates in the hope of raising birth rates. Initially, the party used the sex ratio imbalance and a promise of finding husbands for women to draw female supporters to the party. Observers at the time noted that Hitler gained some of his support from young, single German women by promising them husbands. A feminist wrote: 'the young teacher, too, who used to come in the afternoons to look after my children, would certainly have supported anybody who promised her a husband; for that is what Hitler did, to her and her whole generation' (Thomas, 1943, 26). In an interview published in the *New York Times*, Hitler proudly boasted that his efforts were quite successful: 'the surplus of women is happily diminishing ... our aims encourage women to marry and stay home' (Baynes, 1942, 528). To assist them Hitler advocated early marriage and promised special marriage loans and better chances of promotion for engaged couples (Thomas, 1943).

The party set to work to increase marriage rates almost immediately after the election. Through the Unemployment Act of 1 June 1933, they offered interest-free marriage loans of up to 1,000 Reichsmarks (issued in the form of coupons for household goods) on the condition that the bride leave her job and not return until the loan was repaid. Although actual numbers vary, it was estimated that over 1 million couples received a marriage loan between 1933 and 1938 (Quine, 1996). As a further incentive, the loan was reduced by 25 per cent with the birth of each child: in other words, the loan repayment was cancelled when the couple had their fourth child. In effect, the party provided an economic incentive of 250 marks per child. The absolute number of children born to parents holding marriage loans grew from year to year, so that during 1936 there were 186,654 abatements for births to loan marriages. In that year, which marked the peak of the campaign's success, there were 108.8 abatements for each 100 loans (Kirkpatrick, 1938).

Not only was it designed to boost marriage, but the loan program was also part of the government's initiative to quicken the pace of the recovery from economic depression by reducing male unemployment (Quine, 1996). The fund to pay for the loans came partly from revenue collected from another pronuptial and pronatalist initiative: Germany's celibacy tax on unmarried men and women. In 1934 and 1939 the income tax laws were reformed, so that the income tax for childless couples as well as for single men and women was raised (Bock and Thane, 1991; Frevert, 1989). Himmler stated: 'those who believe they can escape their obligations to the nation and the race by remaining single will pay subscriptions [to the SS] at a level that will cause them to prefer marriage to bachelordom' (Henry and Hillel, 1977, 49). Other pro-birth family policies and material incentives to increase birth rates were implemented.

Pronatalism

German statisticians calculated that in 1933 births in Germany were 31 per cent below the estimated requirements for maintaining a constant population (Kirkpatrick, 1938). They estimated that, at the rate of reproduction in 1933, the 4 million inhabitants of Berlin would dwindle to a scanty 100,000 (ibid.), a prediction, in fact, that was impossible, since cities at the time were primarily maintained not by birth rates but by internal migration. As a result, an increase in births was one of the main goals of Nazi state welfare measures. Yet the government's goal was not simply to boost birth rates across all groups in Germany, but to promote the multiplication and preservation of the German 'race.'

In this phase of their campaign, Nationalist Socialists used both 'positive' and 'negative' measures to boost 'racially pure' birth rates.

The most obvious example of the regime's negative measures was the introduction of what became the most severe legislation against abortion and birth control in all of Europe (Quine, 1996). In May 1933 abortion became 'a crime against the race' and was punishable by a maximum sentence of fifteen years. Punishment became even harsher when, during the Second World War, special courts were established with the power to impose the death penalty for those who performed illegal abortions. Records show that a number of women who were convicted of being abortionists were indeed executed during the war (ibid.).

Other negative measures were introduced to establish and maintain a new racial order based on the idea that hierarchies of human worth existed. Some of these measures involved the systematic deprivation of individual reproductive rights and freedoms, including induced abortions for 'undesirable groups' (Quine, 1996). Thus, where pronatalist policies were implemented to boost birth rates of 'desirables,' antinatalist measures were introduced to limit and diminish birth rates among 'undesirables.' Nazis sought to encourage 'Aryans' to have large families and at the same time to prevent non-Aryans from procreating. The aim was to purify the blood of the German people by wiping out 'contaminants,' who included Jews, Gypsies, Russians, homosexuals, communists, and the mentally and physically ill (ibid.). In 1933 the government quickly passed a bill for the compulsory sterilization of the mentally and physically disabled, but there was nothing particularly 'Nazi' about the Third Reich's sterilization program: it was said to have been inspired by U.S. compulsory sterilization state laws of 1907 (ibid.). Canada also had a pervasive eugenics movement at the time (see McLaren, 1990).

Jews were especially targeted – particularly brutally after 1938. A nationwide pogrom began in earnest on 9 November 1938. The situation became more dire as the years passed. In the summer of 1941 the 'Führer's order' was issued to annihilate German Jews (Ayçoberry, 1999). Years before his rise to power, Hitler had written that 'the mightiest counterpart to the Aryan is represented by the Jew' (1925/1943, 300). During the Weimar Republic, Hitler spoke out fiercely against 'the ethical and moral contamination of the body politic' (Bleuel, 1973, 31). When he spoke of 'contamination,' he was often specifically referring to syphilis, which he believed was a typical Jewish disease, designed to debilitate the German people (ibid.). For example, Hitler wrote: 'with satanic joy in his face, the black-haired Jewish youth lurks in wait for the unsuspecting girl whom he defiles with his blood, thus stealing her from her people. With every means he tries to destroy the racial foundations of the people he has set out to subjugate' (1925/1943, 325). Consequently, according to Hitler, the miscegenation with Jews would result in the contamination of the German 'race': 'It [nature] shows with terrifying clarity that in every mingling of Aryan blood with that of lower peoples the result was the end of the cultured people' (286).

Once in power, Hitler implemented policies designed to ensure 'sexual hygiene,' a goal that had been clearly outlined years before throughout *Mein Kampf*. For example: 'For me and all true National Socialists there is but one doctrine: people and fatherland. *'What we must fight for is to safeguard the existence and reproduction of our race and our people, the sustenance of our children and the purity of our blood, the freedom and independence of the fatherland, so that our people may mature for the fulfilment of the mission allotted it by the creator of the universe'* (1925/1943, 214; original emphasis). Therefore, miscegenation was condemned and precluded, often through brutal means, including forced sterilization. The situation was quite different for those considered to be of the 'proper' racial stock: for them, the party used ideological and economic incentives to boost birth rates. Hitler declared: 'it is no degradation of woman that she should be a mother: that is her highest exaltation' (Baynes, 1942, 532). Furthermore, the party promoted the idea that the activities of women should be restricted to 'traditional womanly' (read 'motherly') pursuits. Comparing mothers to soldiers, Hitler declared that 'every child that a woman brings into the world is [equivalent to] a battle, a battle waged for the existence of her people' (529). To assist her, 'Mothers' Schools' were established to offer courses in household management and infant care, and some women even received training in 'racial science' courses (Quine, 1996). Also implemented was the Nazi Mother and Child Organization, part of the party's welfare services, through which the Nazi party claimed to have created 25,000 racial health centres by 1938, where over 10 million women had received eugenic advice. According to Hitler, 'the programme of our National Socialist Women has in truth but one single point, and that point is The Child' (Baynes, 1942, 530).

National Socialists thus promoted compulsory motherhood for 'valuable' German women and compulsory sterilization for those deemed unfit. They began by promoting the idea that there was joy in sacrifice, and the first sacrifice for women who worked outside the home was to give up their jobs and apply themselves to the business of being good wives and mothers. Through legislation limiting their employment, women were expected and encouraged to marry and bear children. A series of symbolic measures was promoted to encourage families to have many children. One psychological or symbolic incentive offered was to allow mothers who had nine children (or seven sons) to choose any official of the state to be the next child's godfather. By 1936 Hitler had over 12,000 such godchildren (Koonz, 1977).

On every Mother's Day racially pure and especially prolific women were given a medal of honour for their service to the nation. From year to year, on 12 August – the birthday of Hitler's own mother, which he designated Mother's Day – women with four to six children were granted a bronze Mother's Cross, those with six to eight were granted a silver, and those with more than eight children were given a gold. Female party members with many children were encouraged to wear special fertility runes or medals on their uniforms as signs of distinction (Quine, 1996). After 1939 all party youth who encountered these women on the street were required to salute them.

Symbolic and propagandistic measures also worked to lessen the stigma attached to illegitimate children and the women who bore them (Koonz, 1977). ('Illegitimate' children were already protected by the German Civil Code of 1896 and Sections 35–41 of the National Child Welfare Law of 9 July 1922; Friedlander and Myers, 1940.) One such measure included the establishment of the *Lebensborn* Registered Society on 12 December 1935. Although there is a great deal of controversy regarding the true nature of the *Lebensborn*, it was said to have been established by Himmler as a chain of medically supervised maternity homes for racially valued unmarried mothers. Once in the homes, unmarried mothers were given the right to change their names, were officially entitled to call themselves 'Frau' instead of 'Fräulein,' and were given the right to withhold the name of the child's father. All this was done to protect and respect the honour of the pregnant woman (Henry and Hillel, 1977). The message was that all racially pure children were valued and welcomed without stigma, shame, or fear being attached to the mother. Several hundred thousand women were said to have been involved in the organization in some way, and the figure of 12,000 births has been put forward (ibid.).

National Socialists also introduced economic measures to increase the number of 'legitimate' births; one such measure was tax reform in favour of Germans with large families. According to the tax law of 16 October 1934, deductions for the presence of children were raised.

Whereas having one child formerly reduced the family's total income tax by 8 per cent, the new law reduced its total income tax by 15 per cent; for two children it changed from 16 to 35 per cent (Kirkpatrick, 1938). Families with six children would receive a 100 per cent reduction in total income tax under the new legislation, compared with 48 per cent under the old tax laws. Similarly, new property tax laws granted an exemption of 10,000 marks for each child, and the inheritance tax exemption was raised from 5,000 to 30,000 marks for children in the family. Thus, new tax laws favoured families that were more prolific, but many of the subsidies further stipulated that parents had to be Aryan, of good character, and free from mental or bodily defects. On 24 March 1936, by a new decree, a continuous allowance of 10 marks per month for the fifth and later children up to the age of sixteen, was provided (Kirkpatrick, 1938), although it was limited to workers who earned less than 185 marks per month. About 237,000 families were affected by these grants.

Nazi Germany introduced other minor financial favours to large families, including allowing fathers of large families to pay lower contributions to the German Labour Front (fathers with seven children paid a rate four grades lower than their corresponding income; Kirkpatrick, 1938). Educational expenses and transportation rates on German railways were also reduced for parents with large families (ibid.; Quine, 1996), and salary promotions and tenure decisions favoured fathers of numerous children. The situation was very different for mothers.

The National Socialists seriously opposed female employment during the crisis of unemployment from 1930 to 1934. The Nazis took steps during 1933–5 to limit women's access to universities and the professions and to ensure that women's education was strongly biased towards 'female' subjects (Evans, 1976). From 1933 to 1937 the National Socialist attitude towards women and employment was clear and negative. Pierre Ayçoberry (1999) noted that 'the first item of business was to eliminate women from positions they had recently won within the elite of public officialdom and the liberal professions' (172). From the outset, the regime passed legislation against double-income families (Koonz, 1977). The state wanted to remove women from the paid labour force in order to free jobs for unemployed men; thus, in June 1933 legislation mandated the immediate dismissal of all women whose husbands were employed by the government (ibid.). From 1933 to 1936 other laws were passed to limit women's employment. For example, women doctors were allowed to practice only if they merged their practise with their physician husbands (Henry and Hillel, 1977), and women lawyers were removed from judgeships and high state offices. Similarly, women teachers were dismissed in favour of men (Koonz, 1977). New legislation allowed married women civil servants to be dismissed, discriminatory wage structures were prescribed, and prospects of promotion to senior positions were removed for women (Frevert, 1989). As a result, women's labour force participation dropped from 30 per cent in 1933 to 24 per cent in 1935 (Koonz, 1977). To prevent young women from entering the professions, quotas of 10 per cent were imposed on women candidates for higher education (ibid.). The Ministry of Education, which regulated elementary and secondary schooling, banned Latin classes for girls in the first five years of their schooling and banned science in the last three years, replacing these courses with domestic training and language courses (Ayçoberry, 1999).

After the Nazis took office in 1933, women's public roles were severely restricted. For example, while in the Weimar Republic there had been a record number of women in parliament, under the Nazis there were none (Quine, 1996). In this second phase, women gained no political power; efforts were made to remove them from public life; and motherhood, at least for some women, was viewed as their supreme role. After 1937 this state of affairs changed somewhat.

Phase 3. Nazi Attitudes and Policies: Women as Labourers

By 1936 Germany had experienced an economic upswing (Tröger, 1984), and in 1937 Hitler reversed his policy on women and employment, in preparation for the upcoming war. He called upon women to become mothers *and* factory workers, although he did so with some hesitation, since he preferred to have women committed to motherhood above all else. When the decision was made that women were needed as labourers, Hitler also announced that, as compensation, they would never have to work in factories again once the war was over (Ayçoberry, 1999). A series of measures was put in place to encourage women, especially mothers, to take paid employment, particularly after Germany had invaded Poland. For example, throughout most of the 1930s German women (like most women elsewhere) were paid about one-third less than their male counterparts. As women began performing the work of men who had been sent to active service, it became even more apparent that women were being treated unfairly and, unjustifiably, being paid less than men. Thus, in October 1939 the Labour Ministry ordered that women performing 'men's jobs,' such as train guards, bus and tram conductors, and electricity meter readers, would henceforth be paid 'men's wages' (Frevert, 1986).

When war broke out, there were calls for compulsory service for all adult German women, but it was not until the declaration of 'total war' in 1943 that all women aged seventeen to forty-five (later fifty) were obliged to report to the authorities, who would then establish their fitness and suitability for work (Frevert, 1989). Day nurseries and crèches in factories were strongly supported by local and national authorities, and large enterprises hired social workers to deal with personal and family problems of women factory workers (ibid.). All these and similar activities centred around the goal of assisting working wives and mothers in dealing with combining professional and family responsibilities.

By 1939, 6.2 million married women were in the workplace (2 million more than in 1933). At least 35 per cent of married women between the ages of fourteen and sixty-five were combining domestic duties with full-time employment (Frevert, 1989). The proportion of female public officials and blue- and white-collar workers in services, trade, and industry rose after that period. By 1938, when it also became apparent that the military and economic build-up would require more science and academic personnel than were currently being graduated from German universities, women were once again encouraged to study, especially in the humanities and medicine (ibid.). In terms of gaining access to the public sphere, women's situation appeared to be improving. On the other hand, it should not be forgotten that, even throughout the war, it was the 'high duty of German women and girls of good blood to become mothers' (Henry and Hillel, 1977, 39).

Resistance and Vilification of Objectors

The Nazi Party never strayed from its view that German women were expected to bear many children and socialize those children with faith in the Nazi state. Those who did not or could not do so were seen as enemies of the state, especially if they were otherwise deemed to be of good racial stock. There were a number of groups in Germany that were especially targeted as traitors to the cause. Two of those groups that were believed to be of 'good blood' but not performing their duty were 'emancipated' German women and homosexuals. One of the first campaigns against childlessness in which the Nazis engaged immediately after their accession to power was concentrated on the 'emancipated woman.' They included women who were too slim (they were believed to be unable to have many children), women exclusively devoted to their dogs (they were believed to be robbing their future children of love), and women who wore make-up (Henry and Hillel, 1977). Make-up was deemed un-German, and in Berlin women wearing make-up were accosted on buses as 'whores' or traitors (ibid.). Furthermore, emancipated women included middle-class and professional women: they saw their organizations and societies dissolved, their past vilified, and some of their cherished policies reversed under the Third Reich (Evans, 1976). One scholar wrote that the removal of feminism from the German political system 'found its final expression in the physical separation of the leading radical feminists from their homeland' (265). These women, who were said to have been for a long time 'swimming against the political tide,' left Germany and were in exile when the Nazis took over (Evans, 1976).

The campaign against homosexuality also began immediately following the Nazi rise to power in 1933 (Bleuel, 1973). The government distributed propaganda films and supplied youth leaders with prepared speeches on the subject. Repressive measures were taken, because the party was disturbed not so much by homosexual activity per se but by the childlessness that ensued (Henry and Hillel, 1977). The anti-homosexuality campaign was said to have been most vigorously pursued by and within the SS. For example, on 15 November 1941 Himmler decreed that he would lay down the death penalty for any member of the SS or police who engaged in homosexual acts (Bleuel, 1973). It is said that he ordered that his own nephew, SS Obersturmführer Hans Himmler, be 'liquidated' at Dachau for homosexuality (Henry and Hillel, 1977).

Nazi 'Successes' and Failures

In general, there is a great deal of controversy and debate about just how effective and/or detrimental the National Socialist policies on women and families were. Some have argued that Nationalism Socialism 'does not appear to be a "regression" into dark and distant days of discrimination against women' (Frevert, 1986, 250). On the other hand, there are those who believe that, despite what at times appear to be cultural gains, women in Nazi Germany always found themselves to be 'only privates in a civilian army commanded by Nazi men' (Koonz,

1977, 471). Despite considerable disagreement, what remains clear is that this was a unique period, which combined traditionalist tendencies and some novel opportunities and social welfare reforms for women and families. Secondly, it cannot be denied that the Nazi agenda in all its phases held almost absolute control over women's productive and reproductive powers (Tröger, 1984). But were the policies effective in implementing real change in birth rates and in women's status throughout the period?

General fertility rates went from 59 live births per 1,000 women in 1932 to 77 in 1934 (Quine, 1996). The crude birth rate jumped from 14.7 in 1933 to 18.0 in 1934 (Mitchell, 1992). The rates remained high until 1940 (Quine, 1996). At the same time, new tax breaks and favours to large families did not even begin to compensate for the actual cost of rearing children (Kirkpatrick, 1938). Purportedly designed to reduce child poverty, the regime's family allowance scheme was a failure, since few workers gained entitlements (Quine, 1996). Since it never provided parents with enough subsidies, it was a poor incentive to have large families.

The marriage rate did increase somewhat during the Third Reich. There were 15.7 marriages per 1,000 population in 1932; the rate peaked at 22.3 marriages in 1934, but declined between 1935 and 1938 (Mitchell, 1998). As a result, historians have cast doubt on the effectiveness of the marriage loan program, claiming that the marriages would have taken place without the loans (Quine, 1996). The loans themselves did not provide enough economic incentive, since the cost of raising children was not offset by the relatively small amount of financial aid offered (ibid.). The regime also promised but failed to make available a large number of cheap public housing projects in the major cities. In fact, the regime's management of the economy created price inflation, which negatively affected working-class families (ibid.).

Hitler's much publicized expulsion of women from paid work had minimal effects on the absolute number of women employed (Koonz, 1977). The early polemics of Nazis and non-Nazis against women's employment remained largely ineffective (Bock and Thane, 1991). Furthermore, although women could not expect to hold positions of power within the Third Reich, they could aspire to status within the women's bureaucracy. In fact, women were encouraged to belong to one of the women's organizations or services. Clearly, the Nazis separated society into masculine and feminie spheres – and women's spheres were inferior – but the party did create civil service opportunities for women. As a result, in 1935 one out of every ten civil servants was a woman (Koonz, 1977), in part through a policy by which every community with a population of over 3,500 was assigned a full-time paid director of women's affairs. Consequently, about 18,500 communities in Germany had a head of home economics. In addition to these full-time salaried officials, part-time and volunteer workers totalled 2.7 million women by 1935 (ibid.). Furthermore, despite National Socialist attempts to limit the number of female doctors, the newly established organizations designed to assist mothers and children created many jobs for women in the medical profession (Ayçoberry, 1999). Thus, while they sought to curb women's paid employment and return women to the home, the Nazis also created jobs for many of them.

A Recapitulation

Following the First World War, Germany was in a peculiar situation: in the midst of an economic and demographic crisis, it had lost the war, a large portion of its population, and its national dignity. According to Koonz (1981), after November 1918 'nearly two million German soldiers did not return from the front, but six million did, some alienated and others rebellious, but all of them needing jobs' (26). At the same time, the Weimar Republic promoted one of the most socially advanced political platforms in Europe, protecting and advancing the rights and needs of its citizens through a slate of solid social welfare initiatives. Women, in particular, were among the benefactors of the new reforms. They obtained the right to vote and hold office and were granted more sexual freedom and control over their own bodies, and working women were protected by new labour codes. However, many of the new reforms and social welfare initiatives became economically difficult to maintain and demanded profound social change, which many Germans simply would not accept.

Many sought to stem the tide of 'decadence' that they feared was engulfing society. After the National Socialists formed the government, efforts were made to reverse some of the changes, including changes and/or advancements to the status of women in German society. During at least part of their regime, Nazi leaders sought to return 'Aryan' women to their 'natural place' in the homes – as wives and mothers – all the while hoping to alleviate male unemployment. In their brief time in power, National Socialists changed their position on the 'woman question' several times. What remained consistent throughout their mandate was that 'Aryan' women would be used (as party supporters, as workers, as mothers, or as both mothers and workers) for the sake of the nation and that they should have no control or influence on policy-making. Women lost the political power and autonomy they had acquired only a few years before, under the Weimar Constitution. In return, they gained some degree of social status and protection as mothers, although these benefits were limited to those of the 'correct' racial stock.

Some have found it difficult to describe National Socialism as a purely antifeminist movement, since it promoted equal status for unwed mothers and improved maternity benefits (Evans, 1976). As a matter of fact, as historian Richard Evans (1976) stated, 'five years of Nazi rule did more in some ways to help professional women than a decade of feminist pressure in the Weimar Republic' (263). The German Women's Association (Bund Deutscher Frauenvereine – BDF) and other women's groups would not agree. What remains uncontested is that policies and practices that were initiated during the Nazi regime in Germany were implemented without consulting women or granting them a voice on the matter (Koonz, 1977).

3

Nationalism in the Interwar Period: Italy

The Political and Economic Situation Prior to the Rise of Fascism

The First World War highlighted a fracture in the Italian political system. From August 1914 to May 1915 a struggle took place between those who wanted intervention in the war and those who advocated neutrality (DeGrand, 2000; Mussolini, 1928/1998). The interventionists won, and Italy entered what many believed would be a short, victorious war. Instead, over three and a half years, Italy mobilized 5.7 million soldiers, mostly peasants who became part of the infantry. These peasants absorbed 95 per cent of Italian casualties (DeGrand, 2000) and, as a result, felt extremely angry and bitter.

The war split Italy's political parties and citizenry. It revived past woes that dated back to Italian unification, as the ideas behind unification clashed with the practical reality of implementing them. It has been argued that Italian unification in 1870 was the result, at least in part, of the demand for internal reforms 'of a liberal nature' within various Italian states (Albrecht-Carrié, 1966, 28). Mazzini, one of the 'fathers' of Italian unification, who was said to have been interested in 'humanity at large,' believed that nations should be free, and, once free, that their peoples would work in 'harmonious association' (35). His as well as Cavour's and Garibaldi's ideas on unification and liberty resulted in the creation of a new Italy (Albrecht-Carrié, 1966), but this beginning was plagued by financial problems. Nonetheless, they pushed ahead with reforms to local government, education, and social programs (ibid.). For example, Giovanni Giolitti (1904, 1990), reporting to the king on his first year in office, provided a long list of reforms and expenses for among other things, 'the economic transformation of the region of

Basilicata, for the economic and industrial revival of Naples, the transformation of communal debts in the continental portions of the South, and for the prompt construction of aqueducts in Apulia' (23). Italy was also financing extensive militarization and war with Turks in Tripoli, even before the First World War.

While Italy was experiencing many losses in the wars of the period, the Italian parliament made promises of land reform and territorial gains in the Balkans and Africa to pacify soldiers and increase morale. When the First World War ended, promises were broken and unrest ensued; Italian politicians then faced the serious problem of restoring social control over urban and rural working classes (DeGrand, 2000), not an easy task at the time. Italian colonialism had brought few economic rewards, and following the war, Italians suffered from 'an inferiority complex.' The post-unitary and post-war Italian state was seen as 'impotent,' while political life was seen as 'atrophied' and 'morbid' (Quine, 1996). The unprofitable and very costly colonial campaigns and the First World War exposed a 'latent paralysis' in the entire parliamentary system (28). The effect of the war on Italy's economy and society was dramatic: between 1915 and 1918 industrial production expanded rapidly, yet by the end of 1919, after demobilization, unemployment rose sharply to 2 million (DeGrand, 2000). As a result, large segments of the Italian population no longer responded to traditional means of political control: 'The links that held liberal Italy together began to break' (19; Thurlow, 1997). Mussolini (1928/1998) noted: 'the years 1919 and 1920 that immediately followed the end of the war seemed to me the darkest and most painful periods of Italian life'; he added that 'the progress of Italy's unification was threatened ... we were left without any cohesive force, any suggestive heroism, any remembrance, any political philosophy, sufficient to overcome and stop the factors of dissolution' (59, 60). He concluded: 'a sense of humiliation had crawled over our whole peninsula' (76).

Fascism provided an entirely new alternative to suppressing social unrest by creating a private army alongside the existing state apparatus. It did so by mobilizing some of the discontented parties: young officers, students, and professionals in cities and towns; estate managers, small farmers, and some share croppers in the rural areas (DeGrand, 2000). 'Most people who accepted Mussolini at first were interested in restoration of law and order, not in squadrism, syndicalism, or demagogic nationalism' (Tannenbaum, 1972, 43).

The Demographic Situation

From the early 1800s to the Second World War, the European population grew rapidly, from about 200 million to over 500 million, although
the growth was not shared evenly across the continent (Ipsen, 1996). It
should be noted, however, that this growth was a result of declining
mortality, especially in infancy and childhood, rather than of increasing
fertility rates. In fact, after 1914 many European countries feared a loss
of population due to war (Quine, 1996) and declining family size.
Following the First World War it was said that Europe experienced a
'demographic shock' (Ipsen, 1996, 26). However, owing to its still predominately rural economic base, especially in the quasi-feudal south,
Italy's population growth was greater than that of Britain and France. In
1920 its birth rate peaked at 32.2 births, compared with Germany's 25.9,
Spain's 29.5, and England's 25.5 (Mitchell, 1992). Nonetheless, there
was a widely held belief that the Italian population was under threat of
decline and that population growth was essential for nationalization,
mobilization, and industrialization (Detragiache, 1980; Quine, 1996).
Another major source of concern in Italy was migration. At the time,
'Italy became historically the single greatest national exporter of population' (Ipsen, 1996, 21). On the eve of the First World War, Italy faced
continued declines in mortality and fertility, massive emigration, industrialization, and urbanization. Despite considerable debate across
Europe on the population problem, few of the proposed demographic
measures advanced beyond the planning stage in the pre-war period.
The situation changed after 1918.

Women before Fascism

Much like other European statesmen at the time, Italy's leaders hardly
ever spoke of Italian women and women's issues before the First World
War (DeGrazia, 1992). Patriarchal attitudes were enshrined in law. For
example, after Italy's unification (in 1859–60), by law men enjoyed
economic and civil rights denied to women. Italian legislation del-
egated all authority to male heads of households – wives were obliged
to take their husbands' names and reside with them. Women were
under the guardianship of men (Birnbaum, 1986). They were barred
from most commercial and legal acts and from contracting debts or
writing cheques (DeGrazia, 1992). Adultery was an offence for women

but not for men, and courts often annulled marriages if the husband claimed that his wife had not been a virgin on her wedding day (Pugh, 1997). On the other hand, in 1861 Italian women accounted for over half (57 per ent) of the total industrial labour force (Istituto Centrale di Statistice, 1968), while elsewhere in Europe governments passed factory laws and pension reforms to allegedly protect the welfare of women and children and remove them from the labour force. In contrast, since Italy was a relatively 'late industrializer' in Europe, Italian industries continued to depend on women as a source of cheap labour (DeGrazia, 1992).

In the early 1900s about one-third of Italian women, aged fourteen to sixty-five were active in the economy (Istituto Centrale di Statistice, 1968); in 1901 this amounted to a total of 5.385 million adult women. They made up 35 per cent of those working in Italy's industries (ibid.). Italy ranked fourth among industrialized nations at the time in its use of female labour (DeGrazia, 1993). It was only later, as Italian industries developed more rapidly, that the number of women active outside the home began to decrease, except in the rapidly expanding textile industry (Birnbaum, 1986). On the eve of the First World War, women still made up about one-third of the workforce; that is, in 1911 the number dropped somewhat to 5.234 million adult women active in all sectors of Italy's economy, but still made up about 30 per cent of the total. In the industrial sector, the number dropped about 5 per cent, to 30.5 per cent of the labour force (Istituto Centrale di Statistice, 1968), but this was still significant for the time.

It was in this setting, at the end of the nineteenth century, that Italian feminism emerged. The first to speak of women's emancipation were working-class and lower-middle-class women – mainly factory workers, clerks, and teachers who were committed to socialism. This was but one of three main branches of feminism that emerged at the time, whose common goals were civil rights for women but that differed in their purpose, tactics, and attachment to male-dominated associations (DeGrazia, 1992). Thus, along with the salaried, socialist women's organizations, a second group of Catholic women emerged, who separated themselves from the secular women's groups, because of differing opinions on divorce, suffrage, and the church's role in schools. The third branch involved several smaller groups of lay, bourgeois women who later, in the fascist era, came to be known as the 'old feminism' (ibid.).

At the onset of the First World War, these branches were profoundly divided as they found themselves bombarded by critics. High unemployment rates fractured the labour movement and socialist feminists came under attack (DeGrazia, 1992). Frightened by working-class radicalism, middle-class feminists turned away from some women's associations. Furthermore, moral zealots launched campaigns against the degeneration of family life, blaming declining birth rates on urbanization, women's emancipation, and neo-Malthusian birth control practices (ibid.). By the time the Fascist Party came to power, there was ample anti-emancipationist sentiment to legitimate the anti-feminist politics that would ensue.

Early Fascist Policies on Women

In Milan, on 23 March 1919 a new political movement, the Fasci di Combattimento, was founded by the formerly socialist newspaper editor, Benito Mussolini. (The name, meaning 'bundle or bands of struggle,' is derived from the Roman symbol, a bundle of rods, representing strength in unity.) It was said that fascism began as a continuation of leftist interventionism or 'national syndicalism' of the war era (DeGrand, 2000). According to Carl Ipsen (1996), fascism, especially at the outset, was a combination of radical nationalism and revolutionary syndicalism. As a matter of fact, in its early years fascism appeared to be attuned to feminist aspirations. For example, its program of 1919 called for extension of the vote to women and eighteen-year-old men, a new republican constitution, an eight-hour day, and worker participation in management (DeGrand, 2000). In the first two years of his ministry, Mussolini reiterated in speeches his intention to extend voting privileges to women. On 15 May 1925, fascists actually passed a law granting a limited number of women the right to vote in local elections – women decorated for special services to Italy, mothers and widows of war dead, heads of households, those who had a university degree, or those who paid annual taxes (Noether, 1982). Unfortunately, these women did not get a chance to cast their ballots, because subsequent laws in February and September 1926 abolished local elections outright.

When Mussolini came to power, he declared: 'I was anxious to improve, refine and co-ordinate the character of Italians' (1928/1998, 206). However, this 'co-ordination' took root and developed not in large industrial or industrializing towns and cities, but rather in the countless small towns throughout rural Italy where fascism took hold. As a result, it developed as an agrarian reaction against socialist peasant leagues (DeGrand, 2000). Consequently, both Mussolini and the Fascist Party ceded their early position and slid to the political right, abandoning revolutionary socialism.

After coming to power, especially after 1925, 'political, economic, and social stresses propelled Fascism towards an ever more conservative view of women's place in society' (Noether, 1982, 70). At first, the regime appeared to herald a new style of welfarism especially devoted to the protection of women and children. For example, in 1925, ONMI – Opera Nazionale per la Protezione della Maternità ed Infanzia (National Organization for the Protection of Motherhood and Infancy) – was created. ONMI promised to build clinics, nurseries, soup kitchens, and milk dispensaries, and to mobilize new doctors and social workers to care for and educate the public on health and nutrition. ONMI was pivotal in medicalizing childbirth and publicizing new standards of prenatal and post-partum care. They were expected to prevent unwed mothers from aborting or giving birth under clandestine conditions (DeGrazia, 1992). ONMI was also charged with the responsibility of assisting unwed mothers in raising their children. As the cost of administering support services to mothers and children increased and became unmanageable, the Fascist Party sought to make childbearing seem as if it were in the service of the state, with one of the main forms of compensation offered to women being public recognition. Fascist policies increasingly emphasized the traditional role of women as mothers and promoted the idea that women must be brought back to their natural place: in the home (Birnbaum, 1986). Saraceno (1991) argued that though the explicit aim of Fascist measures was population increase, the immediate target was 'the structure of family relationships and the distribution of power and authority in the family' (196). By 1927 Mussolini's transition towards an increasingly conservative position, particularly regarding the roles of women and the family was clear and complete.

On 26 May 1927 Mussolini issued what has come to be known as the Ascension Day Speech, in which he outlined his attempt to deal with Italy's demographic 'problem,' linking it to the country's political and economic health and future. He asked the nation to confront itself and its 'problem' of population decline. It should be noted, however, that at this point Italy's demographic 'problem' was no more severe than that of other countries. His was clearly a nationalist reaction. He declaimed that Italy's demographic strength constituted the basis of the nation's political, economic, military, and moral strength (Mussolini, 1964a).

Mussolini blamed two factors for Italy's demographic decline: industrial urbanism and small property holdings, which gave rise to the fear that having several children would lead to the eventual division of already small land holdings. Mussolini stated: 'there is a type of urbanism that is destructive, that sterilizes the people, and it is called industrial urbanism' (366; my translation). He lamented that if the population declined, Italy not only would have to give up its goal of becoming an empire, but would end up a colony instead. Mussolini boasted that there were 5,700 institutions across the country committed to assisting mothers and their children, but since he lacked the funds to adequately support them, he intended to impose a celibacy tax on bachelors to raise funds for those institutions and encourage population growth. Mussolini believed that twelve children was the ideal for a family (Birnbaum, 1986); therefore, in the years that followed, other measures were introduced designed to boost fertility rates.

Mussolini further outlined his population policies and demographic concerns a year later when he published an article in his newspaper, *Il Popolo d'Italia*, entitled 'Il Numero come forza' (Strength in Numbers), in which he demonstrated that he considered fertility to be a political force – an important resource and weapon to be used for fascist Italy's political resurgence. Mussolini believed that the remedy for the demographic 'problem' lay in a spiritual transformation facilitated by appropriate population policies, including the suppression of birth control, public assistance to mothers and children, and reversal of female emancipation (Mussolini, 1964b). He closed his article with an appeal to fascist families:

And so my discourse is directed squarely at Fascists and Fascist families. This challenge is the purest touchstone against which the conscience of Fascist generations will be measured. We must determine whether or not the spirit of Fascist Italy is irreparably infected with hedonistic, bourgeois, and Philistine values. The birth rate is not simply an index of the progressive power of the nation; it is not simply as Spengler suggests, 'Italy's only weapon'; it is also that which will distinguish the Fascist people from the other peoples of Europe as an index of vitality and the will to pass on this vitality over the centuries. If we do not succeed in reversing this trend, all that the Fascist revolution has accomplished and will accomplish in the future will be perfectly useless, as at a certain point in time fields, schools, barracks, ships, and workshops will be empty. (216)

The Fascists equated declining birth rates with an overall crisis of national vitality. These speeches reveal that the Fascists under Mussolini believed large rural families would offset the trend towards declining birth rates, which was especially apparent in Italy's northern cities. Historians have noted that for the Fascists, urban areas were equated with the vices of individualism, consumerism, and feminism, which the party blamed for the declining birthrates (Quine, 1996).

Fascist Ideology Put into Practice

Fascist ideology is fraught with contradictions. For example, Mussolini stated: 'we shall combat every retrograde idea, technical or spiritual' (Mussolini, 1933, 9); at the same time, he was highly critical of industrialization, especially because it inevitably led to urbanization, and urbanization, he believed, contributed to declining birth rates. As a result, the Fascists promoted an especially anti-modern ruralism (Quine, 1996). For Mussolini, industrial urbanization brought with it 'sterilization of the population' (1964a, 367). His population policies were therefore a response to this phenomenom, policies that carried with them rigid and traditional attitudes towards the roles of women and men in society. Fascist policies sought to re-establish a so-called natural hierarchy between the sexes. In reconstructing Italy's national identity, Mussolini directly repudiated pacifism, promoting instead a form of macho militarism often demonstrated in his speeches with statements like: 'war alone brings up to its highest tension all human energy and puts the stamp of nobility upon the peoples who have the courage to meet it' (1933, 11).

Fascist militarist and pronatalist ideologies often described the Italian 'race' in terms such as 'noble,' 'warrior,' and 'virile.' Men were expected to fill their assigned role as fearless warriors, while women were expected to fill their allotted mission as 'angels of the hearth,' having babies and sacrificing their sons for the nation. Fascist ideology depended greatly on these myths and symbols. That is, the Italian state was destined to triumph and overcome all existing problems, including what was perceived as a demographic problem, if men and women did their part. Men and women should make up two separate, distinct, and complementary parts of the Italian national whole. This dichotomy is evident in Mussolini's observation: 'Fascism, now and always believes in holiness and in heroism' (1933, 13) – presumably women's holiness and men's heroism. As a matter of fact, when the Fascists introduced a national celebration of Mother's Day, they chose Christmas Eve, 24 December, in order to exploit the Catholic cult of the Virgin Mary and to associate motherhood with the Virgin's chastity and sacrifice of her only son (DeGrazia, 1992).

When Mussolini initiated his population policies, his goals were to increase the size of the population and to support a particular notion of family, in contrast the Nazis, whose aim was to improve the 'purity' of Germany's racial stock. While he did state that Italians should take seriously the 'destiny of the race' and begin 'curing the race,' his real emphasis was on increasing its numbers (1964a, 363–4). In one of his speeches he stated: 'let's speak openly: what are forty million Italians compared to ninety million Germans and two hundred million Slavs? ... The fact is that the future of nations is tied to their demographic power ... [thus] the ideal would be: maximum natality, minimum mortality' (364, 365, 366). Furthermore, although he did claim that the 'entire white race can become subsumed by the coloured races [later he specifically mentioned "Blacks" and "Yellows"] that multiply at a more rapid rate than ours' (210), Mussolini initially ridiculed Nazi race policies. He described them as 'one hundred percent racism. Against everything and everyone: yesterday against Christian civilization, today against Latin civilization, tomorrow, who knows, against the civilization of the whole world ... drunk with stubborn bellicosity ... We shall see whether Nazism succeeds in making a pure-blooded "herd." According to the most favourable hypothesis ... one needs six centuries of racial marriages and not less of racial castrations' (1964c, 233; cited in Nolte, 1969, 291). After years of failed attempts to boost Italian birth rates, however, he conceded that the German nation was positively responding to racist appeals.

By the outbreak of the Second World War, Mussolini had commissioned a number of people, including Paolo Orano, to develop a Fascist race ideology. Much of it was built upon anti-Semitism. For example, during the war Mussolini began to speak of 'a world sickness caused by demoplutocracy and Judaism' that must be 'cured by fire and sword' (Nolte, 1969, 308). Nonetheless, it was noted by historians that what was 'entirely absent' in Mussolini's population policies 'was the tendency to classify the body of the nation according to its hereditary biological values, and to declare the progeny of considerable sections of the population to be undesirable' (480). Mussolini continued to press for improving the quantity of Italians, rather than the 'quality of the race,' and when he did speak of improving 'quality,' it was often through promoting the importance of physical fitness (1964a, 361; Frasca, 1983).

In a number of speeches he and other Fascists extolled the virtues of a fecund rural Italy. In their quest to make procreation appear to be a patriotic duty, Fascist youth, particularly boys, were taught to believe, obey, fight, and procreate (Ipsen, 1996). In addition to promoting a pronatalist ideology, a series of proactive measures was introduced in parliament to 'assist' Italy's demographic development. They set a path towards an expected demographic 'success' through a series of concrete pronuptialist and pronatalist policies and practices.

Pronuptialism

Mussolini and Fascist parliamentarians became consumed by demographic statistics and the demographic health of the nation. They spoke about Italy's demographic health as one of the greatest possible disasters of the nation's future. Naturally, they felt inclined to respond to this potential threat with a series of preventative and proactive policies, including pronuptialist measures and initiatives that involved, among other things, a bachelor tax on unmarried men, a levy borrowed from antiquity, when it had been imposed by Emperor Augustus. Effective 1 January 1927, the bachelor – or celibacy – tax was intended to act as an inducement to marriage and to redistribute national income towards families with many children. In his Ascension Day Speech Mussolini (1964a) made direct reference to it, explaining that not only would the tax be used to finance thousands of institutions designed to assist mothers and their children, but it would jump-start or 'whip' the nation's population into action. The tax was calculated on the basis of age and income and was especially hard on men age thirty-five to fifty. In this age group, it amounted to a 25 per cent surcharge on income tax, in addition to a flat rate annually levied (Quine, 1996). Only priests and soldiers were exempt. The bachelor tax was increased in 1928 and again in 1934 and 1936. For example, in 1936 a thirty-year-old bachelor was expected to pay twice the normal income tax, plus 155 lire per year (DeGrazia, 1992), and the tax was applied in the Italian colonies (Ipsen, 1996). Bachelors also were discriminated against in the workplace: hiring and promotional preference were given to married men, especially those with children.

Another important measure was the creation of marriage loans. Newlywed couples, where both partners were under the age of twenty-six and had a combined income of under 12,000 lire, were eligible for loans that ranged from 1,000 to 3,000 lire (Ipsen, 1996). Repayment of the loans would begin six months after the wedding day unless the woman became pregnant. After the birth of the first child, 10 per cent of the loan would be cancelled and its repayment would be put off by one year. Each subsequent pregnancy would result in further postponement and cancellation of the debt: an additional 20 per cent would be cancelled with the birth of the second child, 30 per cent with the birth of the third, and 40 per cent with the birth of the fourth child. By having four children in a period of six and a half years, a couple could avoid repayment altogether (ibid.). The Fascists also legislated a fifteen-day marriage leave for newlywed workers and in 1932 introduced train fare reductions for honeymoon trips (ibid.).

Pronatalism

A series of other pronatalist initiatives was introduced throughout the period of Fascist rule. Many of the measures were symbolic, having to do with the granting of fertility prizes and medals. Using a series of pseudo-scientific arguments, women were declared biologically and genetically superior to men and honoured for these qualities (Noether, 1982). For example, as mentioned above, in 1932 the Fascists established a national holiday, to be celebrated on Christmas Eve, to honour motherhood and infancy (Quine, 1996). Other awards and incentives were monetary, amounting to family subsidies, tax exemptions, privileges, and other rewards. In general, fertility prizes were awarded for each birth – clearly, multiple births received the higher rewards. A 1928 law granted tax exemptions to state workers who had at least seven dependent children (under age twenty-one) or to non-state workers who had at least ten dependent children. It was estimated that there were about 30,000 state workers and 100,000 non-state workers who qualified for the exemptions (Ipsen, 1996). These tax exemptions were followed by other laws, which graduated income tax according to family size and gave hiring and promotional preference to married men with large families.

Employment

In 'defence of the stock,' measures were also put in place to aid working women, which included the 1929 establishment of maternity leave and insurance. Maternity leave was mandatory for a two-month period – one month before and one month after the birth. The pregnant woman's job was guaranteed, and upon her return to work she was allowed breaks for nursing (Ipsen, 1996). Out-of-work mothers qualified for unemployment insurance benefits, and in 1936 maternity insurance was expanded to include agricultural workers, though payments were comparatively low. Despite the apparent benefits to women, these measures increased the cost of female labour to employers, making them less desirable as workers and therefore less likely to be hired in the first place.

While the Fascists appeared to assist women workers with one hand, the other hand was busy promoting policies that sought to remove women from the workplace. In general, the Fascists believed that paid work distracted women from their true and natural calling as mothers and caused male unemployment (note that by then the depression was affecting many parts of Europe). In 1934 Mussolini (1964c) wrote: 'today, machines and women are two major causes of unemployment ... The departure of women from the labour force would undoubtedly have an economic repercussion on many families, but legions of men would raise their humiliated heads ... and hundreds of new families would immediately become part of the nation's life' (311). As a result, there was a push for the gradual elimination of women from offices, factories, and schools. Beginning in 1923, various laws were passed to restrict the number of women employed by the state. In December 1926 a law was passed preventing women from teaching Italian, Latin, Greek, philosophy, history, and political science in secondary schools (Noether, 1982), and in 1933 women were barred from competing in civil service examinations. While such restrictive laws were being put in place, preference in employment to fathers of large families was also introduced (DeGrand, 2000). Furthermore, in 1938 the Fascists attempted to curtail the employment of women by setting a quota of 10 per cent in both public and private enterprises (DeGrand, 2000), and women employees were excluded completely from offices or businesses with fewer than ten employees (Noether, 1982). This law allowed a three-year grace period for phasing women out of the labour force, but before the three years were up, Italy was at war and women filled the vacancies created by enlistment and conscription.

Moral Hygiene and Compulsory Heterosexuality

As the Fascist regime pushed to boost the size of Italy's population, it also sought to safeguard the 'morality of the race,' introducing in 1923 a series of measures to encourage 'moral hygiene.' They effectively extended state control over private life by launching a battle against alcoholism; the trafficking of drugs; venereal diseases; white slavery; and sexual deviance, including pornography, the use of sex toys and contraceptives, and homosexuality (Quine, 1996). The penal code of 1931 outlawed homosexual acts among men (DeGrazia, 1992). Women intellectuals were especially targeted, portrayed as hysterical, perverted, sterile, masculinized, or homosexual (Pickering-Lazzi, 1995). There was also a battle against obscene speech and jokes and the telling of demeaning jokes about Mussolini's baldness or weight (Quine, 1996). By 1926 the sale of contraceptives was banned, since it was seen as an offence against public decency (Durham, 1998).

Italians also saw conservative changes to their abortion laws. After the unification of Italy and the establishment of the Zanardelli Code of 1889, abortion was decriminalized (although it remained illegal and resulted in harsh sentences if performed late in the pregnancy; Quine, 1996). Under Fascism, the state banned abortion, the sale of contraceptive devices, and sex education (DeGrazia, 1992). Article 545 of the Penal Code of 1930/31 (the Rocco Code) prescribed heavy penalties, including jail terms of two to five years, for anyone procuring or abetting abortion and one to four years for women who actually performed abortions (Detragiache, 1980; DeGrazia, 1992). Doctors were ordered to report and register all pregnancies, to ensure abortions would not take place, since abortion came to be seen as an offence against the race and the state. The 1942 Civil Code further reinforced this view and the notion of the Italian family as a social and political institution (Saraceno, 1991).

Resistance to Fascist Policies and Vilification of Objectors

Women, especially mothers, were used as signifiers of Fascist ideology: representing life and death; past, present, and future glory of the nation; morality, chastity, and duty. Feminism, on the other hand, was perceived as a threat to this ideology, since it was seen as sanctioning individualistic propensities that would encourage women to withhold reproductive services from the Italian nation (DeGrazia, 1992). Mussolini was said to dislike 'society women' who pampered their dogs instead of having babies. As a result, he prohibited all newspapers from publishing photos of women with dogs (Tannenbaum, 1972). Women's magazines at the time, such as *Il giornale della donna* (*The Woman's*

Journal), worked to promote Fascist views on women, to delegitimize more modern or feminist views, and to induce women to rethink their true vocations, since feminism had dragged women into a crisis of identity (Graziosi, 1995). Their recurring message was clear: female citizens could become real women only if they stayed home and filled their prescribed roles as mothers, wives, sisters, and daughters (ibid.). It is not clear how many Italian women complied and to what degree.

Some have argued that no real form of feminist resistance actually developed in Italy under Fascism (DeGrazia, 1992), but not all agree. It was a woman who attempted to assassinate Mussolini on 7 April 1926. More subtly, there developed a kind of resistance to Fascist models of gender at the local level (Re, 1995). It is true that many, including women, welcomed the new measures imposed by the Fascists, but there were those who were clearly opposed to them and challenged the image of the 'new' Italian woman through avant-garde and experimental literature (ibid.). Furthermore, there were thousands of invisible dissenters who purchased the tens of thousands of copies of dissident novels and poetry published (and banned by Fascist censors) at the time. One such novel was Alba De Cespedes's (1938) *No Turning Back*, which challenged the prevailing construction of gender and by December 1940 had gone through nineteen editions (Gallucci, 1995). The novel, which included a series of narratives about the complex and diverse lives of its eight female protagonists, challenged women's oppression in the regime and outlined tactics used by the protagonists to subvert rules (ibid.). Other authors and poets wrote and published along the same lines.

Aside from those who expressed their dissent through published material, other women had the courage to voice their concerns directly to Mussolini. My own cursory analysis of a collection of published letters sent to him from 'average' Italian women reveals that some of them included attacks and critiques of the man himself. Although by far most letters were in support of Mussolini's policies and actions, several brave women wrote of their discontent with him and with Fascism. I translate some of their words below.

On 15 June 1940 Lina Romani wrote: 'You inconsiderate one! He who bears a sword will perish by the sword. The blood of many innocent people will pour onto You and your children' (Cederna, 1989, 146). Similarly, Enza N. From Palermo, Sicily, wrote on 28 June 1942: 'Do you not quiver in horror at Yourself for all that you have done? ... What are you waiting for, Duce, to shed a tear on your poor Italy?' (96). Some even openly criticized racial and demographic policies. For example, in December 1938 Dina M. wrote: 'Shame! To the scientists that have discovered the "true Italian race" and to those of you who thought up the measures for the defence of the race. I am still in disbelief and I rest upon the hope that you have not yet realized the monstrosities you are creating in people's minds and actions, which will inevitably have huge consequences and which will painfully divide our large Italian family' (49). These critical voices were few, but they wrote frankly and directly to Mussolini about the hardships he and his policies were creating. It should be of some consolation to these dissenters that, in hindsight, many of Mussolini's policies and practices did not succeed in achieving their goals.

Fascist 'Successes' and Failures

Over the years of Fascist rule, it can be said that one of the biggest accomplishments for women was the establishment of a new respect and dignity for mothers, although much was purely symbolic and ideological. Practically speaking, despite the many efforts by the Fascists to boost birth rates and change the demographic course of the nation, pronatalist policies and initiatives failed. Birth rates continued to decline steadily throughout the period, with only a few years of exceptions: they decreased from 1920 to 1925, increased slightly in 1926 and 1927, but dropped again in 1928 and 1929 (Mitchell, 1998). They remained low throughout the 1930s, and the average number of children per marriage never returned to the 1930 level (3.61 births per marriage; ibid.). In sum, there appeared to be consecutive declines in fertility rates from 1920 to 1937, with the exception of 1926 and 1927, when incentive and punitive pronatalist legislation was first introduced, and 1930, immediately following the introduction of maternity leave insurance (ibid.). Slight increases also occurred in the late 1930s (1938–40), but they were attributable not to the success of Fascist pronatalist policies but largely to the post-Ethiopia demobilization. Fertility rates declined soon after. In fact, numerous authors have commented on the failure of specific pronatalist policies. For example, Quine (1996) declared that the celibacy tax 'proved to be unsuccessful' (41). Similarly, Ipsen (1996) noted that the marriage loan program got off to a rough start, since it became yet another expense imposed on provincial governments that the national government did not reimburse.

Furthermore, there was no wholesale withdrawal of women from paid employment – only a small, temporary decline in the proportion (Tannenbaum, 1972). In fact, overall, after Mussolini's rise to power the number of women working in the industrial sector of the Italian economy increased steadily. Clearly, the proportion of jobs held by women in that sector was declining, dropping from 56.6 per cent female in 1861 to about 20 per cent female in 1951 (Istituto Centrale di Statistice, 1968), but this decrease can also be attributed to the rapid growth in the number of men in that sector, not solely to the decline in the number of women. Nonetheless, it should be noted that the proportion of women never declined to the desired and legislated 10 per cent. The almost constant warfare in which Italy was involved after 1935 (its invasion of Abyssinia/Ethiopia in 1935, its aid to Spanish fascists in 1937, its attack on Albania soon after, and its entry into the Second World War in 1940) minimized the impact of the repressive laws designed to limit the number of women in paid labour. As a result, the laws never really became operative, since women continued to be called upon to fill jobs in the paid labour force.

In retrospect, Fascist pronatalist policies did little to stave off declining birth rates, since Italy's demographic decline mirrored that of other developed countries in the early twentieth century, including those that did not implement such policies (Ipsen, 1996). Fascist attempts to return women to the hearth and home were equally unsuccessful. As a matter of fact, some have argued that Fascist politics and policies actually inadvertently helped women to gain access to the public sphere. For example, although women were specifically barred from taking any political initiatives under Fascism, they were expected to attend meetings and rallies to support the movement, to undertake charitable work, to promote propaganda, to assist the sick and wounded, and to serve as godmothers to newly founded *Fasci di Combattimento* (DeGrazia, 1992). For the first time in modern history, Italian women were mobilized en masse into party cadres and were actually being urged to attend party rallies (Noether, 1982). Furthermore, the Catholicization of Italian civic life also contributed to the growth of women's groups – albeit conservative groups (DeGrazia, 1992).

The majority of Italians were and remained Roman Catholic, but a new relationship was forged between Mussolini and the church following his 1929 signing of the concordat of reconciliation with the papacy. Subsequently, Fascists and the papacy worked hand in hand. For example, in 1930 Pope Pius XI issued an encyclical, *Casti connubi*, which described women's work outside the home as a 'perversion' and a corruption of the role of wife and mother (Birnbaum, 1986).

Regardless of the support in different spheres for Fascist policies, the attempt to encourage women to return to a traditional role as 'angels of the hearth' failed, since women were inadvertently encouraged to enter some aspects of public life. Overall, despite their views on women's place in society, the Fascists 'opened new vistas for Italian women' (Noether, 1982, 77).

A Recapitulation

At the end of the First World War, Italian Fascism appears to have emerged on the political scene as a somewhat enlightened movement that was responding to the turmoil and disappointment of the time. Not long after, the Fascist leadership broadened its social base by appealing to both urban and rural 'masses.' In doing so, it was also compelled to resort to traditionalist discourse, which included attempts to return men and women to traditional social roles. Simultaneously, it appealed to ethnic history and biological preservation. Fascists believed and promoted the idea that citizens, both male and female, must share common values and national sentiments. The series of punishments and rewards designed to 'encourage' citizens to fulfil their national duties clearly contained a double standard. Each sex had to play its role within the national family either as a war hero and father or as a guardian or an angel of the hearth and mother. Numerous measures were introduced – including celibacy taxes, marriage loans, and symbolic and practical assistance to wedded and unwed mothers – throughout the Fascist period, which had both mixed and unintended results.

It should come as no surprise to many that the family became a special focus of attention. As a matter of fact, it has long been argued by theorists like Max Horkheimer (1972) that the family is an important tool for political, moral, and religious movements that often aim to strengthen and renew its unity. In addition to the obvious fact that families continue to be seen as the only legitimate locus of reproduction, Horkheimer noted that these movements are keenly aware that one of the fundamental roles of the family is as creator of 'the authority-oriented cast of mind.' In other words, not only do families produce new members, but in almost all cases, they socialize those new members to accept the current order of things, including faith in a single god and submission to paternal authority, where that is the norm (ibid.). Fascism undoubtedly represented a form of paternal authority and thus depended upon the population's submission to it. As a result, the Fascists fostered a general rigidification of social relationships, which encouraged and tried to sustain (in particular, large) Italian families. The promotion of large, patriarchal families also fostered a renewed commitment to duty, honour, authority, self-sacrifice, obedience, and the unquestioning acceptance and naturalness of a hierarchy of power relations both inside families and in society in general. Average men, especially fathers of large families, were reaffirmed as heads of households. At the same time, Mussolini was granted unquestioned authority as head of the national family. While the Fascists appeared to be quite successful in the ideological re-patriarchalization of families, on a more practical level birth rates continued to decline, and individual men and women either did not or could not simply and easily take their 'natural' places in a large, traditional Italian family.

4

Internationalist Beginnings in the Interwar Period: Revolutionary Russia

Political, Economic, and Social Circumstances prior to the Revolution

For centuries, Russia was ruled as a feudal aristocracy. In the eighteenth century, for example, about half the country's peasants were 'owned' by secular lords, and the other half belonged to ecclesiastical institutions or to the state (Kochan and Keep, 1997). In the mid-nineteenth century, serfs made up roughly 75 per cent of the population of Russia and the gentry less than 1 per cent (Engel, 1977). Even after the emancipation of the serfs in 1861, Russia remained primarily a peasant society (Tilly, 1993). Studies of family estates provide some insight into what serfdom meant to peasants' lives. One account revealed that the main adversaries of the serfs were the forces of nature rather than their seignior or the distant state power. One estate, believed to be typical of others in the nineteenth century, included a number of husband-and-wife work teams (*tyaglo*), cultivating some six hectares each, which yielded enough to support six to eight people (Kochan and Keep, 1997). Peasants' accommodations were crowded, with dirt floors and little room for beds. Owing to many factors, in the 1850s about 45 per cent of the children on this particular estate died before the age of five, and life expectancy for the survivors was forty years. Serfs generally married young: the average age of grooms at the time was 20.1 years and women typically married at 19.5 years (ibid.). As a result of this and other factors, birth rates were exceptionally high compared with those in other parts of Europe at the time. A woman who survived her child-bearing years would normally have six to eight children. Furthermore, the community was said to intervene in domestic affairs to preserve the three-generation household and the authority of the *bolshak* or patriarch (ibid.). Men, who themselves were powerless compared with their seigniors, were said to have taken out their rage on those less powerful: their women/wives and children (Engel, 1977). Patriarchal control was maintained through a series of laws that granted older male serfs power over their families (Hosking, 1998). For example, passport laws gave a husband or father the legal right to forbid women in his family to work, establish residence, or travel without his consent (Rosenthal, 1977).

Following the emancipation of the serfs in 1861, little changed for peasants in general (Kohn, 1957) and peasant women in particular, with the exception perhaps of Cossack women (O'Rourke, 1996). Peasants remained legally tied to the land since they were obliged to accept a land allotment and make annual payments to the provincial government (*obshchina*). Power continued to be held by an elected village elder and the patriarchal head of each family. The patriarch maintained control over his family, including the right to deny family members access to passports needed for travel throughout the country (Kochan and Keep, 1997). Throughout their lives, peasant women were subject to the authority first of their fathers, then of their husbands, then of their sons (O'Rourke, 1996). Couples were still encouraged to marry young and have many children – especially male heirs – while daughters were held to be of relatively little account (Kochan and Keep, 1997). It was believed that the reinforcement of traditional, patriarchal forms of order were used to ensure that peasants would continue to pay taxes and remain tied to the land (Sanborn, 2001; Hosking, 1998). Only industrialization and urbanization, which accelerated in the 1890s, began to undermine the traditional system.

A study in Voronezh province revealed that, as late as 1896, 42 per cent of households comprised two generations and 46 per cent three or more generations (Kochan and Keep, 1997). Slowly, patriarchal authority was being hollowed out. For example, with time, if joint property was divided, married women had a say in how it would be divided (Kochan and Keep, 1997). In many cases, young married women were actually the ones who initiated the division of property, since it was they who were most likely to seek to escape the subordination of their in-laws in traditional family arrangements. In these traditional families, women were allotted a well-defined economic and social role, since they usually had an independent source of income, especially in the autumn and winter months, by spinning cloth and looking after poultry. They were therefore seen by their menfolk as a valuable asset, but they continued to be physically beaten ('disciplined') by husbands, who held patriarchal control over family members. Women were also subordinate to their fathers and mothers in-law in these arrangements (ibid.). Throughout this period, czarist law subjected women first to their fathers and then to their husbands (Engel, 1977).

Industrialization and urbanization helped to separate the extended family into individual households, contributing to the breakdown of the patriarchal stronghold. In the early industrial period (in 1897, for example) women comprised less than 2 per cent of the labour force. Most worked as servants (55 per cent), field hands (25 per cent), industrial workers (17 per cent, mostly textile workers), and in educational and health services (4 per cent), the only fields open to educated women (Rosenthal, 1977). In 1897, 1.867 million Russian women worked in agriculture, forestry, and fishing, 894,000 in manufacturing, and 1.777 million in services (Mitchell, 1992). The number of women in the labour force started to rise, reaching 5 per cent in 1906 and 26 per cent by 1913. It should be noted, however, that their wages averaged about 47.7 per cent of men's daily earnings and they were automatically dismissed if they became pregnant (Rosenthal, 1977).

Many women at the time understood that the struggle for autonomy meant a 'painful break from home and family' (Engel, 1977, 355). Many, especially educated women, did make that break, and feminism grew rapidly in Russia after 1905 (Rosenthal, 1977). Most demanded legal equality, equal access to education, employment, divorce reform, and access to birth control. Women began to organize, strike, and demonstrate. In fact, it is said that women triggered the February Revolution of 1917, which resulted in the abdication of Czar Nicholas II only days later (Lund, 1970). Historical records reveal that on International Women's Day (8 March in the western calendar, 23 February in the eastern calendar), against the advice of all political parties, women textile workers called a general strike. These women appealed to all women workers and housewives standing in breadlines to join them. Apparently, men joined them reluctantly and only after it became clear that the army would not fire on them (Rosenthal, 1977).

It should be noted that Russia had been in economic turmoil for quite some time. The Napoleonic wars had played havoc with the empire's finances, and just as the economy stabilized, it was again ruptured by war. The Crimean War (1853–6) was followed by the Russo-Turkish War in 1877 and the Russo-Japanese War in 1904–5 (Garraty and Gay, 1972); not one year later, in 1905–6, the first Russian revolution took place. Thus, the nineteenth century and early twentieth century in Russia were marked by economic, social, and political instability.

Between the emancipation of the serfs and the 1917 revolution, Russian society altered dramatically. Economic change caused by industrialization coincided with political change brought on by the emergence of a new radical spirit, which was manifested by nihilism, anarchism, and populism, to name a few movements. In addition, the First World War was raging. Inflation ran rampant, and instead of liberalizing state policies, Czar Nicholas II handed over supreme power to the reactionary empress and to Rasputin (Riasanovsky, 1984), who was put in sole charge of the government. He was said to have distributed jobs to the husbands of women who slept with him and turned out of office the husbands of women who refused him. It was also said that 'the high offices of the Church itself were filled with charlatans and political priests he had chosen' (Moorehead, 1958, 104). No one who opposed him was safe.

With Nicholas II and most of the army away at war, demonstrators (including women textile workers) stormed St Petersburg (renamed Petrograd during the war, later renamed Leningrad) and turned to the Duma for leadership. Under these circumstances, Czar Nicholas II abdicated, and a new provisional government was established, which lasted about eight months. During this period a general state of crisis and unrest persisted (Riasanovsky, 1984), and the provisional government seemed struck by paralysis (Kochan and Keep, 1997). In October 1917 the Bolsheviks decided to set up a military revolutionary committee in Petrograd. The city fell to the Bolsheviks in a bloodless coup, the provisional government was overthrown, and the new Soviet era began.

The Russian Revolution

The Bolsheviks espoused communism, a variant of Marxism as developed by Lenin (Riasanovsky, 1984). Lenin, like Marx, believed in the imminent worldwide overthrowing of the capitalist system by professional revolutionaries and the establishment of a classless society, which would end human exploitation and inequality. Lenin emphasized the role of the party and the dictatorship of the proletariat (Riasanovsky, 1984). In fact, one of the goals was the internationalizing of the proletarian movement for emancipation (Lenin, 1970). Although communism after the revolution involved the nationalization of industry and almost all other aspects of economic life, its ideology remained internationalist in nature. According to prominent thinkers like Alfred Cobban (1969), in the beginning 'Marxism was the enemy of nationalism' (188). Most communists, at least ideally, claimed to be internationalists or outright anti-nationalist. For example, Alexandra Kollontai – communist revolutionary, member of the first Bolshevik cabinet in 1917, and the first woman ever (in the modern world) to have been appointed ambassador – stated that she felt it was a socialist's duty to struggle against the First World War. Lenin, too, noted that socialists had 'always condemned war between nations as barbarous and brutal' (1970, 4). Speaking about her own experiences, Kollontai remarked that the intoxication of patriotic feelings 'has always been something alien to me, on the contrary I felt an aversion for everything that smacked of super-patriotism' (1971, 23).

While most communists claim to be anti-nationalist, the first Soviet government proclaimed the right of peoples to self-determination. It might appear contradictory that they supported the right of nations to self-determination while at the same time promoting internationalism. However, Lenin argued that 'socialists cannot achieve their great aim [international dictatorship of the proletariat] without fighting against all oppression of nations' (1970, 26). He added that the championing of this right to self-determination, far from encouraging the formation of small states, would lead, on the contrary, to the freer, fearless and therefore wider and more widespread formation of very big states and federations of states, which are more beneficial for the masses and more in keeping with economic development. At the same time, the languages and cultural activities of minorities received 'every encouragement' (Cobban, 1969, 206). It is interesting that, in the non-Russian districts intermarriage was common and formed a bond of union between nationalities (Cobban, 1969).

When national independence movements in the former Russian empire began declaring independence (as early as 1917), the Soviet government deemed the movements to be bourgeois and counter-revolutionary, and on 30 December 1922 the Union of Soviet Socialist Republics (a multinational state) came into being as a federation of Russia, the Ukraine, White Russia, and Transcaucasia (Riasanovsky, 1984). In the first two decades of the twentieth century, much had changed in the region; according to Tilly (1993), the New Economic Policy, for example, produced 'substantial economic recovery' (222). In a few short years, political and social life were also radically and dramatically altered.

Bolshevik Policies on Women

Domestic Roles: Family Law, Housework, and Motherhood

Very soon after the Bolsheviks took over, they set out to remove all legal barriers to equality between Russian women and men. As early as December 1917, only two months after their rise to power, the new government began to repeal all czarist laws governing marriage and divorce. After that date, only civil marriages were valid. The Family Code of October 1918 erased all distinctions between children born in or out of wedlock by abolishing inheritance rights for everyone. The code also prohibited adoption, gave each parent equal authority over children, and gave children more rights vis-à-vis their parents. It also legislated that men and women controlled their own earnings, allowed a woman to retain her own name after marriage, establish her own residence, and have her own passport (Rosenthal, 1977).

The civil codes of 1918, and their revision in 1926, facilitated divorce by allowing one partner simply to send the other a postcard stating that the relationship was at an end. As a result of the changes, the divorce rate in the early 1920s was twenty-six times greater in the U.S.S.R. than in the United Kingdom, and in Moscow at the time there was one divorce for every two marriages (Kochan and Keep, 1997). After the first changes to the divorce laws in 1918 husbands more often than wives initiated divorces, often leaving working-class mothers with young children in penury (Kochan and Keep, 1997), since alimony was abolished, except in cases of physical disability, exemptions for which men also qualified (Rosenthal, 1977).

The revisions to the Family Code in 1926 sanctioned common-law marriages and changed the law regarding alimony and child support, in order to protect destitute women and children from broken marriages. Not only were alimony and child support payments reintroduced, but they were actually enforced for one year in the case of both marriage and common-law union dissolution. As a result of the 1926 revisions, divorce rates rose rapidly: for example, 450 per cent in Petrograd and 300 per cent in Moscow (Rosenthal, 1977). It was found that women now were initiating over 60 per cent of divorces, particularly in cases where they sought compensation after men had deserted them. The courts tended to allot one-third of a man's wages for support, but many men simply did not pay (ibid.). The revised code also gave 'illegitimate' children the same right to support as 'legitimate' children, and women could file paternity suits. If the mother did not know who the father was, she could name all possible men and each would then be partially responsible for child support, thus allowing children to have several legal fathers (ibid.). This provision, as well as the fact that multiple divorces were quite common, made support payments and multiple payments difficult to administer and enforce. Nonetheless, it should be noted that efforts were made to recognize women as equals of men and to retain some autonomy and control by women over their domestic and sexual lives.

The Bolsheviks had liberal views on sexuality. For example, Kollontai (1971), in her speeches and practice, promoted women's sexual freedom and challenged conventional patriarchal morality and its sexual double standards. Russians were also quite tolerant of homosexuality; in fact, shortly after the revolution, Soviet Russia was the first country to legalize homosexuality (Mamonova, 1989). It is said that during the 1920s 'the situation for Soviet homosexuals was relatively bearable and many gays and lesbians (such as Kuz'min, Kliuev, and Parnok) played a major role in Soviet culture' (Riordan, 1996, 160). However, in December 1933 (under Stalin) the government introduced a bill making 'buggery' a criminal offence, punishable by deprivation of freedom for a term of up to five years (Riordan, 1996). Until the Stalin era, political commitment to various forms of equality was quite obvious.

In revolutionary Russia, both state policies and political speeches made attempts to address 'the woman question' and issues surrounding women's equality. For example, on 8 March 1921 (International Working Women's Day) Lenin published a supplement to *Pravda* (the Bolshevik newspaper) in which he wrote that under capitalism half the human race – namely, women – were doubly oppressed. He stated that, first, they were deprived of rights granted to men (because laws did not give them equality with men), and, secondly, they remained in 'household bondage,' since they continued to be 'household slaves,' 'overburdened with the drudgery of the most squalid, backbreaking and stultifying toil in the kitchen and the family household' (Lenin, 1977, 32:161). He boasted that no party or revolution in the world had ever 'dreamed of striking so deep at the roots of oppression and inequality of women as the Soviet, Bolshevik revolution is doing' (161). In this essay, Lenin recognized that one of the loci of women's oppression was the home and domestic labour.

Lenin noted: 'laws alone, of course, are not enough' (1977, 30:43). He stated: 'notwithstanding all the laws emancipating women, she continues to be a *domestic slave*, because *petty housework* crushes, strangles, stultifies and degrades her, chains her to the kitchen and the nursery, and she wastes her labour in barbarously unproductive, petty, nerve-racking, stultifying and crushing drudgery' (429; original emphasis). He added, 'the real *emancipation of women*, real communism, will begin only where and when an all-out struggle begins ... against this petty housekeeping, or rather the *wholesale transformation* into a large-scale socialist economy begins (ibid.; original emphasis). Thus, he recognized that women's equality must begin by re-evaluating and changing the nature of domestic work and family relations.

When addressing a group at a conference in 1925, Trotsky similarly noted: 'for many decades to come it will be possible to evaluate a human society by the attitude it has toward women, toward the mother and toward the child' (1970, 42). In an article published in *Za Novyi Byt* in that same year he added that the most accurate way of measuring revolutionary Russia's advance would be to evaluate 'the practical measures which are being carried out for the improvement of the position of mother and child' (45). In conclusion, he stated: 'it is impossible to move forward while leaving the women far behind' (48). Like nationalists in Italy and Germany, Trotsky spoke of women as 'mothers of the nation,' but his suggestions on how to improve their position in society were quite different and antithetical to nationalist policies and practices: 'From the enslavement of women grow prejudices and superstitions which shroud the children of the new generation and penetrate deeply into all the pores of the national consciousness. The best and most profound path of struggle against superstition of religion is the path of all-sided concern for the mother. She must be raised up and enlightened. Freeing the mother means cutting the last umbilical cord linking the people with the dark and superstitious past' (48). The party's views on 'the woman question' were also clearly outlined in an article entitled 'Is Soviet Russia Fit to Recognize,' published in January 1933 in the American magazine *Liberty*, in which Trotsky responded to a series of fourteen questions submitted to him in advance. A few of his answers provide interesting insights into Bolshevik attitudes towards the sexual, political, and domestic status of women in Russia. For example, he was asked (question no. 4): 'Is Bolshevism deliberately destroying the family?' He replied, 'If one understands by "family" a compulsory union based on the marriage contract, the blessing of the church, property rights, and the single passport, then Bolshevism has destroyed this policed family from the roots up' (52). He added, 'If one understands by "family" the unbounded domination of parents over children, and the absence of legal rights for the wife, then Bolshevism has, unfortunately, not yet completely destroyed this carryover of society's old barbarism' (52–3). Furthermore, 'if one understands by "family" ideal monogamy – not in the legal but in the actual sense – then Bolsheviks could not destroy what never was nor is on earth, barring fortunate exceptions' (53).

Question no. 8 enquired: 'Is it true that divorce may be had for the asking?' Trotsky answered 'Of course it is true. It would have been more in place to ask another question: "Is it true that there are still countries where divorce cannot be obtained for the asking by either party to a marriage?"' (1970, 54). Question no. 9 asked: 'Is it true that the Soviets have no respect for chastity in men and women?' Trotsky responded: 'I think that in this field it is not respect but hypocrisy that has declined ... The Soviet Government's abolition of a number of laws which were supposed to protect the domestic hearth, chastity, etc., has nothing to do with any effort to destroy the permanence of the family or encourage promiscuity. It is simply a question of attaining, by raising the material and cultural level, something that cannot be attained by formal prohibition or lifeless preaching' (54–5). According to Trotsky, 'to alter the position of women *at the root* is possible only if all conditions of social, family, and domestic existence are altered' (45; original emphasis). In his 1936 article entitled 'The Revolution Betrayed,' Trotsky wrote that the revolution 'made a heroic effort to destroy the so-called family hearth – that archaic, stuffy, and stagnant institution in which women of the toiling classes perform galley labor from childhood to death' (61). For the Bolsheviks this effort was to include (at least ideally), the replacement of the family as a 'shut-in enterprise' by a 'system of social care and accommodation,' which included 'maternity houses, childcare centres, kindergartens, schools, social dining rooms, social laundries, first-aid stations, hospitals, sanatoria, athletic organizations, moving-picture theatres, etc.' (61). This goal included no less than the complete absorption of housekeeping functions by institutions in a socialist society. Thus, it was recognized that women's 'liberation' involved a variety of measures both inside and outside the home. Lenin noted that 'owing to her work in the house, the woman is still in a difficult position. To effect her complete emancipation and make her equal to the man it is necessary for the national economy to be socialized and for women to participate in common productive labour' (Lenin, 1977, 30:43).

Public Roles: Women's Employment and Political Life

One of the first steps taken by the Bolsheviks after their rise to power was to mandate equal pay for equal work, a concept that was completely unknown in the rest of the world (Rosenthal, 1977). Doctors at the time analysed the impact of industrial work on women and 'did not recommend that women leave the factories to become full-time mothers' (Hyer, 1996, 112). In fact, the Bolsheviks forbade the dismissal of pregnant women, instituted paid maternity leave, and introduced on-the-job nursing breaks. Furthermore, they extended labour codes to protect women's health on the job by prohibiting hot, heavy, or hazardous work as well as night work and overtime (Rosenthal, 1977). The female share of the workforce grew slowly after the revolution, reaching about 30 per cent by 1929 (Kochan and Keep, 1997). On the other hand, most women continued to be employed in the textile industry and other traditionally 'female' (low-paid) jobs.

Bolsheviks also made serious attempts to increase women's political involvement. This initative, too, enjoyed mixed success. In a 1920 *Pravda* address to working women, Lenin boasted that the Soviet government was the first and only government at the time to completely abolish old bourgeois laws that placed women in an inferior position compared with that of men. He seemed particularly proud of the fact that women were not only allowed but also encouraged to become involved in politics: 'in order to be active in politics under the old capitalist regime special training was required, so that women played insignificant parts in politics, even in the most advanced and free capitalist countries. Our task is to make politics available to every working woman' (Lenin, 1977, v. 30, 44). He urged working women to take a bigger part in Soviet elections and in the administration of both socialized enterprises and the state. He also urged the general population to elect more women to the Soviet: 'send more working women to the Moscow Soviet! Let the Moscow proletariat show that it is prepared to do everything, and is doing everything, to fight for victory, to fight the old inequality, the old bourgeois humiliation of women! ... The proletariat cannot achieve complete liberty until it has won complete liberty for women' (30:372). Despite the party's encouragement, only 8 per cent of party members were women in 1922, and by 1927 they accounted for only 12 per cent (Kochan and Keep, 1997). It is interesting that under Stalin women started working their way up in the party, increasing their membership from 8.2 per cent in 1925 to 15.9 per cent in 1932. By

1933 girls were half the members of *Komsomol* (Young Communist League) (Rosenthal, 1977).

Despite slow beginnings, women did hold positions of power within the party. Its most accomplished female orator in 1917 was Alexandra Kollontai, who later filled key posts within the government. She was one of the first women in modern European history to hold cabinet rank (Clements, 1997). As the first commissar of social welfare, Kollontai devoted special attention (in vain) to establishing model nurseries and parental care facilities (Rosenthal, 1977). She resigned in March 1918, when economic hardship precluded the expenditure of funds for communal facilities, which she considered essential for women (ibid.). Kollontai was then appointed the first woman ambassador, a post she occupied for three years.

Roles, Status, and Treatment of Feminists / Female Revolutionaries

The rise of feminism in Russia preceded the 1917 revolution. As a matter of fact, Russia had a strong feminist movement dating as far back as the 1860s. At the time, there were 'individualistic' feminists or 'bourgeois' feminists, whose primary goal was achieving their own autonomy and freedom (Engel, 1977), and 'radical' feminists or revolutionaries. The radicals were typically young, impoverished gentlewomen who shared many of the goals of the individualistic feminists but were becoming increasingly attracted to broader political action and ideology, which included nihilism, communism, and anarchism (ibid.). Many of these feminist radicals played key roles in bringing Bolsheviks to power and continued to play roles within the party. The *Bolshevichki*, as they were called, engaged in all the activities that prepared the way for their party's seizure of power in 1917, including making speeches, writing articles, serving as Duma delegates, and so on (Clements, 1997).

To facilitate the politicization of women, the *Zhenotdel* (Women's Department) was formed within the party. Under Kollontai's leadership, it concerned itself with the education and socialization of children, the recruitment of women into the communist movement, and the organization of women workers and peasants. Its activities ranged from selecting and training women for election to local soviets to helping them to obtain divorces (Rosenthal, 1977). Unfortunately, not long after the beginning of the Stalin era (in 1928) the Zhenotdel was abolished (in 1930). In fact, earlier proposals of free love, communal living, and collective child rearing were disavowed, and instead premarital chastity and the traditional nuclear family were endorsed (Clements, 1997). Under Stalin, the party did not officially reject the idea that women should be equal participants in society, but in the 1930s it adopted the notion that women should also find fulfilment in taking care of their families.

The new Soviet constitution enshrined equality between men and women (see Article 122 of the 1936 Soviet constitution; Mosse et al., 1957), and a significant number of women became doctors, engineers, and scientists. However, reversals of previous policies that had assisted women were also made: for example, divorce became difficult to obtain; the policy on illegitimate children was revoked, reattaching stigma to illegitimacy; and women lost their right to file paternity suits (Rosenthal, 1977). The goal was to create a 'stable social climate' deemed conducive to large, nuclear families. Under Stalin, special honours were provided, including cash subsidies for large families (ibid.). In sum, the rise of Stalin marked the end of the revolutionary dream of equality between men and women. His takeover resulted in the expulsion of Trotsky, the promotion of forced-draft industrialization, and the rapid growth of a civilian administration and politicized secret police (Tilly, 1993). National glory and militarism became part of the new vocabulary and ideology in the 1930s and beyond.

The Revolution's Successes and Failures

The revolutionaries attempted to change not only the nature of women's activities in society, but also their roles, including conventional expectations of what those roles should be, particularly in public.

The massive numbers of married women with children entering the labour market was expected to produce fundamental and consequential changes, but after the initial utopian-revolutionary aspirations were abandoned and found to be economically infeasible, married women generally found themselves carrying the double burden of old (traditional) household responsibilities and new, wage-earning responsibilities (Hobsbawm, 1995). While it is true that 'family and gender relations were fluid during the first decades after 1917' (Northrop, 2001, 191), there were no fundamental changes in relations between the sexes in either the public or the private spheres.

Eric Hobsbawm (1995) has argued that the reasons why women entered the labour force were varied and not always connected to revolutionary or emancipatory principles: 'the reasons why women in general, and especially married women, plunged into paid work had no necessary connection with their view of women's social position and rights. It might be due to poverty, to employers' preference for female over male workers as being cheaper and more biddable, or simply to the growing number ... of female-headed families' (313). On the subject of women's paid employment, it was noted that protective legislation backfired on women. In some instances, managers did not want to hire and/or train women because paid maternity leave and nursing breaks made women more costly to employ. Furthermore, many men came to resent female workers who went on maternity leave, since it was seen as a paid vacation for women, but not for men. As a result, in some places of employment, women were the last hired and the first fired (Rosenthal, 1977).

Trotsky acknowledged that the Soviets had failed in their promise to liberate women from the drudgery and isolation of domestic work; in 1936 he wrote: 'up to now this problem of problems has not been solved' (1970, 61). He noted that, at the time, 'the forty million Soviet families remain in their overwhelming majority nests of medievalism, female slavery and hysteria' (61–2). He blamed the poor state of the Soviet economy for the failure, explaining that 'the real resources of the state did not correspond to the plans and intentions of the Communist Party. You cannot "abolish" the family; you have to replace it. The actual liberation of women is unrealizable on the basis of "generalized want"' (62). In other words, what was accomplished was often inadequate. For example, Trotsky noted that the total number of steady accommodations in childcare centres amounted to about 600,000 in 1932 and seasonal accommodations, during harvest season and so on, to 'only about 4,000,000' (63). Although numbers increased over the next few years, he explained that they amounted to only an insignificant part of the total needed. Even the existing childcare centres in large cities such as Moscow and Leningrad were 'not satisfactory' (63).

Economic hardship prevented the state from funding the proposed communal facilities that were considered essential for women. The communal agencies that did develop were inadequate, beyond serving as emergency or crisis measures: 'Instead of communal restaurants – soup kitchens; instead of especially designed dormitories – requisitional homes where workers slept on the floor; instead of model nurseries – emergency shelters for homeless children where many died' (Rosenthal, 1977, 379). Dreams of progress were further thwarted by the two years of civil war that began in 1918.

Although they were equally entitled to vote and to hold office, women were underrepresented in leadership positions, and the party's women's department did not have an influential voice (Kochan and Keep, 1997). Furthermore, despite legal changes in the status of women, in the countryside patriarchal norms were still adhered to: marriages were arranged by elder kin and young women without families were regarded with suspicion by potential in-laws. Similarly, despite the repeal of laws barring women from gaining an education, the proportion of female students in higher education did not surpass the level achieved in 1913 (ibid.), although literacy rates among women rose.

A Recapitulation

Equality between the sexes was a central tenet of the Russian revolution, since the goal was a classless society that facilitated economic, social, intellectual, and cultural equality. The revolution sought to implement the Marxist ideology of internationalism, equality, and a dictatorship of the proletariat. Despite serious attempts, especially early on, little of this goal actually was achieved.

One of the first moves by Bolshevik revolutionaries after their rise to power was to wipe out any traces of inequality between men and women that existed in marriage and family laws, including those concerning children (Lenin, 1977, v. 32). Laws were changed, to make divorce attainable for both men and women who found themselves in unsatisfactory or conflict-ridden marriages. Lenin noted, however, that it was not enough to change the laws; domestic life must be restructured as well, and the Bolshevik solution involved the establishment of communal kitchens and childcare and other measures designed to liberate women from domestic drudgery. Unfortunately, civil war, economic hardship, and Stalin's rise to power, prevented the implementation of these initiatives, and traditional ideas about gender roles were reinstituted in law and in practice.

5

Multinational Beginnings in the Interwar Period: The Kingdom of Yugoslavia

Political, Economic, and Social Circumstances prior to Its Establishment

For some time Yugoslavia has been a unique polity/region that has fascinated many. One of its most interesting, and at times enigmatic, qualities is its combination of eastern and western cultural and religious traditions. It was and to some extent continues to be simultaneously traditional and modern, European and Asian, as a result of its geographic location and history. Located on the Balkan peninsula, it has been described as the gateway to Asia or a bridge between Europe and Asia, and its position has tempted many powers to invade and control the area. At one time, a person could travel by train from Paris to Constantinople across Yugoslavia on the fashionable Orient Express.

The Slavs migrated south into this region in the middle of the first millennium A.D. (Singleton, 1994) and began establishing their own states when the Byzantine Empire started to weaken. During the fourteenth century the Ottomans (so named after their founder, Sultan Osman), a group composed of many nations but with a Turkic majority, began their victorious missionary drive westward. By the fifteenth century the Ottomans had advanced through Bosnia and Serbia, and five hundred years of Ottoman rule in parts of the peninsula had begun (ibid.). As the 'Turks' pushed towards the centre of Europe, the Habsburgs of Austria (Christians) became a counter force. The Habsburgs regained control of parts of the Balkan peninsula. As a result, half the Slavs were under Turkish domination, inside the Ottoman Empire, and the other half became Christian and Austrian. This was the situation in the Balkans for centuries. By the eighteenth century the Ottoman Empire was weakening, and by the early nineteenth century the Serbs had defeated the Turks and declared their independence. It took the rest of the century to 'resolve the Oriental question' in the Balkans (Erlich, 1966).

The Austro-Hungarian monarchy maintained control of Croatia and Slovenia, its possessions in the Balkans, until the First World War. During the war, a South Slav committee in London prepared the foundations for a new, unified state in the region. After the defeat and fragmentation of Austria in October 1918 the Austrian-controlled South Slav regions united with Serbia and Montenegro, previous possessions of the Ottoman Empire, to create a new common state: the 'Kingdom of Serbs, Croats and Slovenes,' renamed 'The Kingdom of Yugoslavia' (1931) and later renamed 'Yugoslavia.' The word 'Yugoslav' or 'Jugoslav' literally means south ('jug') slav. Some have argued that the formation of this new Yugoslav state was the direct result of the events of the First World War, since the collapse of the Habsburg monarchy had left Slovenes and Croats with little alternative but to ally themselves closely with Serbs (Shoup, 1968; Fitzgerald, 1946). It should be noted however, that the South Slavs in the Ottoman Empire (Turkish) and those in the Habsburg Empire (Austrian) had acquired distinct political and cultural features; thus, the proposed unification was not without many opponents. As a matter of fact, there was considerable opposition to the proposed unification, particularly in Croatia and Slovenia (previously Austrian possessions), where many suspected and feared that the unification would simply create a larger, Serb-dominated state, or Greater Serbia (Vucinich, 1969; Fitzgerald, 1946). Furthermore, the new country would have to construct a polity in which its three major and often clashing religious groups – Orthodox, Roman Catholic, and Muslim – could coexist (Vucinich, 1969). The Serbs, Macedonians, Montenegrins, and some minorities were Orthodox Christians; the Croats, Slovenes and some minorities were Roman Catholic; the Albanians, Turks, and Islamicized Slavs in Bosnia and Herzegovina were Muslim (ibid.).

This new polity would also have to unify relatively economically advanced regions, such as Slovenia, Croatia, and Vojvodina (part of Serbia), with the less economically advanced regions of Montenegro and Macedonia. The remaining parts of independent Serbia fell somewhere between them. An ethnographic study of a Serb village revealed that Serb villagers were acutely aware of their relatively less developed economic status compared with other parts of Europe, but one villager explained. 'Give us twenty years without a war and we'll make of our Šumadija [the name of the village] a little America' (Halpern and Halpern, 1972, 66).

Modernization had begun in the more prosperous northern regions and major urban centres, but the traditional way of life prevailed in most other parts of the country, regardless of its history and religion. Two features were similar in practically all parts of what became Yugoslavia: a predominantly agrarian lifestyle and a distinctive organization of family life. About 14 million people lived in Yugoslavia in the interwar period, most of whom were peasants. In fact, Yugoslavia had the highest percentage of agrarian population in Europe: Yugoslav statistics showed that 76.5 per cent were peasants, and League of Nations statistics revealed that 83 per cent lived in rural communities (Erlich, 1966). At the centre of rural life was the extended family, or *zadruga*, a dominant family form throughout both eastern and western parts of Yugoslavia (ibid.). The word *zadruga* in Serbo-Croatian means 'the joint family,' 'cooperative enterprise' (Halpern, 1969), association, or community.

Rebecca West, a member of the British gentry, provided an extensive eyewitness account of her travels throughout Yugoslavia in 1937. In the 1,000-page account of her travels throughout the country, she confirmed that the *zadruga* had been the basis of much of the Slav social system for a long time. West also noted that some radical political views in Yugoslavia emerged from the 'ancient Slav communist tendencies' of the *zadruga* system (West, 1941, 543). Family scholars have been struck by the fact that all the Croat, Serb, and 'Muslem-Slav' *zadrugas* from the same region showed essentially similar characteristics, aside from specific religious customs (Halpern, 1969).

Family Life before the Founding of Yugoslavia

According to Vera St Erlich (1966), who conducted extensive research during the interwar period on family life in Yugoslavia, the basic principle of the *zadruga* was its patriarchal and patrilocal structure. An extended family, it functioned as a joint production and consumption unit (Halpern, 1969; Mitterauer, 1996), with common property holdings as its foundation. The *zadruga* was governed by a hierarchical system, in which every member had a rank, determined by age and sex; sex was the stronger of the two criteria, which meant that all men in the household were superior to all women. At the top of the hierarchy was the *domaćin* (from 'dom,' meaning home) or *starešina* (from 'stari,' meaning old one), or oldest male, who represented the *zadruga* in public life, arranged marriages for children and grandchildren, organized the household economy, and was final arbiter in family dealings (Erlich, 1966). It should also be noted, however, that it was not enough to be the oldest male: the *starešina* was expected to be vigorous and industrious, as in the old folk saying 'he who cannot work cannot give orders' (Halpern and Halpern, 1972, 19). Furthermore, he did not have absolute power over the family, since all married men had a right to participate in decisions, and the head could be removed if he proved incapable.

The female head of the home, or *domaćica*, was the *domaćin*'s wife; she administered domestic matters, planning and coordinating all women's work throughout the household (Halpern, 1969). All other women (daughters-in-law) and unmarried girls and women were subordinate to the female head (Erlich, 1966). Children were given their own tasks and responsibilities and were considered to belong to the commune as a whole, not to individual couples.

Marriage was seen as a partnership defined by formal inequality (Halpern, 1969). Women had no legal status as individuals: a married woman had no right to govern her own property; she could not be guardian of her own children; she could not undertake any legal matter that concerned inheritance without her husband's consent; and, if a husband had any legal heir, his wife inherited nothing (Emmert, 1999). The law also forbade paternity investigations (ibid.). Law 920 of the Serbian Civil Code forbade certain adults from administering property, including 'the insane, the good-for-nothings (*propalice*), those heavily in debt, and married women while their husbands were still alive' (37). Other than clothing and small objects, there was no private property or private ownership of any kind within the *zadruga*. Furthermore, according to the Serbian Legal Code of 1844, property was passed from the husband, first through kinship on his paternal side and then through kinship on his maternal side before his wife could inherit anything (Emmert, 1999). Such inheritance laws were designed to protect the *zadruga*.

There were, of course, some variations in the rules governing the *zadruga*, especially across regions. In regions formerly belonging to Austria, it took the form of a military unit and was much more likely to be based on more clearly defined written codes. On the other hand, peasants living under Ottoman rule, especially in Muslim districts, did not favour the *zadruga*, because separation of the wife from others in society was an important Muslim principle (Erlich, 1966). Furthermore, in these regions the *zadruga* was not bound by legal codes, since the Ottoman Empire was not regulated by formal written laws. Among the Montenegrins and Albanians, it was more common to find a tribal system consisting of several clans or brother groupings, which varied in size (ibid.). This was the state of family affairs in the part of the Balkans that, after the First World War, came to be known as Yugoslavia.

The Establishment of the Kingdom of South Slavs

Throughout the First World War groups both inside and outside Croatia, Slovenia, and Serbia raised the idea of future unification of the South Slavs, which became possible after the end of the First World War and the defeat of the Habsburg Empire. The most important group involved in the creation and organization of Yugoslavia was the Yugoslav Committee, whose headquarters were in London. This group, as well as the Slovenian People's Party under Korošec and the Serbian government under Pašić, convened in October 1918 to form the National Council of Slovenes, Croats, and Serbs. The organization declared its support for the establishment of a state composed of South Slavs, to be organized as a monarchy with a democratic basis (Jelavich, 1997). A provisional assembly was appointed, whose members were drawn from the Serbian Assembly, the Zagreb National Council (Croatian), and other bodies that represented the various nationalities. The new state's multinational character was encoded in its treaties, constitution, and laws. For example, Article 2 of the 'Treaty of Peace between the Allied and Associated Powers and Austria, Saint-Germain-en-Laye,' which was signed on 10 September 1919, clearly stated: 'The Serb-Croat-Slovene State undertakes to assure full and complete protection of life and liberty to all inhabitants of the Kingdom without distinction of birth, nationality, language, race or religion' (Trifunovska, 1994, 164).

The new multinational organization and cooperation did not proceed smoothly, however (Jelavich, 1997), and the diversity proved difficult to manage. For months after the war, several currencies (dinar, perper, kruna, lev) circulated in Yugoslavia; not until 1920 was the new dinar established as a national currency. The provinces and regions constituting the new Yugoslavia had to be given uniform legal, judicial, economic, financial, educational, and political systems, but sweeping aside old national loyalties and creating genuine devotion and sacrifice among Yugoslavs, and Yugoslav patriotism was difficult. The new state remained a loosely configured collection of diverse regions distinguished by national rivalries and sporadic outbursts of ethnic violence. Furthermore, the Yugoslav movement could never point to an authentic national leader (Shoup, 1968).

Unification did not and could not forge a new homogenized state; in fact, it took place only on the condition that a generous measure of autonomy was conceded (Fitzgerald, 1946). Thus, the new interwar Yugoslavia, with its plurality of nationalities, was characterized by complex political, economic, and social issues. According to historian Fred Singleton (1994) 'religion, local customs and traditions were part of the heritage which provided bonds of cultural identity far stronger than the abstract concept of a nation' (133). The few changes that resulted from unification had little impact on the lives and attitudes of most peasants in the new country. Willingly or unwillingly, the new South Slav state permitted a broad degree of local autonomy, in recognition of and in response to the diversity of cultures in the region (Singleton, 1994).

Family and Civil Policies under the New Regime

We have already noted that from the Middle Ages to the nineteenth and early twentieth centuries, the area that came to be known as Yugoslavia was roughly divided, both politically and culturally. Historian Barbara Jelavich (1997) explained that 'Yugoslavia had the most complex internal history of any Balkan nation at the time' (143). As a result, civil and family law were also quite diverse throughout the territory. Family life in northern and western regions were bound by the Austrian Civil Code of 1811. The Serbian Civil Code of 1844 (closer to the Napoleonic Code) governed parts of the eastern regions, and Montenegro had its own customary law (Chloros, 1970). As a result of this diversity, the codification of family law after 1918 was problematic. Interestingly enough, the new state allowed for the various regions to maintain their own, often very diverse, family codes simultaneously throughout the different parts of the new country. In effect, the new multinational state permitted considerable choice (not personal choice, but local/regional choice) in legal regulation of marriage, ranging from 'the almost formless civil to the strictest religious celebration' (50). For example, in Vojvodina and other northern parts of Serbia, where Hungarian law was in force, civil marriage was compulsory. In Slovenia, Dalmatia, and Istria (the latter two are parts of Croatia), according to the Austrian

Civil Code, civil marriage was permissible only in certain circumstances (Chloros, 1970). It was not until 1946 that the unified Basic Marriage Law was enacted, which purported to introduce a general law and framework for marriage relations (ibid.).

In addition to national or ethnic diversity, the region's complex history resulted in much religious diversity. The Kingdom of Yugoslavia brought together large groups of Orthodox Christians, Roman Catholics, and Muslims. Thus, in Serbia and Macedonia (both Orthodox Christian) and Croatia and Slovenia (both Roman Catholic), a religious ceremony for marriage was the rule. In Serbia and Macedonia, marriages were governed by the Serbian Civil Code of 1844 *and* the rules of the Serbian Orthodox Church. The Roman Catholic minority in Serbia and Macedonia (where the majority were Orthodox) were subject to (their own) rules of the Catholic Church and the Serbian Civil Code of 1844 as far as property rights were concerned (Chloros, 1970). Similarly, those living in Bosnia and Herzegovina were subject to the Austrian Civil Code on civil matters, but they retained their religious privileges. In this case, along with Orthodox and Roman Catholic Christians, there were a large number of Muslims of Slavonic, Albanian, and Turkish origin, who were subject to *Mejelle*, a code of Islamic Law.

Article 10 of the 10 September 1919 treaty, which effectively proclaimed the kingdom's existence, officially stated: 'The Serb-Croat-Slovene State agrees to grant to the Mussulmans in the matter of family law and personal status provisions suitable for regulating these matters in accordance with Mussulman usage' (Trifunovska, 1994, 167). As a result, Muslims in all parts of the new country were entitled to have disputes on family law or succession determined by *Shari'a* or Islamic Law. Thus, in the new state it was still possible for a polygamous marriage conducted under Islamic Law to survive or for the dowry to have legal consequences (Chloros, 1970). Clearly, the new state was attempting to recognize the ethnic *and* religious diversity of its citizens as both majorities and minorities in various regions. In other words, diversities that had preceded unification were allowed to prosper after 1918, and there was minimum regulation by the state, in the forms of taxes and its demand for military service (Halpern, 1969).

After the establishment of the Kingdom of Yugoslavia, local ethnic and religious groups were allowed to retain their own rules and customs surrounding marriage and family life, which meant that women were still subject to traditional patriarchal domination by their ethnic and religious brethren. At the time of unification Yugoslav women were not exposed to new laws and policies designed to alter their lives. The state made no attempt to legislate changes to their living conditions, and thus they continued to be subject to what Sylvia Walby (1996) called 'private patriarchy,' as opposed to the 'public patriarchy' that Italian and German women were exposed to at that time. According to Walby (1996), public patriarchy involves domination imposed by the state, while private patriarchy is characterized by the domination of the patriarchal relations in the home, where the 'mode of expropriation of the woman is individual, by the woman's husband or father' (243).

When the kingdom's new citizenship guidelines were codified and enshrined in law, they stated that the Serb-Croat-Slovene State 'admits and declares to be Serb-Croat-Slovene nationals *ipso facto* and without the requirement of any formality' (Trifunovska, 1994, 164), unless, of course, one was a married woman, in which case the 'option by a husband will cover his wife' (165). In other words, individuals had the right and option to declare themselves nationals unless they were married women, in which case their husbands decided for them. Similarly, the law stated that Serb-Croat-Slovene nationals living in another country had the choice and right to 'cease to be considered as Serb-Croat-Slovene nationals,' but the article clearly added: 'In this connection a declaration by a husband will cover his wife' (165). Thus, while the new state remained only a distant reality in the everyday lives of its citizens, the laws clearly reinforced 'private patriarchy' by granting individual men the right to make decisions on behalf of their wives. Despite their diversity, the main legal systems across Yugoslavia similarly proclaimed the husband as the legal head of the family. A Yugoslav scholar explained: 'He directs the household, wields alone parental powers, selects the residence of the family; the wife takes the husband's name, obeys his orders, the husband is presumed to be the manager of the wife's possessions and is legally not responsible to her for his management, possessions acquired during the marriage belong to the husband if not expressly stipulated otherwise, in case of death of the father the mother cannot be the legal guardian of her children' (Halpern, 1969, 335).

Not until the legal system was changed in 1946 were women legally entitled to escape this type of patriarchal control. The reforms of 1946 proclaimed the legal equality of women. For example, possessions acquired by the economic activity of husband or wife during marriage were owned in common. The wife was free to retain her maiden family name. The mother had equal parental rights with the father, and, in case of the death of the father, she was the legal guardian of the children (Halpern, 1969). Throughout the 1920s and 1930s women in Serbia, for example, who had continued to be bound by the Serbian Civil Code of 1844, had had no right to govern their own property or undertake any legal matters that concerned inheritance without the consent of their husbands (Emmert, 1999). The new governments that emerged following the founding of the Kingdom of Yugoslavia made no effort to change the code, which granted women no legal status as individuals, even though there were numerous women's groups that fought to change the laws (ibid.).

A study of the feminist movement in Serbia in the 1920s revealed that a large number of women's societies and feminist groups sprang up throughout Serbia following the First World War and the founding of the Kingdom of Yugoslavia. By 1921 some 205 organizations, representing over 50,000 women throughout the Kingdom of Yugoslavia, were part of a national alliance whose goals included national unity, equality with men in private and public life, equal pay for equal work, equal educational opportunities, and a single moral code for both women and men (Emmert, 1999). For the most part, however, women's groups were ignored or dismissed. For example, when representatives from a number of newly formed political parties were invited to speak as part of a series of lectures in the first half of 1926, with few exceptions and in patronizing ways each of them assured his listeners of his party's respect for women and commitment to providing new opportunities for them (ibid.). When it came time to support women's rights, however, few parties were willing to do so. Women were expected to remain loyal and submissive and to continue to fill traditional roles (ibid.). The new constitution essentially denied women basic civil rights.

Nonetheless, the structure and function of families in the new multinational state did begin to change, as a result not of legal, constitutional, or official policy changes, but of economic shifts following unification. The new states' goals included attempts to unify and modernize an effectively disunited cluster of regional powers. Industrial development in Slovenia, Croatia, and Serbia proper had begun in the nineteenth century, but the communication and rail networks developed at the time were oriented outside the regions, reflecting their historical (colonial) links to foreign capitals (Singleton, 1994). Slovenia's roads and railways were linked to Austria; Croatia's were oriented towards Budapest (Hungary); communication within the former Turkish territories was directed southward through Macedonia to the Greek port of

Salonika and to Istanbul and Vienna (ibid.). It was the task of the state to reorient, unite, and develop new communication routes and to support the growth of industry and promote modernization. Government policies encouraged the development of railways and small industries throughout Yugoslavia. 'The boom years of 1918–1925 were followed by a period of slower growth during the next five years, but steady progress continued until the effects of the world slump hit Yugoslavia in the early 1930s' (153).

One of the first acts of the new government in 1918 was to promise and enact land reforms, beginning with the abolition of any remnants of feudalism and followed by a royal Manifesto to the People that read, 'every Serb, Croat and Slovene should be the full owner of his land. In our free state there can only be free landowners' (Singleton, 1994, 154). Of course, 'his land' literally referred to men only.

The state strongly emphasized industrialization (Halpern, 1969), along with the implicit negation of village and communal *zadruga* life. The process of modernization that ushered in paid employment greatly altered the traditional structure of this patriarchal family form (Erlich, 1966; Halpern, 1969). The large, extended family was slowly being replaced by smaller household units characterized by even harder work lives (resulting from the loss of kin as workers who contributed to the household) and a stricter division of labour between the sexes (Halpern, 1969).

The rate of economic change varied across regions and times, leaving villages and families at different stages in the process, but some general trends were identified. Most peasants were unprepared for the degree of change and the extent of difficulties that they encountered. The introduction of a money economy was seen as a foreign element, which once introduced would disrupt patriarchal traditions. In fact, in many areas the family structure collapsed suddenly (Erlich, 1966) and the entire subsistence economy broke down. These dramatic changes brought about economic insecurity, which only worsened as Yugoslavia was hit by depression and the outbreak of the Second World War in the 1930s. Family hierarchies began to crumble as young couples sought to achieve economic independence. The establishment of the money economy was clearly challenging the collectivist trend that was said to have dominated the region from time immemorial (ibid.).

Economic change was accompanied by a decline in the importance of extended kinship ties and the rise of individualism (Halpern, 1969). The authority of the husband waned, and an abundance of children was seen as a burden to the family. As a result, average household size declined consistently; for example, in one village, household size decreased from 8.3 individuals in 1844 to 6.9 in 1890 to 4.5 in 1953 (ibid.). At the same time, relationships between young men and women became freer (Erlich, 1966), and the school system developed and illiteracy declined. Dragolioub Yovanovitch (1929/1990), writing on the effects of war in Serbia, noted that in the interwar period peasants 'enlarged their horizons' and 'women in particular changed greatly' (86). While peasant men adopted small elements of European costume (shedding elements of their national costume), women were 'more radical, particularly the younger ones' (87). Clearly, changing dress coincided with changing attitudes, particularly among peasant women.

On a more negative note, it was said that 'under the changing conditions, the status of dependent family members rose,' yet at the same time, 'the storm tosses the women between dependence and revolt, between the husband's tyranny and his indifference, between heavy economic pressure and the temptation to spend money' (Erlich, 1966, 420–1). Brutal beatings of wives by husbands appeared to be on the rise, especially while men were drunk (Erlich, 1966). Therefore, during this period the complex of traditional customs, norms, and attitudes began to disintegrate quickly, with both positive and negative outcomes. It should be noted, however, that although the economic changes were initiated by the new regime, many of the changes to family life were not direct products of the policy changes it had implemented.

A Recapitulation

The establishment of Yugoslavia in the interwar years provides an interesting example of how one multinational polity differed from nationalist polities that existed at the time, particularly concerning their treatment of gender issues and family life. As a matter of fact, the new Yugoslav state was primarily preoccupied with the task of unifying very diverse regions characterized by linguistic and religious complexities as well as formidable administrative differences. For example, there were six customs areas, five currencies, four railway networks, three banking systems, and, for a time, two governments, one in Zagreb and one in Belgrade (Singleton, 1994). One of the primary goals at the time was to develop economic unity while simultaneously allowing the various regions to maintain their cultural diversity. Marriage, family, and other civil laws remained local, not national(ized), for a long period. As a result, women were not directly affected by public patriarchy, as was the case in Fascist Italy and Nazi Germany at about the same time, but instead remained subject to local, domestic, or private patriarchy.

In failing to promote national family policies, and instead focusing on national economic development, the new Yugoslav state indirectly altered gender relations and family life. The traditional (extended) Yugoslav family, the *zadruga* (the predominant family form throughout the otherwise diverse regions) was reshaped and transformed by the substantial economic changes taking place in many parts of the country. Of course, the transformation process was different in each region, and numerous villages were at different stages in the process, but change was almost inevitable and ubiquitous.

In the Yugoslav case it is clear that women and families were not areas of concern for the newly emerging state. At this point, women were not seen as vital to the construction and maintenance of a 'Yugoslav' identity, nor were they seen as 'reproducers of the nation.' Thus, while under Italy's and Germany's nationalist regimes women were a central focus of the nation-state, in multinational Yugoslavia women were virtually ignored by the state. They did, however, continue to be subordinate to their male counterparts and subject to localized and domestic forms of patriarchy, which varied, of course, according to the ethnocultural and religious characteristics of the group.

This first attempt to unify Serbs, Croats, and Slovenes in the Kingdom of Yugoslavia was a failure; during this period the Serbs attempted to establish a centralized Serb state and the Croats and Slovenes vigorously resisted them (Langer, 1987). The new state was completely preoccupied with the problem of amalgamating diverse and often reluctant political groups under an unsatisfactory arrangement, where Serbs were believed to dominate. As a result of the difficulties of uniting this multinational smorgasbord, everyday life in various regions was allowed to proceed under a multiplicity of locally applicable social systems.

Part II
The Post-1989 Period

6

Nationalist Revival in Post-1989 Russia

The Political and Economic Situation before the Break-up

Lenin's revolution was primarily political (Seton-Watson, 1965). It resulted in the destruction of imperial Russia and the establishment of a dictatorial socialist regime that accomplished great social change. Following the 1917 revolution, Lenin set himself to resolving three principle issues: establishing peace and dealing with the claims of workers and peasants' demand for land (ibid.). Lenin was not in power long before his death in 1924, but the succession struggle had begun over one year earlier. Joseph Stalin emerged victorious following a power struggle primarily between him and Leon Trotsky.

Stalin's 'revolution' was said to have been more 'drastic' than Lenin's (Seton-Watson, 1965; Tilly, 1993). Stalin destroyed the independent peasant and smallholder as a class and introduced large collective farms. At the same time, he created vast industries through massive mobilization and systematic exploitation of the working class (Seton-Watson, 1965). Most citizens experienced a drop in personal incomes that was only slightly offset by the introduction of free education and health services (Kochan and Keep, 1997). Many families in the 1930s had two bread-winners, since both husbands and wives were obliged to work to make ends meet. By 1939 women comprised 43 per cent of all industrial workers; many performed heavy industrial labour, including coal mining, where they made up one-quarter of the workforce (Kochan and Keep, 1997; also see Mitchell, 1992). At the same time, a massive adult education drive was initiated; the new elite that emerged would dominate Soviet affairs for the next half-century. For example, during this period Leonid Brezhnev, who led the country from 1964 to 1982, entered an agricultural academy that had been created as part of this drive (Kochan and Keep, 1997).

During the Stalin era, family policies also became more traditional in terms of gender roles: divorce became harder to obtain and abortion was criminalized (Michaels, 2001). In response to the rising tendency of non-Russian ethnicities to fight for 'local' nationalism, Stalin introduced a policy that identified two crimes: nationalism and cosmopolitanism (Deutscher, 1949/1976; Seton-Watson, 1965). He declared that a non-Russian was guilty of nationalism if in any way he stressed the differences that separated his nation from the Russian nation (Seton-Watson, 1965). Following his death, the nationalities policy was modified but was not dramatically changed.

Under Stalin, a brutally repressive police apparatus emerged to purge the U.S.S.R. of dissenting voices (Khrushchev, 1956/1972; Brzezinski, 1961). It included deportation to the Gulag, a highly developed forced-labour system under which very few lives were spared (Moore, 1954). In a speech delivered at the Twentieth Congress of the Communist Party of the Soviet Union in February 1956, Nikita Khrushchev (1956/1959) reflected publicly on a conversation he had had with Nikolai Alexandrovich Bulganin: 'once when we two were traveling in a car, he [Bulganin] said, "It has happened sometimes that a man goes to Stalin on his invitation as a friend. And, when he sits with Stalin, he does not know where he will be sent next – home or to prison"' (184). It was noted by many that, between Lenin's death (1924) and his own death (1953), there was hardly a time when Stalin did not 'have a whip hand over his rivals, internally' (Kennan, 1961, 250). Meanwhile, his external rivals, capitalism in general and the United States in particular, grew in power in the post-war period. According to Deutscher (1949/1976), the new balance of power 'would require that the United States should reconcile itself to Russian ascendency in the East and Russia to American ascendency in the West' (550). The result was an inevitable clash. In the years after 1948 the term 'cold war' came to describe a web of international tensions deriving from the bipolar antagonism of the two emerging superpowers.

The death of Stalin in March 1953 did not end the cold war, but it did lead to a series of changes within the Soviet Union. After the Cuban missile crisis in 1962, relations between the U.S.S.R. and the United States appeared to be changing, and perhaps even improving, under Khrushchev's leadership (Garray and Gay, 1972). Meanwhile, within the U.S.S.R. Khrushchev was waging a campaign to reduce the central bureaucracy and 'replace terror by mobilizing the masses to participate in political process' (Hosking, 1985, 347). He also intended to move from socialism to full communism, but much of this plan was undermined by administrative reorganization, resulting in disruption and mixed results (Kotkin, 2001). This failure along with numerous other problems and disappointing yields in agriculture eventually led to Khrushchev's removal from power.

Brezhnev was selected as Khrushchev's successor in 1964. He reversed some of Khrushchev's reforms but did not seek to change Soviet institutions; instead, he kept the system 'ticking' while reinforcing the U.S.S.R.'s military might. He also did what he could to make life more comfortable for members of the medium- and upper-level state apparatus (Hosking, 1985). By the 1970s spreading corruption had done much to undermine Communist Party's rule. Agencies were put in place to suppress abuses of power, but to no avail. The KGB, under the leadership of Yuri Andropov (1914–84), later general secretary of the party, after Brezhnev's death, began to gain more power throughout this period. In fact, Andropov was said to have had a strong influence on policy-making, behind the scenes for as long as Brezhnev's illness was concealed and then quite openly, until Brezhnev's death. Andropov himself was in power only three years before he died of severe emphysema.

During this period the U.S.S.R. was marking time and stagnating. The agricultural sector was in disarray; crop yields were improving but much food went to waste because of inadequate storage and transport facilities. Similarly, in the industrial sector under Khrushchev workers' incomes had grown throughout the early 1960s, but the rate of increase tailed off in the 1970s (Hosking, 1985). Attempts to improve the system of planning and management also 'ran into the sand' (Kochan and Keep, 1997, 482).

By the time Gorbachev came to power in 1985, the Soviet Union was economically in decline (Kotkin, 2001). Too much political tension had built up beneath the surface (Kochan and Keep, 1997) and the economy needed more than reforming: the U.S.S.R. could not simultaneously modernize, boost output, improve quality, and produce new types of goods without running into further debt. Furthermore, it had to withdraw from its 'outer empire' in eastern Europe. Even before Gorbachev took the reins, he delivered an address in December 1984, which used three terms that became the hallmark of his policy: democratization, *glasnost* (openness), and *perestroika* (reconstruction). Gorbachev initiated changes that 'had consequences as unintended as they were overwhelming' (520). This speech marked a new era in Soviet history – but also marked the end of the union (Lapidus, 1993).

Women and Families in the Soviet Union

In early communist ideology, soon after the 1917 revolution, a woman was accepted as 'a comrade of special qualities.' Women comrades were perceived to differ little from men, even sporting short haircuts, pants, and smoking cigarettes – 'a style of behaviour that turned them into "their own boys"' (Lissyutkina, 1993, 277). Women were ideologically reconstructed as 'sexless figures in boots as road workers, construction workers, vegetable farmers, etc.' (277).

Gender equality was a basic tenet of Marxist-Leninist theory, but it manifested itself mainly in the absorption of women into the socialist economy (see Article 122 of the 1936 Soviet Constitution; Mosse et al., 1957). After the economic and demographic problems resulting from the First World War and the Civil War/Russian Revolution, the goal of the Bolshevik government was to draw women into the emerging industrial labour force. Among other things, it set out to protect the employment rights of pregnant women, since pregnancy could no longer be cited as a reason for refusing women employment, nor could women be dismissed from work when they became pregnant (see Article 139 of the 1960 Russian Soviet Federative Socialist Republic RSFSR Criminal Code; Belyakova et al., 1978). In fact, women were legally entitled to request a transfer to lighter work, and pregnant women and new mothers could not be sent on business trips without their consent (Ilic, 1996). Furthermore, paid maternity leave was introduced and was not to be deducted from a woman's continuous work record. Paid leave of eight weeks before and eight weeks after birth was introduced for industrial workers and six weeks before and after birth for white-collar workers (ibid.). Maternity grants were offered to mothers to help to offset the cost of baby clothes and other related purchases, nursing mothers were allowed a minimum half-hour break every three hours to feed their babies (see Article 169 of the Fundamentals of Labour Legislation of the USSR, 1970; Belyakova et al., 1978), and nursing mothers could request a transfer to employment closer to their place of residence (Ilic, 1996; see the Decree of the Presidium of the Supreme Soviet of the USSR of 8 July 1944; ibid.).

Gender equality at the time was believed to be best achieved by introducing socialized child care and housework and establishing a 'socialist comradery' between the sexes (Morvant, 1995). Under Stalin, however, the emphasis placed on women's liberation by the Bolsheviks came to an end. The socialization of housework proposed by Lenin and Trotsky and the like never got off the ground. Nonetheless, women continued to become involved in paid employment, all the while raising children and maintaining a household. By 1970 women accounted for 51 per cent of the working population (Morvant, 1995; also see Mitchell 1992).

At no time in its history was the U.S.S.R. a truly egalitarian society (Heitlinger, 1979). In theory, women in the Soviet Union enjoyed full equality with men, but in practice they, like most women elsewhere, bore the triple burden of paid employment, domestic work, and childcare. Furthermore, in spite of formal equality, women faced considerable discrimination at work. For example, in 1956 a decree of the Presidium of the Supreme Soviet ratified Convention 100 of the International Labour Organization of 29 June 1951, which granted equal renumeration for men and women workers for work of equal value (Belyakova et al., 1978). Nonetheless, throughout the Soviet era, women were paid less than men and were under-represented in senior positions, despite having, on average, higher levels of education (Morvant, 1995; Lissyutkina, 1993).

During the Soviet period controversy surrounded women's control of reproduction. Policy on abortion, for example, underwent considerable change: abortion was legalized in 1920, deemed illegal in 1936, and then legalized again in 1955 (Michaels, 2001). As mentioned above, during the Stalin era family policies became more traditional compared with those in force under Lenin, and divorce became harder to obtain. Following Stalin's death, family policies were liberalized. Abortion became legal again in November 1955 after the law 'On Abolishing the Prohibition of Abortion' permitted abortion on request during the first three months of pregnancy as long as it was carried out by qualified medical personnel (for the actual Decree see Belyakova et al., 1978).

A unique feature of Soviet society was ideas on the socialization of children. Traditionally, when 'family' was defined by academics and researchers, the definition included a list of functions a family was supposed to perform; in most cases the list included 'the physical reproduction of new individuals, the nourishment and maintenance of these individuals during infancy and childhood, and the placement of these individuals in the system of social positions' (Davis, 1959, 394–5) or some variant of these functions. In Soviet society, in most cases the socialization of children was expected to take place outside the family, in institutions (Zimmerman et al., 1994). In fact, parents were generally discouraged from raising children 'privately.' For example, according to A.S. Makarenko (1937/1967), who wrote one of the most widely read practical guides for parents raising Soviet children, 'Our family is not a closed-in collective body, like the bourgeois family. It is an organic part of Soviet society, and every attempt it makes to build up its own experience independently of the moral demands of society is bound to result in a disproportion, discordant as an alarm bell' (xi). In other words, parents were encouraged to be guardians of their children but to leave some of the work of raising them to the state. Makarenko did suggest that a parent be more than a guardian, by advising: 'you must also be organizer of your own life, because your quality as an educator is entirely bound up with your activities as a citizen and your feelings as an individual' (17).

One researcher noted that, whereas the major goal of family policy in the United States was the well-being of family members, the official goal of family policy in Soviet society was the successful functioning of the family as a social institution that supported the welfare of the larger society (Zimmerman et al., 1994). Consequently, 'women were perceived primarily as workers rather than mothers' (Ilic, 1996, 236), since, at this point, women were needed to be economically productive. It was later argued that women in the Soviet period had been forced to develop personality traits more appropriate to the workplace than to the home, and that children were 'abandoned' to the impersonality of state crèches and kindergartens (Attwood, 1996).

During the Soviet period, because it served the state's economic interests, women were not defined simply by traditional roles. For example, women were encouraged to become involved in politics, and their participation in legislative bodies was ensured through quotas. The arrangement resulted in their one-third representation in the Supreme Soviet (Issraelyan, 1996). Women also made up 28 per cent of the Communist Party membership, 52 per cent of the Young Communist League, and 36 per cent of the Central Trade Union membership (ibid.). There has been considerable debate about the amount of 'real' power women held in these organizations.

The Rise of Nationalism and the Break-up of the Soviet Union

It has been argued that the 'nationality crisis' coupled with the economic crisis were the main threats to the survival of the Soviet empire

(Zaslavsky, 1993; Lapidus, 1993; Suny, 1993; Tilly 1993). The deepening economic crisis undermined the status and power of the Soviet Union, in general, but it also served to weaken the state's ability to manipulate nationality and ethnic relations. In other words, its weakening administrative structures ceased to have the power to impose formal ethnic cohesion. Feodor Burlatsky (1998) noted that 'Boris Yeltsin together with other representatives of the "opposition" was stirring up the nationalist sentiments of the Russian people' (141). David Reynolds (2000) stated that Yeltsin 'cultivated Russian nationalism, especially after he gained election as chairman of the republic's new Supreme Soviet in May 1990' (571).

According to Zaslavsky (1993), 'with the advent of *perestroika* and the collapse of centralized control, nationality emerged as the most potent base of social mobilization' (72). The first two fault lines that emerged divided the Baltic republics from the Slavic ones and the southern Muslim republics from the northern non-Muslim ones. By 1990 the overwhelming majority of autonomous republics unilaterally raised their status to that of union republics and were well on their way towards independence. Even in traditionally imperialist Russia, the nationalist idea quickly 'gained the upper hand in the mass social consciousness of Russians' (80). The national identity of the majority of Russians historically had been based on an imperial idea, but in the new circumstances of *perestroika*, nationalist movements underwent rapid modification towards separatism (Zaslavsky, 1993; Drobizheva, 1993; Tolz, 1998; Pain, 2000; Gorenburg, 2001). 'Isolationism and separatism were emerging as the one platform unifying all the major strands of Russian nationalism' (Zaslavsky, 1993, 86).

Gorbachev pronounced illegal the first declarations of sovereignty by autonomous republics. Yeltsin, on the other hand, strongly supported policies promoting at least Russian sovereignty, while offering a larger degree of self-rule to the autonomous republics (Tilly, 1993). Feodor Burlatsky (1998) explained that 'Gorbachev, as always, sought compromise and balance,' and 'ceded to Yeltsin's pressure' (141). By December 1991 the leaders of Russia, Ukraine, and Belorussia pronounced the end of the U.S.S.R. (ironically, these nations were founding members of the Soviet Union). They simultaneously pledged to found a loose association of independent states that would welcome the remaining republics.

By most accounts, the new Russia faced formidable difficulties in moving from a centrally planned economy to a market economy (Central Intelligence Agency, 1996). In January 1992 President Yeltsin launched a series of economic reforms, freeing all prices, slashing defence spending, eliminating the centralized distribution system, completing an extensive privatization program, establishing private financial institutions, and decentralizing foreign trade (ibid.). These measures had a serious impact on the lives of individual Russians and on women in particular.

At the outset, it was said that none of the political leaders during *perestroika* had formed a program for or were interested in women (Lissyutkina, 1993). But a deeper analysis reveals that this statement was not completely accurate. The misery and general social breakdown created by the dramatic political and economic changes were especially negative for women (Filtzer, 1996); in fact, women became a focus of much, perhaps unwanted, attention from politicians, the national crisis in Russia being manifested in an 'intensification of maternal metaphors' (Goscilo, 1996, 34). The political and economic changes that took place at the time were accompanied by a 'celebration of masculinity' and the 'denigration of the strong capable woman worker glorified in the first decades of Soviet history' (Attwood, 1996, 255). According to Rebecca Kay (1997) '"over-emancipation" of women in Soviet Russia is blamed for a whole myriad of contemporary social problems' (82).

This period of national revival coincides with serious economic crisis (Marsh, 1996). As a result, Russian nationalism at this time did not construct an ethnic 'other'/nemesis, as is commonly the case with the rise of nationalist sentiment. Instead, since Russian male identity was threatened by joblessness (Meshcherkina, 2000), domestication of women, not the quest for racial purity, was presented as a solution (although there were some, like the leader of the Russian Party, Nikolai Bondarik, who argued that only those with 'Russian blood' should be represented in government; Tolz, 1998).

According to Goscilo (1996), articles, essays, and letters to the editors in numerous Russian newspapers echoed the message: 'the solution to the country's anomie rests in mothers' tender hands. Crime would decrease, men would recover their masculine dignity (not to mention sobriety and sexual potency), disaffected adolescents would buckle down to meaningful activities, and the breakdown of the family would fade to a memory) – were women to reprise their predetermined function in the maternal metaphor of nationhood' (35-6; see also Tartakovskaya, 2000). Consequently, a series of proposed policy changes, specifically aimed at the aggressive re-masculinization of post-Soviet Russia (Attwood, 1996) and a 're-feminization' and 'domestication' of women, were introduced. At first, many women greeted these changes with enthusiasm, since they were perceived to provide relief from the 'double burden' of juggling paid and unpaid labour, but their response soon changed (Lissytkina, 1993; Issraelyan, 1996).

Women and Family Policies in Today's Russia

The constitution of the Russian Federation, adopted in 1993, proclaimed equality between men and women. Russia also signed international agreements pledging to eliminate all forms of sex discrimination. On the other hand, 'instead of equality between men and women, there has been a lowering of both sexes to poverty and the deprivation of political rights' (Lissyutkina, 1993, 283). Furthermore, women burdened by both paid and unpaid labour were in no position to take advantage of new opportunities for political and economic initiatives opened by *perestroika*, and worse: 'ideology suggested that they should not try' (Waters, 1993, 288). In other words, *perestroika* was met with mixed emotions and experiences. A feminist researcher suggested: 'the Soviet people have found themselves at the epicenter of a social cataclysm known as "perestroika"' (Lissyutkina, 1993, 280). It was characterized as having and promoting at least three cultural value systems: communist ideology, the traditional conceptions and values of pre-revolutionary Russia, and western values (democracy, individualism, private enterprise; ibid.). Much of the remainder of this chapter will present and evaluate the second of these systems, the traditional values, which have been especially relevant to the lives of Russian women.

A Return to Domesticity

In his book *Perestroika*, Gorbachev began a section entitled 'Women and the Family' by stating that women should become more actively involved in the management of the economy, but only two paragraphs later he wrote: 'But over the years of our difficult and heroic history, we failed to pay attention to women's specific rights and needs arising from their role as mother and home-maker, and their indispensable educational function as regards children. Engaged in scientific research, working on construction sites, in production and in the services, and involved in creative activities, women no longer have enough time to perform their everyday duties at home – housework, the upbringing of children and the creation of good family atmosphere' (Gorbachev, 1987, 117). Some have noted that Gorbachev did not have a malicious intent, but instead was responding to the idea that under Soviet rule Russian women 'felt crushed by emancipation' (Goscilo, 1996, 9). Nonetheless, Gorbachev was writing that, since women were 'distracted' with productive and paid work, they were burdened by their duties in the home as mothers and homemakers. He went on to say: 'We have discovered that many of our problems – in children's and young people's behaviour, in our morals, culture and in production – are partly caused by the weakening of family ties and slack attitude to family responsibilities. This is a paradoxical result of our sincere and politically justified desire to make women equal to men in everything' (1987, 117). Others amplified Gorbachev's words, by stating: 'the country was experiencing a crisis of spirituality ... which could be traced to the breakup of the family and to the absence of proper homes and of proper women to organize them' (Waters, 1993, 288). Researchers noted that the vast majority of Russian politicians and reformers appeared to view the 'domestication' of women as a necessary precondition for the establishment of a liberal democratic government (Koblitz, 1995).

What these voices seemed to be saying is that the socialist goal/ideal of granting women equality with men, although a noble concept, was a mistake. Gorbachev (1987) proposed to 'correct' this paradox or mistake by devising policies designed to return women to their homes to fulfil their 'womanly duties' as housewives and mothers: 'Now, in the course of perestroika, we have begun to overcome this shortcoming. That is why we are now holding heated debates in the press, in public organizations, at work and at home, about the question of what we should do to make it possible for women to return to their purely womanly mission' (117). It is important to note, however, that during Gorbachev's rule, relatively little was accomplished towards this goal. It was not until after Yeltsin had declared Russian sovereignty that things started to change. For example, in a speech broadcast on International Women's Day in 1995 President Yeltsin described women as 'more cultured than men.' He explained that 'women are clearly made in such a way as to create naturally an atmosphere of spiritual warmth and cordiality around them' (Kay, 1997, 84).

The official and unofficial ideology of post-Soviet Russia came to emphasize the domestic roles of women and a 'return to the family' campaign (Issraelyan, 1996). For example, Aleksandr Solzhenitsyn, the famous Russian writer and winner of the Nobel Prize for Literature, when writing on the changes that were taking place in his country, noted: 'normal families virtually ceased to exist in our country ... [but]

the family has a fundamental role in the salvation of our future' (1991, 42). He proposed to 'save' the family, and thus the nation's future, by stating that women 'must have the opportunity to return to their families to take care of the children; the salary earned by men must make it possible' (42). In other words, the return to the traditional nuclear family would result in the salvation of Russia's future.

The image of women and men as partners in the building of socialism began to be replaced by that of the 'traditional functionalist family in which men and women have different but supposedly complementary roles: a single male breadwinner battles with the world of work, and comes home to the loving care of a wife who devotes herself to home and children' (Attwood, 1996, 256). An article in a Russian newspaper explained that the most successful 'type' of woman is one who 'reasons delicately and realistically. She lets a man feel the necessity of his leadership in life, lets him take charge in the family but always under her hidden control' (Kay, 1997, 83). Lissyutkina (1993) explained that during the period of transition, 'While economically oppressed and spiritually crushed, Soviet men are forced to conform to the traditional roles of the head of the family and master of his wife' (283). Both conservatives and radicals in Russia were said to share the essentialist view that women's place was in the home (Waters, 1993). Debates in the post-Soviet period have clearly emphasized women's roles as mothers rather than workers (Ilic, 1996). Caiazza (2002) similarly noted that in policy debates in the Duma women were defined primarily as mothers.

Russian sociologist Igor Bestuzhev-Lada had long been a protagonist in the campaign to return women to the home. He received a chance to help implement such a change when he became one of the government's advisers on a new bill (Attwood, 1996). Bestuzhev-Lada's vision of the restoration of the patriarchal family, now in a free-market economy, found concrete expression in the draft bill 'For the Protection of the Family, Motherhood, Fatherhood and Children.' At first glance, the bill appeared to be quite progressive, proposing, for example, that an employer pay a female employee on maternity leave no less than twice the minimum pay; if he was unable to transfer her to lighter work during her pregnancy, according to a law enacted decades earlier, he would have to release her while continuing to pay her an average wage. Furthermore, it proposed that women with children under the age of fourteen should not be allowed to work more than thirty-five hours per week (ibid.). The bill appeared to be protecting women, especially mothers, from a harsh work environment, but a closer look revealed that the proposed laws placed women at a disadvantage in the labour force and contained a sexist double standard.

According to the bill, if a woman had three children, she could *not* declare herself unemployed if she lost her job. That is, a mother of three could not register at the labour exchange, receive unemployment benefits, or appear on any list of people seeking work (Attwood, 1996). Furthermore, employers would hesitate to hire a woman, fearing that she might become pregnant and therefore an economic liability to the company. The proposed laws effectively limited mothers with children under the age of fourteen to the status of part-time worker; worse, they enshrined women's dependence on their husbands, because despite the fact that 'fatherhood' appeared in the title of the bill, nowhere was the role that fathers should play in raising children discussed. It was assumed that father was synonymous with breadwinner. Needless to say, it was also assumed that women with children were in heterosexual, two-parent households, where the husband/father/man was the breadwinner and his income was adequate to support the family. None of these assumptions adequately reflected social reality. Divorce, lone-parenthood, underemployment of men (and women, for that matter), and inadequate wages were facts of life in the new Russia.

Many have noted that the decline in the standard of living in Russia in the early 1990s meant that many families needed – now more than ever – the income of two adults to make ends meet (Morvant, 1995). Furthermore, there was an increase in the number of divorces, a drop in the number of marriages, and a rise in the proportion of children born out of wedlock, meaning that there were more single mothers and women dependent solely on their own wages (ibid.). By the end of 1992, 42 per cent of families with children under eighteen were living either on the brink of poverty or below the poverty line: for families with one child, the figure was 34 per cent; with two 47 per cent, and with three or more 72 per cent (Sargeant, 1996). Therefore, the proposed bill's goal to (re)establish the traditional nuclear family as the Russian ideal was virtually impossible.

The bill also proposed to elevate the social value of child-rearing through the recommendation that non-working parents responsible for the care of three or more children receive a sum of money no less than the minimum wage (Ilic, 1996). The bill hoped to provide a solution to both the demographic (low birth rates) and economic (chronic underemployment and unemployment) problems of the nation by redefining women primarily as mothers (ibid.).   Furthermore, according to the draft legislation, the main 'functions' of family were reproductive and economic, which among other things meant that if a couple did not want or could not have children, they would not be defined as a family (Sargeant, 1996).

The draft bill 'had many critics, and although it received second reading in February 1993, it was not passed before the confrontation between Yeltsin and parliament in October 1993. However, despite the fact that this particular bill was not passed, by the beginning of 1994 the government had drawn up about thirty different programs and decrees on the protection of mothers and children. None of them was implemented, owing to a lack of funding and coordination (Sargeant, 1996). Economic hardship became a fact of life for the new Russia and its people.

Pronuptialism and Pronatalism

According to Tolz (1998), partly in response to the growing assertiveness of non-Russian republics, Russians began to feel resentful about having taken on an excessive economic burden. Accompanying this resentment was the perception of a threat to the biological survival of Russians (ibid.). As a consequence, a number of titles like 'Is Russia Dying?' started appearing in the Russian press (Sargeant, 1996). The fact was that because many young people in post-Soviet Russia could not afford to have children, the number of marriages significantly declined. For example, in 1987 there were 1.443 million marriages registered in Russia, while the number for 1992 was 1.054 million (ibid.). This trend intensified in 1993 and 1994. The state felt it had to do something to encourage families to stay together and to have children. One of the president's decrees was entitled 'On Measures of Social Support for Families with Many Children.' Among other things, the decree stipulated that local authorities should give plots of land to large families, and large families were allowed to obtain prescription medicines free of charge (ibid.). The decree proved to be ineffective. Only a tiny fraction of the families were given land, since banks were unwilling to offer interest-free loans to large families, as stipulated by the decree. When approached by large families, banks simply declared that they did not have the money. On the other hand, they found the money when businessmen requested loans to be repaid at 200 per cent interest (ibid.). Similarly, pharmacists would tell large families looking for free prescription medication that they did not have the medicine, but the same medicine was available to families willing and able to pay for it (ibid.). In order to encourage Russians to marry, remain married, and have children, it was also suggested that the Russian government should introduce home-purchase loans for newlyweds. The proposed loans would include a provision to write off parts of the loan after the birth of each child (ibid.). Again, profound economic crisis has prevented this plan from being implemented.

These failures have not hindered efforts to achieve the national goals through other means. For example, in March 1994 the Russian government issued bureaucratic directives designed to increase birth rates and reduce abortions. One of the directives was to remove most abortions from medical insurance coverage and introduce fees for them (Parfitt, 2003; Sargeant, 1996). In 1995 for-fee abortions cost approximately 150,000 rubles or $33, which was a significant sum, given that the monthly household incomes of some women were two to three times the cost of an abortion (Rankin-Williams, 2001). Removing most abortions from medical insurance coverage would make it virtually impossible for many women to afford the procedure. Furthermore, one of the 'unforeseen' consequences might be that women would opt for illegal abortions, which could result in the death of many women, as was the case in Romania in the 1980s (see Baban and David, 1994). Simultaneously, in post-Soviet Russia, a largely male, vocal, anti-abortion movement began (Vanden Heuvel, 1993; Koblitz, 1995). Some have noted that, since the abortion procedure in the Soviet Union was brutal, seeking to ban it was justified. The question remains: why not push for improvements in the procedure rather than for an outright ban?

Women's Participation in Public Life: Employment and Political Life

During the first few years of *perestroika* there was increased nostalgia for traditional female roles centred on the home and family (Morvant, 1995). In the 'more relaxed atmosphere of glasnost' the question of the role women should play in contemporary Russia received considerable press coverage. Numerous articles suggested that it was somehow unfeminine for women to be active politically or professionally (ibid.). Furthermore, following the collapse of the Soviet Union, the demographic imperative behind returning women to the home was reinforced by the belief that women had no business working as long as men were without jobs. For example, when asked about the problem of women's unemployment in 1993, Labour Minister Gennadii Melikyan replied, 'Why should we employ women when men are out of work? It's better that men work and women take care of children and do housework. I don't think women should work when men are doing nothing' (5). Clearly, following the political and economic changes that fell upon Russia in the early 1990s, attempts were made to return women to the private sphere. Women were told that the democratization and economic revitalization of Russia was a man's job.

Many have noted that women were especially economically hard hit by changes that took place in Russia over the last decade of the twentieth century. Surveys done throughout this period reveal that there was increasing gender discrimination in pay, recruitment, promotion, and dismissal as well as a growing tendency towards the feminization of poverty (Issraelyan, 1996). It is estimated that between 70 and 80 per cent of those officially recognized as unemployed were women (Attwood, 1996), and those especially hard hit were women with high levels of education, a significant proportion of whom were under the age of thirty (Issraelyan, 1996). Furthermore, statistics show that the number of underemployed women was almost as high as the number of unemployed (ibid.). In addition, the wage gap between men's and women's employment was increasing. One feminist researcher noted that in 1936, when Stalin officially proclaimed women's emancipation achieved, women earned 70 cents to every man's dollar. In the 1990s the wage gap widened, women earning as little as 40 cents for every man's dollar (Richardson, 1995). It appeared that one of the underlying objectives of this disparity was to drive women out of the paid labour force, since it was believed that withdrawing women en masse from the workforce would not only ease the economic crisis, but in the words of Solzhenitsyn (1991) would 'play a fundamental role in the salvation of our future' (42).

Yeltsin's wife, Naina, was believed by some to be the model of the ideal post-Soviet woman, as wife and servant. In one of the few interviews she gave, she stated that she was not 'the first lady' but rather the wife of the Russian president and a housewife: 'I choose his ties, I take care of his shirts and suits' (Attwood, 1996, 258). She declared that unlike Gorbachev's wife, Raisa, she did not undertake public or social work and had no power to affect change. In fact, she added, 'there is an unbreakable rule in our family: I must never ask my husband about anything that relates to his work' (258). In other words, the Russian male is/should be the head of the household, and the Russian female is/should be his private supporter and keeper of the hearth.

Women in Soviet society had every reason to be dissatisfied with the impotence of the roles they filled in the Communist political system, but the situation did not improve in the new system that emerged in the 1990s. Women continued to hold minority positions of power, particularly in the executive branch of government. One of the first consequences of the fall of Communism was the sharp drop in women's political representation (Gigli, 1995). In the post-Soviet era quotas on women's participation in legislative bodies were lifted, which resulted in a dramatic drop in their representation. United Nations data reveal that in 1987 women occupied 34.5 per cent of parliamentary seats in the U.S.S.R. (1991a). This proportion fell to 13 per cent in the Russian Federation in 1995 and 10 per cent in 1999 (United Nations, 2000b). Women accounted for only 5 per cent of parliamentarians in the upper chamber in 1994 (United Nations, 1995).

The position of women in government improved in the December 1993 elections because of successes achieved by the Women of Russia movement. Women's organizations, including the Women's Union of Russia, the Association of Women Entrepreneurs, and the Russian Navy Women's Association, combined forces to win over 8 per cent of the votes and set up a women's faction in the state Duma (Issraelyan, 1996). Even with this unexpected success, women constituted only 10 per cent of deputies (Morvant, 1995). By early 1995, there were sixty-nine women in the Federal Assembly, making up 11 per cent of parliamentarians (Issraelyan, 1996). While the role of women in the Communist system may have been largely symbolic, with democratization, the number of women elected to national and local offices decreased. This fact probably reflects the underlying sexism that some have identified as lurking in the Russian media and popular culture.

Resistance and Vilification of Objectors and 'Deviants'

According to Attwood (1996), with the fall of Communism and Russian independence, a plethora of articles appeared in the popular press with titles such as 'Where Are the Real Man and Woman?' and 'The Bitter Fruits of Emancipation' (255), which outlined a range of alarming social trends. Women were featured in public debate as the root of social ills (Waters, 1993). The 'bitter fruits of emancipation' supposedly included children abandoned to the impersonality of state childcare services, men robbed of their traditional masculine roles, high divorce rates, and low birth rates (Attwood, 1996). Others have noted that in the so-called 'progressive' Russian literature oriented to the ideals of modernization and westernization, another cliché was persistently presented and projected onto women, that of the 'female traitor' (Lissyutkina, 1993). Lissyutkina explained that 'for the Russian thinker, a woman stands only as a deceptive symbol of Russia' (285). She noted that Russian women were breaking radically from the past, and Russian men were condemning this as 'betrayal.'

Evaluating the Russian Government's 'Successes' and Failures

According to Christopher Williams (1996) the 'rise of neo-fascist and right wing ideologies in the early to mid 1990s has led to the continuation of conservative attitudes towards women, a hostility to female emancipation and a failure to accord any priority to women's issues' (150). Similarly, others noted that before *perestroika*, a woman's main role was that of worker and active builder of Communism, 'but after perestroika she was urged to fulfil her traditional function as housewife' (Sargeant, 1996, 270). Fortunately, or unfortunately, the Russian state was in neither the economic nor the political position to be able to implement many of its proposed changes.

The new Russia's vision of returning women to 'a purely womanly mission' as Gorbachev put it, was unrealistic and unattainable. In a single year, from 1991 to 1992, the number of divorces in Russia increased by 7 per cent. In 1992 alone, there were 640,000 divorces, compared with 580,000 only five years earlier, in 1987 (Sargeant, 1996). Between 1990 and 1993, 68 per cent of all marriages ended in divorce (Seager, 1997). Furthermore, in that year, as a result of family break-ups, 569,000 children under the age of eighteen began living with one parent instead of two. Financial constraints and an increasing number of single women and single mothers meant that only a small proportion of women were 'genuinely free' to choose whether or not to work outside the home (Morvant, 1995).

Regarding the state's attempts at pronatalism, the number of abortions being performed was decreasing. For example, in 1992 there were three million registered abortions, compared with two million only one year later, but the ratio of abortions to births remained the same: three to one, which meant that birth rates were declining at the same time as abortion rates (Sargeant, 1996). In other words, women were avoiding both 'registered' abortions and childbirth, resulting in falling birth rates.

A Recapitulation

At the beginning of the twentieth century, the Communist ideals that were to become the foundations of a new society following the Russian Revolution stressed equality between men and women. The reality that followed the revolution was quite different. Economic necessity and Soviet ideology drove women into the paid labour force, but once there, they continued to experience discrimination and a double burden. During the Soviet era women were encouraged to seek self-actualization through their public roles, particularly in paid employment, but they were still expected to fill their roles in the home. In post-Soviet Russia at the end of the twentieth century, there was an ideological shift: nationalist and economic interests attempted to redefine women and womanhood. 'Righting' the Communist 'wrongs' that supposedly had defeminized women and contributed to the destruction of the Russian family and persuading women to return to their 'purely womanly mission' in the home were now emphasized. These goals were said to include the 'reassertion of women's "true feminine nature"' (Kay, 1997, 83).

One of the main barriers encountered by post-Soviet Russian leaders in 'persuading' women was the economic reality that made it virtually impossible for Russians to survive in traditional nuclear families. Where two-parent families existed, men's wages were inadequate to support them. A rise in divorce and lone-parenthood contributed to the impossibility of realizing such an ideal. It may seem quite positive that the Russian state was unable to implement many of its proposed changes in its attempts to re-patriarchalize Russian society, but at the same time the economic reality that has crippled the Russian state has weighed heavily on the nation's women; they continue to struggle to feed their families and make ends meet. What remains clear is that, in national reconstruction, women's actual needs and issues are placed on the national political 'back-burners.' Women are forced and 'encouraged' to move in and out of the labour force. Their image is defined and redefined, moulded and idealized – like a circus contortionist – all for the sake of the nation. Whether they *want* to conform, are *able* to conform, or outright *reject* the new models becomes almost irrelevant, because the economic and social realities of post-Soviet Russia force them to cope with a great deal of turmoil.

7

Nationalist Revival in Post-Yugoslav Croatia

The Political and Economic Situation before the Break-up

For Yugoslavia, the Second World War was characterized by occupation, partition, resistance, and revolution (Singleton, 1994). Aside from fighting on the Allied side against Germany and Italy during the War, Yugoslavia found itself in the middle of what appeared to be a very bloody civil war between Croatian nationalists/Nazis (Ustaša), Serbian Royalists (Četniks), and Communist-led Partisans. Of the 1.7 million dead in Yugoslavia, 1 million were killed in the struggle between various groups of Yugoslavs rather than by foreign enemies (ibid.). At the Teheran Conference in November–December 1943, Churchill, Roosevelt, and Stalin agreed to support the Partisans, led by Tito, as the only effective Yugoslav resistance movement. Tito and his (Communist) government ruled Yugoslavia for the next thirty-five years (see Hitchcock, 2003).

Yugoslavia under Marshal Tito was not like other Communist countries at the time. In the summer of 1948 Tito, though still proclaiming himself a Communist, rejected Russian/Soviet dictatorship and initiated a 'highly important line of future development' (Garraty and Gay, 1972, 1075; Tudjman, 1981; Lichtheim, 1999). In the 1950s Yugoslavia turned to political and economic alliances with newly independent ex-colonial nations of the 'Third World,' including Egypt, India, and Burma. These nations were geographically far apart, but their political situations were quite similar: 'All wanted to steer clear of the power blocks which had developed in the world, and they did not want to be forced to choose between communism and capitalism' (Singleton, 1994, 238). They came to believe that the solution to the problem of independence for small nations could be found in non-alignment and collective self-help.

The economic reforms of the mid-1960s also involved the removal of barriers to the free movement of peoples across frontiers, making Yugoslavia the only eastern European country in which citizens were able to travel freely for both work and leisure. They were also the only ones to be allowed to buy and read western literature and foreign newspapers (Singleton, 1994).

Another significant and unique characteristic of Yugoslavia in this post-war period was connected to the principle of self-management, which was introduced in 1950 (Ramet, 1999a). Self-management involved a system of elections of delegations drawn from occupational and interest groups. Self-management bodies in the economy and society would represent the entire working population, including blue-collar workers in the corresponding political structure (Denitch, 1976). Workers' councils acted as organs of power, which bargained and spoke for the workers who elected them. The elected members of delegations sat in various chambers of the Assembly at federal, republican, provincial, and communal levels and were subject to recall by the body that elected them (Singleton, 1994). Tito considered this arrangement to be a guarantee that the direct democracy of workers would prevail.

While nationalist sentiments were simmering beneath the surface from its post-war inception (Tudjman, 1981), by the late 1960s it became apparent that nationalists, especially in Croatia, were not happy with the amount of autonomy granted to the republics. In the period between 1968 and 1971, a period known as the 'Croatian Spring,' many were openly demanding 'democratization' *and* independence for Croatia. While constitutional changes in 1963 and 1968 allowed national groups greater autonomy (Reynolds, 2000), outright independence was seen as out of the question. The response from Tito was swift and stern.

Aside from nationalist 'outbursts' in the early years, the 1970s were deemed to be a period of political and economic stability; in fact, some have argued that the late-Tito era was one of optimism, or 'a kind of golden age' (Ramet, 1999a, 5). The situation began to change by 1979: the economy started to deteriorate, Vice-President Kardelj died in 1979, and Tito died in 1980, not only leaving a power vacuum, but also depriving the country of unifying symbols. Financial problems, political decay, and escalating Serb-Albanian tensions in Kosovo created an environment of crisis in which the legitimacy of the Communist system was questioned (Ramet, 1999a). The Communist Party as a whole was weak and disunified, members joined out of sheer opportunism, and other political bodies were charged with unconstitutional practices, corruption, rampant inefficiency, and being unresponsive to people's needs (ibid.).

Serbian and Croatian 'national revivals' sprang up throughout the 1980s, and by 1986 a Pandora's box of nationalism had (re)opened in Yugoslavia. Slovenians began advancing a 'Slovenian national program' that included talk of political independence. By late 1990 about 88 per cent of Slovenes believed secession was their best option for the future, and in May 1991, 94.3 per cent of Croats voted for independence: 'In Slovenia, Croatia, Bosnia and Macedonia, it was the dissidents of yesteryear who took hold of the reins of power in 1990' (Ramet, 1999a, 53). For example, the leaders of Croatia and Bosnia, Franjo Tudjman and Alija Izetbegovic, had spent time in prison, under Tito's rule, for their promotion of Croatian nationalism and Islamic fundamentalism, respectively. Between 1989 and 1991 civil turmoil spread throughout the country, giving rise to its eventual break-up. In the early months of 1991 the six Yugoslav republics constructed a series of summit talks to avert civil war, but by then Slovenia, Croatia, and Bosnia had already declared their sovereignty and were making preparations for independence. By the middle of 1991, close to 100 per cent of Slovenes and Croats favoured secession (Ramet, 1999a).

Women and Families in Socialist Yugoslavia

The socialist system that emerged following the end of the Second World War proclaimed equality between men and women and opened the possibility for the political participation of women. As a matter of fact, women's participation in the war effort, national liberation, and the Partisan movement from 1941 to 1945 became a source of 'spontaneous emancipation of women' from the traditional patriarchal system of domination characteristic of Yugoslav family life (Morokvašić, 1998, 73), particularly the zadruga (extended family/clan) system. The official figure released by the Yugoslav government for women's participation in the Partisan cause was two million (Jancar-Webster, 1990). About 100,000 of these women were said to have been soldiers in the Partisan forces, approximately 2,000 achieving officer's rank. It was estimated that about 280,000 died in the concentration camps of Nazi Germany and Croatia (ibid.; Hitchcock, 2003).

Women fought alongside men in the front lines, but they also organized behind the lines to provide support for the war effort. Many did so through an organization known as the Anti-Fascist Front of Women (AFZ), which in 1942 spread throughout the liberated territories to include some 40,000 women (Jancar-Webster, 1990). Clearly, women played significant roles during the course of the national liberation struggle during the war. As a result, some patterns of traditional authority common in towns and villages were shattered. For example, as the Partisans recruited young people from the villages and towns, the traditional authority of the extended family or clan was challenged, effectively 'speeding up the entry of women into modern society' (Denitch, 1976, 50).

Their efforts in the war resulted in formal, institutional gender equality in the civil and political arenas. In fact, even during the war, the Communist Party began to implement some of the women's pre-war demands for increased autonomy and equality (Jancar-Webster, 1990); for example, women were given the right to vote. This right was confirmed in the Yugoslav constitution of 1946, which also guaranteed women's political and economic equality; Article 23 declared that 'all citizens, regardless of sex, nationality, race, creed, degree of education, or place of residence, who are over eighteen years of age have the right to elect and be elected to all organs of state authority' (Trifunovska, 1994, part II, 214). Article 24 is even more direct: 'women have equal rights with men in all fields of state, economic and social-political life' (215).

The new socialist state, under Tito, that emerged after the Second World War gave women the right to employment, abortion, and increased power within marriage – at least on paper. According to Yugoslav feminists, there were few changes within the family, since women were stuck with the well-known double burden (Morokvašić, 1998, 73); nonetheless, marriage and family were placed under the protection of the state. Civil marriages were introduced, legally placing relations between marriage partners on an equal basis.

Under the Family Act of 1946, parental authority was assigned equally to both mother and father, legal discrimination against 'illegitimate' children was abolished, and property acquired after marriage was considered to be owned jointly by both partners (Chloros, 1970). Under the citizenship law, women (like men) were given the right to declare their own nationality (Jancar-Webster, 1990). In other words, the formal legal structure was egalitarian.

It should be noted that, despite the fact that socialist Yugoslavia attempted to implement national policies on family life, regional, ethnic, and religious affiliations continued to contribute to diversity within the country. Nonetheless, a number of general tendencies can be seen as characteristic of family life in socialist Yugoslavia. Through urbanization, industrialization, and social mobility, the large, patrilocal *zadruga* (extended family), which had been typical throughout rural Yugoslavia, declined in frequency and importance (Simić, 1999). What remained from this corporatist and anti-individualistic family form was the idea that even when children did leave their natal homes, they continued to consider their parental households their 'real loci of residence' (ibid.; Reeves, 1995).

Women also became more highly visible in the economy. For example, in 1939 women made up about 27 per cent of the industrial labour force, while between 1945 and 1948, their participation increased to 47 per cent (Jancar-Webster, 1990). There were myriad women professionals, doctors, engineers, and dentists. According to data collected before the break-up of Yugoslavia, women accounted for 39.6 per cent of the total employment in the socialized economy (except agriculture; Milić, 1995). However, this number conceals the fact that there was a great deal of variation within the country. For example, women's employment rate in Slovenia was 46.1 per cent, while in Kosovo it was 23.0 per cent (ibid.).

Women were also increasingly involved in political life. According to statistics collected by the United Nations (1991a), 15 per cent of parliamentary seats in the former Yugoslavia were occupied by women in 1975; this proportion increased to 18.8 per cent in 1987. The political representation of women in the federal parliament before the country's disintegration was 55 per cent; however, in the assemblies of the republics women held only 2 per cent of seats (Morokvašić, 1998). One researcher noted that Yugoslavia did no better, but certainly no worse, than other industrializing nations in improving women's economic and social opportunities (Jancar-Webster, 1990).

Yet the situation was not without its problems and critics. For example, one female former Partisan colonel noted that during the difficult times during the Second World War, when guerilla warfare was necessary, women were considered capable, but in peacetime there was a tendency to retire women officers as soon as possible (Denitch, 1976). In most cases, women were relegated to the same lower-skilled occupations as they had filled before the war. Furthermore, by 1954 women's labour force participation had dropped to 25 per cent (although during the 1970s their share of the workforce rose again to approximately 35 per cent) (Jancar-Webster, 1990).

Many of the changes and improvements in the status of women were more apparent in cities and in areas with modern industries; in the cities, women made considerable headway in the professions, especially in medicine and academic life. Among the working class, however, particularly in rural areas, little had changed for many women (Singleton, 1994), and, as society normalized after the Second World War, traditional patterns tended to reassert themselves (Denitch, 1976). Furthermore, Yugoslavia remained a heterogeneous polity, where the actual status of women varied dramatically, not only between urban and rural settings, but along ethnic, religious, and other lines.

For the most part, women's equality was achieved on paper only. For example, in socialist Yugoslavia, the government actively monitored the level of economic inequality and reserved the right to intervene. Yugoslav employers guaranteed permanent tenure on the job to both men and women, dismissing employees only if they committed serious offences (Reeves, 1995). In addition, men and women with similar jobs in a firm earned equal pay; in socialist Yugoslavia it was not what one did, but where one worked that determined income. However, contrary to state policy, sex discrimination in the workplace was quite common. For example, if a man and a woman applied for the same job, his chances of getting the job were often better than hers (ibid.). Furthermore, an analysis of 1981 census data revealed that women did not receive the same occupational rewards as men (ibid.). With time, 'consciously or unconsciously, men were advanced in Yugoslavia until they had recovered their former numerical strength in the public and economic sphere' (Jancar-Webster, 1990, 167).

Women were especially hard hit by the economic crises that struck Yugoslavia in the 1980s after the death of Tito. They struggled with purchasing problems created by 200 per cent annual inflation and scarcity of basic foods and merchandise (Jancar-Webster, 1990). They were particularly affected when the economic crisis slowed the development of the day-care and other childcare services that they needed to allow them to enter and remain in the labour force (ibid.). According to Ana Tankosava-Simic, chair of the Yugoslav Conference for the Social Activities of Women, over 90 per cent of the economic organizations had restaurant and childcare facilities, but about 65 per cent of women were employed in non-economic or social service organizations that did not offer such services (ibid.). Women were the first to be laid off and the last to be rehired. One Yugoslav feminist noted that 'by the mid eighties, when the new wave of nationalism came, women were already driven away from work by an economic crisis, and the nationalist rhetoric had been nurturing the myth of women as mothers of soldiers and as custodians of national virtue' (Iveković, 1995a, 11).

Yugoslav women in the 1980s experienced modern and egalitarian 'public' rules combined with paternalistic private rules (Reeves, 1995). In other words, in Yugoslav socialism women had *de jure* equality, but they did not achieve *de facto* equality. Many authors have noted that the position of women in socialist Yugoslavia was not as favourable as it seemed on paper, but it deteriorated even further in the 'new democracies' that emerged after the break-up of the country.

The Rise of Nationalism and the Creation of 'New Democracies'

1990 brought many changes to Yugoslavia, one of them being multiparty elections, which provided a boost to existing nationalist tendencies across the country. Individual republics grew in power at the expense of federal unity. Not one year later, the republics (especially Slovenia) explicitly rejected the federal body, seeking territorial revision and outright independence. The complex multinational undertaking known as Yugoslavia ceased to exist in 1991, and the independence of most of the new republics was recognized internationally by 1992. National dreams had been realized and 'new democracies' were born, but not without considerable violence, intense ethnic enmity, systematic rapes, and numerous casualties (Tindemans, 1996; Grant, 1993).

The six republics of Yugoslavia became six independent states: Milošević ruled the new, smaller Yugoslavia (Serbia, Vojvodina, Kosovo, and Montenegro), Kučan became president of Slovenia, Gligorov was president of the Former Yugoslav Republic of Macedonia, Izetbegović came to rule Bosnia and Herzegovina, and Tudjman became president of Croatia. Although there were many differences in how the new republics were governed by their respective leaders, similarities also existed, particularly in the position of women (Rener and Ule, 1998). In the 'new democracies,' they found themselves 'more and more excluded' (Morokvašić, 1998, 74), and 'women were pushed to the very margins of public life' (Duhaček, 1993, 134). While in the ideology of socialist societies women were used as symbols of emancipation and revolutionary change, in post-socialist societies 'they became the targets of redelegation into "mothers who should ensure the biological survival and moral progress of the nation," "the guardians of the home," and the "guardians of privacy"' (Rener and Ule, 1998, 121). Women became a focus of attention when they came to be viewed primarily as 'mothers of the nation.' This shift began when, according to one feminist, 'the self-proclaimed masters of life and death set up coordinates of right and wrong, black and white, true and false' (Ugreši , 1998, 6), in other words, when nationalist leaders succeeded in creating ethnic 'others' of people who had once shared Yugoslav nationhood. Croats were expected to hate Serbs, Serbs were expected to hate Croats, both were expected to hate Muslims, and so on.

Ethnic 'purity' seemed to be a common nationalist goal, and leaders set out to achieve it in earnest. In the case of Croatia, feminist Dubravka Ugrešić (1998) noted that there was hardly a newspaper article or television broadcast that did not include the word 'clean'; she added: 'in addition to external enemies (i.e. the Serbs, who were waging, and because of whom we are waging, this dirty war), the spirit from the bottle – like the diligent Mr Clean or Meister Proper – has in recent months been cleansing all sorts of things in Croatia' (60). According to Ugrešić, 'they have cleaned the school curriculum of everything 'undesirable' ... Mr Clean Croatian Air has entered the libraries,' and 'following the indistinct instructions of the Croatian Minister of Culture, patriotic librarians are quietly putting books by Serbian writers into the cellars ... [and] a nicely designed strip, with a folk motif, has appeared on books by Croatian writers' (62). 'Blood' was another feature that according to nationalists, needed cleansing. Ugrešić noted that this line of thinking in Croatia was begun by the president himself when he publically announced that 'he was glad his wife was neither a Serb nor a Jew (but a Croat)' (60). This statement, and subsequent family policies, had serious implications for all women.

Croatian feminist Rada Ivekovi– (1995a) noted that, under nationalism, 'women are losing one after another of their 'human' rights formally acquired during socialism' (12). She added that the new nationalist regimes in parts of the former Yugoslavia were really not democracies for women, since the 'nationalist backlash has flung women backwards by at least half a century' (13). In the remaining sections some of this marginalization and archaization in nationalist-ruled Croatia will be traced.

Women and Family Policies in Independent Croatia

Pronatalism

On 27 December 1994, roughly three years after Croatia achieved its independence, President Franjo Tudjman gave a 'State of the Nation Address,' in which he which expressed, among other things, the country's need for demographic renewal. Tudjman began this segment of his speech with: 'Esteemed deputies of both chambers of the Croatian Assembly, from this position, I dare say, the gravest and most devastating consequence of the subjugation of the Croatian people, the unnatural communist system, and the anti-Croatian Yugoslav state is the most worrying demographic situation in Croatia. It is such that the Croatian people would face extinction if we were not to take resolute steps' (Foreign Broadcast Information Service, 1994, 67). The most enthusiastic response Tudjman received, in the form of a standing ovation, came after the following statement: 'Mothers of four or more children should be given the average salary earned by her social equals, so that she is able to devote herself to bringing up her children and be financially provided for for life. [applause]. Families with more children should be given concessions when it comes to the resolution of their housing issues. Single people should pay higher taxes' [standing ovation] (68). This was not the first time women were the focus of special attention by Croatia's new political leaders. In the spring of 1992 the Ministry for Renewal established a Department for Demographic Renewal. The Croatian government's 'Program for Demographic and Spiritual Renewal' proclaimed motherhood as the highest vocation and profession for women and sought to develop strategies to boost an 'ethnically clean' birth rate in Croatia (McKinsey, 1992; B.a.B.e., 1995). This policy for demographic renewal called for, among other things, a definition of womanhood that attempted to compel women to make household and family their priorities in life. In their efforts to 'assist' women to become 'heroic child bearers,' the Croatian government passed a law that recognized women with four or more children with the paid status of 'mother educators' (*Narodne Novine-Sluzbeni*, 1995, 1185). Article 63 of Croatia's Labor Act, which went into effect in January 1996, stated that mothers of four or more children would be given their title and an unspecified sum of money (1185).

The Croatian government considered a variety of ways to increase its birth rate, including a suggestion to tax unmarried adults or married adults who did not have children (Germinal, 1995). It also tried to make abortion difficult to obtain, a strategy employed across the republics of former Yugoslavia, but with less success. For example, Rener and Ule (1998) explained that when nationalists began to rule the new republics, programs for increasing birth rates and against abortion appeared. They noted that in Serbia a 'Resolution on Population Renewal' failed, and in Slovenia, feminists succeeded in preventing the implementation of a proposal for the prohibition of abortion. Croatia's nationalist push for the 'demographic renewal of the population' was relatively more 'successful,' since it was promoted by powerful and conservative Catholic priests.

Their message was echoed in ideological campaigns. For example, one feminist noted: 'in Croatia the streetcars carried posters reading: "each unborn baby is an unborn Croat," whereas after a political meeting brother Croats were urged to "go home and make a new Croat"' (Morokvašić, 1998, 76). Although abortion was still legal, doctors in many hospitals refused to perform them (B.a.B.e., 1994b). According to Croation feminist author Slavenka Drakulić (1993), prohibitions on abortion took hold in Zagreb in November 1991, when the largest hospital in Zagreb prohibited its doctors from performing abortions, despite there being no law against abortion. Furthermore, at that time in Croatia contraception became unavailable, the cost of abortions skyrocketed, the number of anti-abortion groups increased, and state and church officials were given a great deal of public space for advocating demographic renewal (B.a.B.e, 1994b).

The phrase 'Everyone has the right to life' was inserted into the new Croatian constitution (Constitution of the Republic of Croatia, 1991, (Article 21/1), which feminists believed was obviously in preparation to outlaw abortion outright (B.a.B.e., 1995). Meanwhile, although they were still not illegal, it became more difficult for women to obtain abortions in the new 'democratic' Croatia than it had been in the previous socialist republic (Morokvašić, 1998). That is, in the former socialist Yugoslavia, all women were entitled to free health care during pregnancy, childbirth, and after childbirth. Employed women had from 180 days to one year of maternity leave, shorter work hours, and other entitlements under the old system (Reeves, 1995). Abortion was legal, and in the most populous areas of socialist Yugoslavia abortion was the most commonly selected form of birth control. Following the country's break-up, changes were enacted in all forms of health care for employees and their families. Abortion was one medical service for which the patient was now expected to pay full cost, and the fee was twice a woman's average monthly wage (Milić, 1995).

Women's Participation in Public Life: Employment and Political Life

According to Slavenka Drakulić (1993), in the media women were praised as mothers, but were ignored in other situations: 'there were no articles or discussions about the fact that they form the largest percentage of the unemployed, that they are underpaid, and that they are in a very difficult position if they are single mothers' (127). Under the new economic conditions, the labour market became highly selective. At the same time, under new nationalist rhetoric, a woman's 'national duty' was linked to her accommodation to domestic life (Milić, 1993).

According to a Croatian women's rights group, women faced an increased risk of poverty as a result of the political, economic, and social restructuring (B.a.B.e., 1995). Aside from the problem of women's unemployment that resulted from the restructuring of society, many entrepreneurs took advantage of the economic crisis and began hiring women for below-market wages and without offering benefits or protection (ibid.). Since much of this work was illegal, these women were left with no public mechanism for protesting sexual harassment, discrimination, and other abuses (ibid.).

Although the post-Yugoslavia 'new democracies' promised improvement to the population in general, 'the status of women deteriorated as far as employment rights and the possibilities of employment are concerned' (Morokvašić, 1998, 73). Indeed, 'their political passivity and absence from public life is very evident' (Rener and Ule, 1998, 122). Rener and Ule explained that this lack of participation was a product of the contradictions in ideology within post-socialist countries. They noted that these contradictions included reprivatization, the establishment of nation-states, the desired entry into Europe, and the return to traditional values.

Many of the party platforms that emerged around the time of the first multi-party elections did not include women's issues: 'Most party leaders presented an extremely aggressive, masculine image ... [which] significantly reduced women's participation and contributed to their orientation towards the parties they knew' (Morokvašić, 1998, 75). Milić (1993) similarly noted that women disappeared from the political scene once the elections were over. This has led many to concluded that women's position in the public sphere has worsened, owing in part to economic deterioration and in part to assumptions about women's proper place being the home (Morokvašić, 1998).

Resistance and Vilification of Objectors and 'Deviants'

According to Ramet (1999b), the family, as defined by Croatian nationalists, was expected to be heterosexual and authoritarian. As evidence, Ramet points to the May 1992 law drafted in Croatia, which exempted violence within the family from prosecution. Hyper-masculinity, 'manliness,' and courage were celebrated, and any man who departed from this ideal or questioned the patriarchal order was deemed a coward, was said to act like a woman, or was considered homosexual – homosexual pornographic caricatures in newspapers, for example, were common (Ugrešić, 1998, 118). Those who deviated from the newly established norm, or who refused to abide by it were labelled 'faggots.'

Throughout this period, feminists, as well as non-nationalists and pacifists, were labelled the 'internal enemy' and treated as subversives. For example, Catholic priest and nationalist Don Bakovic reportedly asked his followers: 'which is more important for us, Croatia's future or 13 existing women's organizations which have not given birth to 13 children altogether' (B.a.B.e., 1995, 11). Many feminist activists reported being harassed in the streets, portrayed as subversives, and demonized by state-owned and controlled media. (Although Croatia's constitution and laws guaranteed freedom of expression, the main source of information in the mid-1990s was the state-owned and controlled Croatian Television Company.) Human Rights Watch/Helsinki (1995) reported that, since assuming power in 1990, Franjo Tudjman's government had taken steps to assume greater control over publicly owned media: 'the government owns and retains a controlling interest in the primary media sources in Croatia' (58). Human Rights Watch / Helsinki was especially concerned that fear of losing their jobs had resulted in self-censorship by journalists.

Feminist, Rada Iveković (1995), who herself was harassed, wrote that, in the hands of nationalists, the national media was used 'to conduct witch-hunts, and to proceed with ideological and intellectual cleansing' (11). She noted that female intellectuals and artists were regular and easy targets. One case in particular gained a great deal of attention, even outside Croatia, when Meredith Tax, the president of the Women Writers' Committee of International PEN (a world-wide organization with national branches, which works in the defence of writers), prepared a 'casebook,' containing summaries of newspaper articles demonstrating a particular nationalist, anti-feminist campaign against five feminists and journalists from Croatia, whom the press had labelled the 'five witches.' The 'five witches' were Rada Iveković (professor of philosophy and writer), Jelena Lovrić (journalist), Slavenka Drakulić (writer and journalist), Dubravka Ugrešić (writer), and Vesna Kesić (journalist and founding member of B.a.B.e. [Be active, Be emancipated], a women's rights organization).

The 'right of centre' (according to Human Rights Watch/Helsinki, 1995) weekly newspaper, *Globus,* and other Croatian newspapers first harassed the women and then accused them of mounting a scandalous conspiracy to degrade Croatia, when they made the harassment public at a PEN Congress in Rio de Janeiro (Tax, 1993). Meredith Tax (1993) revealed that the media campaign against these women included the printing of derogatory remarks about the writers' physical appearance, choice of marriage partners (Iveković and Drakulić were targeted for having been married to Serbs), and political views. Ugrešić, one of the 'five witches,' had her home phone number printed in a Croatian newspaper along with an obscene sexual characterization. One newspaper wrote: 'without that totally made-up "status" they would be what they really are: a group of selfish middle-aged women who have serious problems with their own ethnic, moral and human intellectual and political identity!' (Tax, 1993, 9). At least three of the 'five witches' have continued writing against the nationalist and anti-feminist stand in Croatia. For example, one recently noted: 'In Croatia, women – journalists, writers, intellectuals – have written against the war, against nationalism and chauvinism, against hatred, against the infringement of human rights, against corruption, against stupidity, against the totalitarian mentality, against rape, against the undemocratic system in Croatia, against numerous mistakes of Croatian politics and the Croatian governing bodies. In "democratic" Croatia those women have been proclaimed "traitors"' (Ugrešić, 1998, 124). The labels 'traitors' and 'amoral beings' did not stop many of these activists. Many women's organizations were not in line with the state or with its nationalist propaganda. Many also kept their networks across the newly established borders in spite of the communication blockade (Morokvašić, 1998). One problem that has remained is that their activities have been limited to big urban centres, and their voices have been virtually ignored on the political scene.

Nationalist 'Successes' and Failures

The government's attempts to 'domesticate' women were not without opposition, problems, and contradictions. Some working-class women temporarily welcomed the chance to end their double burden (paid outside work and unpaid domestic work), but the resulting low family income and loss of personal independence would not allow them to remain occupationally inactive for long (Milić, 1995). Rener and Ule (1998) noted that the withdrawal of women into the domestic sphere would not be complete because of the economic crisis and low incomes that plagued the new republics: 'women, as always, will be forced to supplement the family budget by working outside their homes' (124).

Anti-abortion campaigns also were not very successful. True, the number of abortions registered each year in Croatia did decline following its independence, but abortion rates throughout Europe at the time were also declining. The number of registered abortions in 1991 was 53,351, dropping to 26,223 in 1992, 25,179 in 1993, and 19,673 in 1994 (United Nations, 1997). More important, anti-abortion campaigns resulted in the rise of feminist lobbies, in protest. In Croatia, feminist organizations such as B.a.B.e. were founded to lobby for the recognition and improved status of women. One of B.a.B.e's goals is to ensure women's rights over reproductive choices (B.a.B.e., 1994a). Similarly, in Slovenia, feminists succeeded in preventing the implementation of a proposal on the prohibition of abortion (Rener and Ule, 1998). Milić (1993) noted that women became more politically involved in response to this proposed prohibition of abortion. Soon after independence in Serbia, for example, the first and only party of women, the Women's Party (ZEST), was founded, as were the Women's Lobby and a Women's Preliminary Parliament in Serbia (Milić, 1993). Although the parties were short lived, their timely reaction was effective.

On the other hand, the crude birth rate in Croatia did register a slight fluctuation when Croatian nationalists came to power. Just prior to its independence, the crude birth rate was 10.8 (in 1991). It declined to 9.8 in 1992 but increased to 10.2 in 1993 and 1994 (United Nations, 1997).

A Recapitulation

Since its advent, in the aftermath of the First World War, Yugoslavia was clearly unique. Its uniqueness is a product not only of its multinational character, which resulted in numerous ethnic conflicts, but of its socio-political organization as well, particularly after the Second World War. Under Tito, Yugoslavia was characterized by socialism, the non-alignment movement, self-management, and an intolerance of nationalism. This combination began to unravel following Tito's death, which also happened to take place during a period of economic crisis and ethnic unrest.

As long as the unusual constellation of factors was in place under socialism, women, at least on paper, enjoyed equality with men. Family laws granted women legal equality with their husbands, many were encouraged to enter the labour force, and some became involved·in self-management and political life. On the other hand, women's political and economic activities were taking place, for the most part, in the lower strata of political and economic life. Nonetheless, the rhetoric of socialist Yugoslavia was egalitarian. This changed with the creation of the 'new democracies' that sprang up following civil war and Yugoslavia's disintegration in the early 1990s.

During the attempt to create nationally homogeneous entities, women were 'encouraged' to take on new symbolic roles within the emerging nations. Croatia, for example, promoted the trinity of 'home, nation and God' and a return to traditional values and roles, including both practical and ideological transformations that advocated the 'return of women to family.' According to Rener and Ule (1998), this advocacy is closely related to national-ideological rhetoric that promotes the idea that 'only women who have dedicated themselves exclusively to their families are capable of preserving traditional values and the national consciousness of new generations' (124). They added that this ideal seeks to return women to pre-modern social conditions. The only heartening sign is that, overall, these attempts have not been very successful, thanks in part to the efforts of individual feminists and feminist organizations.

8

Post-Reunification Germany

The Political and Economic Situation before Reunification

The Second World War officially ended on 2 September 1945. The western parts of Austria were divided into three zones, administered by the United States, Great Britain, and France. A similar partition was implemented in the non-Russian-occupied parts of Germany. The American zone in Germany was the largest of the three (about seventeen million people), followed by the British, which included less land but a larger population than the American (about five million more), and the French, which was smallest in both size and population (five million people; Gilbert, 1984). The line that was drawn between the Russian zone and the three zones held by the western powers eventually became the boundary that separated East Germany (eventually called the German Democratic Republic – GDR) and West Germany (the Federal Republic of Germany – FRG; Keylor, 2003). At that point, the Russians also occupied Poland, Czechoslovakia, and the eastern part of Austria. In Germany, they were given an occupation zone that extended beyond the Elbe into central Germany, including Thuringia (East, 1992).

At the outset, Berlin, the German capital, was intended to be occupied and administered by all four countries (United States, Britain, France, and Russia) in common. Eventually, the four powers became the Big Three (United States, Great Britain, and Russia), and the three became two, since Churchill and Stalin were inclined to divide the globe into spheres of influence, with both sides having concrete areas in mind. The weakened and financially strained Britain was unable to take control of its side of the divide, leaving room for the United States to take its place. What remained was Soviet Russia under Stalin on one side and the United States under Truman on the other.

The Americans were convinced that the only way to make western Europe secure against communist domination would be to economically revive West Germany (Keylor, 2003). Thus, in late 1947 and early 1948 the American and British governments assisted in rebuilding the economy of West Germany. To prepare Germany's participation in the European Recovery Plan, the English and American zones were united. German political life was also revived through the establishment of a parliament and government for the whole of West Germany. West Germany was much more powerful in population size and mineral resources than Russian-occupied East Germany. On 24 July 1948 the Russians halted all rail and road traffic between Berlin and the west. At this point, Berlin was still administered under the common control of the United States, Great Britain, France, and Russia. The 1948 'Berlin Blockade' is said to mark the beginning of the cold war. East Berlin and West Berlin had entirely separate administrations; in contrast to the 'bleak-looking' East Berlin, life in West Berlin 'appeared rather splendid' (Gilbert, 1984, 392).

The Marshall Plan provided a spark that ignited widespread industrial production throughout Europe. By the end of 1949 West Germany had surpassed its pre-war level of industrial production (Keylor, 2003), and by the mid-1950s it had more than doubled it. Volkswagen (automobiles), Grundig (radio manufacturing), and Bayer (chemical/pharmaceutical) expanded rapidly into industrial giants. In contrast, by 1955 (the initiation of the Warsaw Pact), East Germany had gained full membership in the Soviet alliance, which included, among other things, the stationing of Russian troops on its territory and the establishment of a Communist regime. Furthermore, because Soviet leaders saw the economic recovery of their own country to be of foremost importance, they began to dismantle some East German industrial installations to transfer them to Russia (Hobsbawm, 1995; Reynolds, 2000), which inevitably led to economic hardship in East Germany. In time, however, the situation changed: there was considerable economic growth in parts of eastern Europe, and Communist East Germany led the way (Volgyes, 1989; East, 1992). Economic growth nonetheless lagged behind the non-Communist Federal Republic of Germany (Hobsbawm, 1995). The gap between East and West Germany became more pronounced, as economic conditions worsened in the 1960s in East Germany, and improved rapidly in the west.

Many German cities, in both east and west, were thoroughly destroyed during the Second World War (Reynolds, 2000). Germans were left with a huge task of reconstruction and faced a scarcity of goods of all kinds. In the west, this scarcity proved to be highly profitable, since Germans consumed everything they produced – driving the economy forward and virtually eliminating unemployment. The economy of West Germany was capable of absorbing 'refugees' from parts of East Germany and also benefited from their presence. By 1960 only 0.5 per cent of West German workers were unemployed, despite the absorption of 2.5 million 'refugees' from the east (Gilbert, 1984; Hitchcock, 2003).

The shortage of workers and demand for goods made employers in West Germany willing to accept improvements demanded by labourers. The economic circumstances gave workers a greater share in the management of industry and resulted in the creation of an extended social security system, including the provision of pensions (Gilbert, 1984). Employers' willingness to improve conditions for labour and workers' eagerness to work, avoid strikes, and rebuild their lives resulted in West German goods' regaining a strong position in foreign markets (Hobsbawm, 1990). The Federal Republic of Germany had drawn strength from its weakness and defeat in the war and was said to have been experiencing a 'Wirtschaftswunder' (economic miracle). During this time of prosperity, the Christlich-Demokratische Union (Christian Democratic Union) became the largest political party in the post-war parliamentary elections in West Germany, which were first held in 1949. The party obtained an absolute majority by 1953, and Konrad Adenauer, its leader, was West German chancellor from 1949 to 1963. Over that period he led the Federal Republic of Germany as it moved towards and through economic development and prosperity.

The 1960s and early 1970s were seen as an economic 'Golden Age,' anchored in the economies of a few capitalist countries of which the Federal Republic of Germany was one (Hobsbawm, 1995). West Germany became a significant economic power, international in scope. For example, the German chemical company Hoechst was connected to 117 plants in 45 different countries, and by the mid-1960s Volkswagen had built car factories in no less than ten countries around the world, including Nigeria, Ecuador, and Egypt (ibid.). By the end of the 1970s West Germany had become a leader in social spending and support of the welfare state, earmarking more than 60 per cent of total public outlays for welfare (ibid). Between 1960 and 1980 the number of students educated in the FRG multiplied by four and five times (ibid.). Germany appeared to be one of the more 'progressive' western, capitalist nations.

In the meantime, East Germany continue to be ruled by a strong Communist government whose leaders feared that, if the regime weakened, West German influence could endanger the east. Walther Ulbricht, a close adherent of Stalin, remained in power from 1946 to 1971 (East, 1992). During that time, he pursued an orthodox line characterized by a planned economy, industrial development, and the collectivization of agriculture. Eventually, East Germany became, industrially, the most important country in the eastern bloc. One of the biggest obstacles it faced was the steady depopulation of the country, as approximately 2.5 million East Germans fled to the west between 1950 and 1962, including a rising number of skilled workers, professionals, and intel- lectuals. This represented a huge loss of labour, particularly since its total population at the time numbered approximately 17.2 million (Gil- bert, 1984; East 1992; Hitchcock, 2003). Because the loss threatened to destroy the economic viability of East Germany, the government de- cided to stop the migration by building a wall to separate East and West Berlin. The 'Berlin Wall' was erected on the night of 12–13 August 1961, and by the 1980s this system of walls, electrified fences, and fortifica- tions extended 28 miles (45 km) through Berlin and a further 75 miles (120 km) around West Berlin, separating it from the rest of East Ger- many. This wall, at the very least, made escape – migration to the west – difficult and dangerous. As a result, the GDR remained cocooned and isolated (Hitchcock, 2003).

In 1969 Willy Brandt's socialist government came to power in West Germany. Brandt initiated more legislation granting West German work- ers co-determination, or a voice in the management of large industry, but his greatest efforts and concern were for foreign policy. Brandt's policy of *Ostpolitik*, for example, sought to improve relations between east and west (Keylor, 2003). He was quite successful and played a significant role in both domestic and foreign policy until his sudden resignation in 1974. Brandt was replaced by Helmut Schmidt, who led a coalition government linking the Socialists and Free Democrats. Schmidt played a key role in strengthening the European Economic Community (EEC) (Deighton, 2002).

Although not as hard hit as other countries, West Germany's unem- ployment rate had increased dramatically throughout the 1970s, reach- ing 8.2 per cent by the second half of 1982, and inflation reached 6 per cent. Schmidt's decision to increase taxes in order to fund programs designed to decrease unemployment rates seem to have cost him and his party dearly. In the fall of 1982 West Germany's government took a turn to the right when Helmut Kohl and his Christian Democratic Party replaced the left-of-centre Schmidt.

Clearly, in their four decades of separation the two Germanies emerged as extremely distinct political and economic units. As a result of their profound differences, a number of social policies that were equally diverse emerged. It is interesting to note that East Germany, despite its lower per capita GNP, was more willing and able to support costly social services.

The Status of Women before Reunification/*Wende* in both Germanies

The 1949 constitutions of both German states contained sections guaranteeing the equality of men and women. For example, since its inception in 1949 the Federal Republic of Germany's constitution had relatively comprehensive clauses guaranteeing equality between women and men. Article 3 included (paragraph 1) the guarantee that all people are equal before the law; (paragraph 2) the guarantee of equal rights for men and women; and (paragraph 3) the prohibition of discrimination on the basis of sex (BIJUS, 2002). It should be noted, however, that the FRG constitutional court rarely used Article 3 in cases of unequal treatment between men and women (Trzcinski, 1998).

Similarly, the German Democratic Republic's 1949 constitution guaranteed equal rights for women and men. By 1968 it was amended to guarantee a more extensive definition of equal rights. The additional clause in effect granted women and men equal rights and an equal position in regard to rights in all areas of social, state and personal life. The GDR constitution (Article 20, paragraph 2) stated that the promotion of women, especially in employment, was a state and social responsibility. This guarantee was not part of the FRG constitution. As a result of these and a number of other differences in the political and legal systems of the two Germanies, the lives of women on the two sides of the wall varied considerably.

Family Policies and Women's Issues in the German Democratic Republic

The GDR's policies towards women were derived, in spirit, from the writings of Marx and Engels (Ketelhut, 1995), but more directly from the work of socialist feminist, Clara Zetkin (Rosenberg, 1996). In general, Marxist ideology included the belief that gender equality is achieved mainly through equal participation in paid labour (see Trappe and Rosenfeld, 2000). Zetkin's goal was to establish the legal and economic conditions necessary to allow the family, as a love-based, monogamous, egalitarian, lifetime partnership, to thrive. She envisioned that this paradigm would include full legal rights and equality for men and women, equal conditions for women and men in the workplace, state support for childcare and education, equal responsibility for housework, and socialization of reproductive labour through state institutions (Zetkin, 1984). Zetkin also advocated for full reproductive rights for women.

In response to this vision, women in the GDR were guaranteed legal and economic independence regardless of their marital status, tax laws were gender neutral, divorce was simple to obtain and inexpensive, and child support payments were automatically deducted from wages and transferred to the custodial parent's account (Rosenberg, 1996). From the outset, the GDR constitution explicitly dealt with marriage and family by placing marriage, family, and motherhood under the protection of the German state (Trzcinski, 1998). Pregnancy and maternity leaves, special medical care, material and financial support at birth, and children's allowances were guaranteed in the GDR constitution (Article 20, paragraph 3).

Not only was the state committed to the promotion and support of nuclear families, but also it provided special support to large families and single parents. The family code was immediately amended to abolish the category of 'illegitimate' for children born outside wedlock. In other words, the position of children of single mothers was equal to that of children of legally married, two-parent families. The children of single mothers had special priority for placements in childcare facilities (Trzcinski, 1998). This was not the case in West Germany.

Further changes to the family code included the removal of the absolute right of the husband/father to control his wife and/or child(ren) and its replacement by the idea of shared parental responsibility (Rosenberg, 1996). Although the family was deemed irreplacable for rearing children, socialization of children was seen not as the sole responsibility of parents, but as a job undertaken cooperatively with the state (Dennis, 1999). Furthermore, while marriage was regarded as the most desirable type of family relationship, the GDR's divorce laws were very lenient; divorce was free and easy to obtain (Adler, 1997) – for example, in 1955 irreconcilable differences constituted grounds (Trzcinski, 1998). On this matter, the GDR was decades ahead of most western nations. The GDR's policies, at least in principle, appeared committed to the reshaping rather than the protection or restoration of the traditional patriarchal family.

Women in the GDR were defined by and expected to fill two key roles: mothers and workers. One researcher noted that 'women had not only the right but, as a rule, the duty to hold a job' (Nickel, 1993, 139). Thus, within a year of its founding, the GDR also rewrote its labour code to guarantee women access to training and employment, explicitly including non-traditional trades and professions (Ferree, 1993; Rosenberg, 1996). According to some social analysts, the GDR's employment policies directed at women could be grouped into distinct periods or stages (Ferree, 1993; Trzcinski, 1998). Ferree named two periods: 'Stage-One – Equity Politics (1949–1972)' and 'Stage-Two – Mommy Politics (1970s–1990),' while Trzcinski identified three.

The first period, from 1946 to 1965, was characterized by a general shortage of labour and an interest in the large-scale deployment of women in the labour force (Trzcinski, 1998). Women's full employment was seen as critical to the GDR economy (Trappe and Rosenfeld, 2000). In this period, businesses were required to hire women and provide the social infrastructure for their employment (Ferree, 1993). Important features included the building of childcare centres and the provision of other 'incentives,' such as paid sick days to care for sick children, the designation of one day per month as a 'household day' for taking care of home duties, and the introduction of a year-long, unpaid maternity leave (Trzcinski, 1998).

The second period, from 1966 to the early 1970s was marked by a shift in focus towards improving women's educational and technical training (Trzcinski, 1998). Businesses were encouraged to provide opportunities for working women to obtain ongoing training and education, to work in male-dominated jobs, and to serve in managerial positions (Ferree, 1993). The result was less occupational segregation along gender lines, but also a pronounced decline in birth rates (Trzcinski, 1998).

The third period, from the early 1970s to 1990, was defined by a political reaction to the sharp decline in birth rates, which triggered a political response that concentrated on facilitating the combination of women's employment and motherhood (Ferree, 1993; Trzcinski, 1998). Among the measures were extended *paid* maternity leave; an increase in children's allowance; the shortening of the work week, without a reduction in salary, for women with three children (ibid.); and the 'baby year' (1976), which extended paid maternity leave to one year for women having their second and third children (Trzcinski, 1998). If childcare was not available, a mother's paid baby year could be prolonged up to three years (Ferree, 1993). By the late 1980s over 90 per cent of East German women (ages sixteen to sixty) were employed, most working full time and most returning to work after the end of the baby year (Dennis, 1999).

The dual characterization of women as mothers and workers did not automatically result in equality between men and women. As a matter of fact, women in the GDR, like other women, continued to experience inequality on a number of fronts. East Germany continued to have a strongly gender-segregated labour market (Ferree, 1993; Nickel, 1993). Despite attempts to encourage women to enter male-dominated professions, they continued to constitute a large majority of workers in education, health, and social services. Virtually all the secretaries, nurses, and preschool teachers as well as most textile and electronics assembly workers were women (Ferree, 1993).

Although both men and women in the GDR were expected to be in the paid labour force, there was not a similar expectation that both should partake in domestic work and family obligations. Despite the GDR's embracing of socialist ideology of equality, the responsibility for children, family, and housework was 'naturally' viewed as women's work (Nickel, 1993).

Women in East Germany also earned less than men: in 1987 women with full-time jobs on average earned 75.5 per cent of men's salaries. In 1987 women in full-time jobs earned an average of DM 762, compared with men's DM 1009 per month (Ferree, 1993). Although women were much more likely to be concentrated in low-paying jobs and poorer sectors of the economy (Nickel, 1993), in East Germany they contributed a higher proportion of total household income (40 per cent) compared with women in West Germany (18 per cent) (Ferree, 1993).

Family Policies and Women's Issues in the Federal Republic of Germany

West German family policies were influenced by competition with and rejection of the GDR's policies. In contrast to the GDR, West Germany chose to reinforce and support the 'bourgeois patriarchal family' through legal and social measures that provided women with few options for economic security beyond economic dependence on husband/father as breadwinner (Rosenberg, 1996). In other words, the West German state adopted policies whose goal was 'restoration of the family.' For example, FRG tax structure and family policies promoted and supported only legally married, two-parent families, not other family forms such as lone-parent families and unmarried couples with children (Adler, 1997). Two-parent, single-earner households were especially privileged, being given the most favourable tax treatment. Similarly, a child-rearing allowance was paid (during the first two years of a child's life) to two-parent, legally married, heterosexual couples, where one parent remained at home as the primary, full-time caregiver (Trzcinski, 1998).

Unmarried mothers were subject to a series of controversial measures. The *Jugendamt* (Office of Youth) automatically assumed official 'curatorship' for every child born to an unmarried woman (Trzcinski, 1998) and would 'safeguard' the interests of the child in regard to determination of paternity, the child's right to a legal name, inheritance, and child maintenance obligations. A mother was obliged to register the child's father's name, or she would forfeit her right to the state's child allowance. Even if she did not require state social assistance, the *Jugendamt* still had the right to attempt to establish paternity, in the child's interest (ibid.).

To further encourage and support the legally married, heterosexual two-parent family, divorce procedures in the FRG were quite complex and very costly (Adler, 1997). As a result, West German women were less likely than East German women to initiate divorce. For example, in 1985 about 70 per cent of all divorces were initiated by women in the GDR, compared with 58 per cent in the FRG (ibid.). Furthermore, while in East Germany irreconcilable differences became recognized as grounds for divorce in 1955, it was not introduced as grounds for divorce in West Germany until 1977.

In contrast to the GDR, where being a woman meant being a worker and a mother, in the FRG womanhood was almost exclusively connected to the role of mother/wife. For example, a 1953 constitutional ruling stated that equal rights in marriage meant that both partners would contribute 'what they are capable of.' The courts interpreted this to mean that work outside the home was men's domain and housework and childcare were women's (Rosenberg, 1996). Even the Social Democratic Party agreed that 'married women should be wives, wives should be mothers and mothers should not work outside the home' (45). Article 3 of the FRG constitution, (equality between men and women) did not originally apply to equal rights of men and women in marriage. In fact, until 1 July 1977 FRG law clearly stated that a wife was entitled to employment as long as she could combine work with her marital and family obligations (Trzcinski, 1998). Thus, a wife was *legally* required to maintain the household and was allowed to seek outside employment only if it could be combined with her duties to marriage and family *as determined by her husband* (ibid.; Rosenberg, 1996). The conservative Adenauer administration applied family, labour, civil, and tax law to remove women from the workforce and commit them to the traditional patriarchal family (Rosenberg, 1996). To further discourage employers from hiring women, the first government-organized and legally regulated recruitment of foreign 'guest workers' was introduced in 1955 (ibid).

In 1977 FRG family law was changed. At that point, gender-neutral language was introduced; the law stated that when deciding the choice and practice of paid employment, each spouse must take into account the interests of the 'other' spouse and the family (Trzcinski, 1998). In reality, very little changed in the lives of average Germans. For example, when married adults with children applied to collect unemployment insurance, before they could receive benefits mothers, but not fathers, were required to provide documentation that childcare was available for their child(ren) (ibid.), which indicated that the recipient of benefits was ready to re-enter the labour force at any time.

In FRG law, biological differences between men and women were used to legally justify labour restrictions placed on women. Women were banned from working at night or after 5 p.m. on Sundays and holidays. They were excluded from working in specific occupations and industries (such as mining) and were prohibited from performing work that required them to lift more than ten kilograms (Trzcinski, 1998). On the other hand, businesses that were dependent on female labour, such as hospitals, restaurants, and hotels, were exempt from the restrictions. Some have argued that, given that the bans were not always applied, the actual intent of the regulations was less about the protection of women and more about protecting men from competition (ibid.).

Because of many legal and ideological factors, there were sharp differences in the lives and experiences of women in the two Germanies. Women in the GDR were much more likely to be employed than their FRG counterparts: in the years leading up to unification, women in the GDR made up 49 per cent of the labour force, compared with 39 per cent in the west (Adler, 1997). Women in the GDR were also more likely to work full time: 91 per cent worked full time, compared with 58 per cent in the FRG (ibid.). Furthermore, GDR women who were employed full time were much more likely than FRG women to be mothers: 62 per cent of married mothers and 89 per cent of single mothers in the GDR were employed, compared with 28 per cent of married mothers and 45 per cent of single mothers in the FRG (ibid.).

In the late 1980s approximately 90 per cent of GDR women aged fifteen to sixty-five were employed, compared with 54 per cent among their FRG counterparts (Ferree, 1993; Nickel, 1993; Rosenberg, 1996). Furthermore, the GDR's women's occupational biographies were far less subject to discontinuity than those of the FRG's women (Rosenberg, 1996). While GDR women did interrupt their employment to have children, virtually all of them returned to the labour force after their maternity leave. In contrast, in the FRG only one-third of women re-turned to the labour force at the end of their maternity leave; one-third of these returned after long absences, while the rest never returned (ibid.; Dennis, 1999). Furthermore, despite the persistent wage gap between men's and women's wages in both the GDR and the FRG, the GDR's women's earnings constituted a considerably higher proportion of family income than was contributed by women in the FRG: 40 per cent versus 18 per cent (Ferree, 1993).

Employed women in the GDR were also much more likely to have completed some kind of educational training (Nickel, 1993). In fact, girls in the GDR reached parity with boys in years of secondary school education in the early 1960s, and women accounted for 48 per cent of university students by the mid-1970s (Rosenberg, 1996). In West Germany, parity in secondary school education for girls was achieved fifteen years later, and in 1989 women still comprised only 38 per cent of university students in the FRG (ibid.). On the other hand, higher educational credentials among GDR women often resulted in a higher likelihood of their being overqualified for their job (Trappe and Rosenfeld, 2000).

Owing to the differences in divorce laws, as outlined above, the GDR's divorce rates were higher than those of the FRG, but they were countered by higher rates of marriage and remarriage in the GDR. Second marriages in the GDR tended to be formed with children of both spouses, in contrast to the common FRG pattern, where men remarried younger women and started new families and divorced women remained unmarried (Rosenberg, 1996). Furthermore, women in the GDR married and had children at younger ages than their West German counterparts. In the years preceding unification, the average age of marriage of women in the GDR was 23.2, compared with 25.7 in the FRG, and the average age of the birth of a first child was 22.9 in the GDR, compared with 26.7 in the FRG (Adler, 1997). It is important to note that in the GDR the average age of marriage was higher than the average age of a woman at the birth of her first child. This difference reflects the fact that in the GDR a higher proportion of births were to women under the age of twenty (11 per cent in the GDR, compared with 4 per cent in the FRG), and the higher proportion of births to unwed women (33.6 per cent in the GDR, compared with 10.2 per cent in the FRG) (ibid.). These figures can be interpreted as an indication of GDR women's relatively high degree of independence from male partners, compared with the FRG's family policies that favoured married, two-parent families (ibid.).

The differences between women in the GDR and those in the FRG became very clear following the collapse of the Berlin Wall. The unification of Germany resulted in an inevitable need to reconcile or at least understand these differences and provided a unique opportunity to tackle 'women's' issues and to push towards a more egalitarian society. Whether these goals have been achieved has been greatly debated in feminist circles.

Unification and Beyond

The Economic and Political Situation

On 9 November 1989 the East German government opened the country's borders with West Germany (including West Berlin). Access points were established in the Berlin Wall through which East Germans could travel freely to the west, and in the first month some 133,000 East Germans moved to West Germany. The wall henceforth ceased to function as a political barrier between east and west. In March 1990 the first free elections were held in the GDR, which resulted in a pro-unification government under the leadership of Prime Minister de Maiziere (Steinberger, 1992), and within months the GDR had ceased to exist as an independent state. On 3 October 1990 the German Democratic Republic was formally joined with the Federal Republic of Germany (FRG) in a political, social, and monetary union called Bundesrepublik Deutschland (Federal Republic of Germany) (CIA, 1996), but the two former republics continued to be referred to as East and West Germany.

Although reunification was greeted with a wave of euphoria (Dölling, 1993), it was not without problems. By the 1990s Germany was one of the greatest economic powers in Europe, but reunification imposed tremendous strains (Reynolds, 2000). Some argued that the FRG simply underestimated the cost and difficulty of absorbing the sixteen-million citizens of the German Democratic Republic (Hobsbawm, 1995) (total financial aid to East Germany from 1991 to 1995 was DM 615 billion). However, it was a series of events – including reunification, consolidation of the European Common Market, and 'liberation' of eastern Europe – that combined to produce this economic strain. An alarming result was the abrupt rise in unemployment, which it reached 10.6 per cent nationally and was 16 per cent (and more in some parts) in the eastern German states (Trzcinski, 1998). It was generally agreed that expenditures would have to be cut. Consequently, the elaborate network of social welfare provisions developed in the post–Second World War period were under attack. Some of the measures proposed were to raise the retirement age for women from sixty to sixty-five years, beginning in the year 2000, and reduce the amount payable during sick leave. It is also important to note that the treaty of 18 May 1990 on the Monetary, Economic, and Social Union of the two Germanies contained an article (2) according to which conflicting provisions of the GDR's constitution on the fundamentals of its long-standing socialist order would no longer apply (Steinberger, 1992). In other words, when there were contradictions or differences between the two constitutions, the FRG's constitution would apply. This also meant that the socialist policies and practices found in the GDR were null and void, which had serious implications for the lives of women, particularly working women from the eastern states.

Women and Family Policies in Post-Reunification

East German workers were especially hard hit by reunification: between 1990 and 1994 the number of employed East Germans fell from ten million to six million (Trzcinski, 1998). Several sources have noted that this decrease disproportionately affected women (Nickel, 1998; Weedon, 1995; *Women's International Network News*, 1995b; Kolinsky, 1999). Work outside the home was central to women's sense of self in the GDR. By 1994 it was clear that the unemployment rate for women in the eastern states was climbing at a faster rate than that for men was, and women comprised over two-thirds of all unemployed workers (*Women's International Network News*, 1995a). In February 1994 the unemployment rate for women was over 23 per cent, while that of men was about 13 per cent (ibid.; Trzcinski, 1998). Female-dominated industries, already more likely to have been in lower-paying sectors of the

East German economy, were especially hard hit after reunification (Adler, 1997; Trzcinski, 1998). Women also had been well represented in public administration in both states prior to reunification, but this sector was downsized by at least 25 per cent following reunification (Trzcinski, 1998). Furthermore, many of the administrative skills held by eastern (Communist) bureaucrats were rapidly deemed obsolete. To make matters worse, many of the jobs becoming available to East German workers required long commuting times to western German states. Owing to the persistent belief that family work is women's work (even in eastern Germany), many women were unable to travel long distances for employment while juggling childcare and family responsibilities (ibid.).

The post-reunification cuts to or outright removal of parts of the social infrastructure particularly common in the east made it even more difficult for women to combine employment and household responsibilities. Public policy that had existed in the former FRG and remained in place after reunification did not adequately support the social infrastructure required for employees (particularly women) to combine paid and unpaid work. For example, when East German women lost access to previously available (state-subsidized) school and factory hot midday meals, they were faced with an increase in shopping, cooking, and other related domestic work (Rosenberg, 1996). Women in the eastern states were especially negatively affected by the loss of access to affordable childcare (Weedon, 1995; Kolinsky, 1999). In 1989, for example, between 80 and 95 per cent of GDR children under the age of ten had been in free childcare facilities (Adler, 1997). In 1988 in the FRG only 3 per cent of children under the age of three could be accommodated in kindergartens (Ketelhut, 1995), whereas in 1989, 80.2 per cent of children under in the GDR had attended nurseries (Nickel, 1993).

State subsidies for childcare were phased out in 1990. There are still many day-care centres available for German children (perhaps of much better quality than before), but their numbers have been much reduced, and the high costs have made them inaccessible to many (Kolinsky, 1999). Childcare, like many other social services previously available to families in the GDR, has moved from being publicly funded to being seen as a personal responsibility. What is clear is that post-reunification family policies reflect the new state's view that marriage and childcare are predominantly private matters (ibid.; Adler, 1997). This privatization is also based on the assumption that unemployed, unpaid women should perform tasks that were previously performed by female public employees.

In the new Germany, the families that benefit most from state-sponsored child support through tax breaks and child allowances are two-parent, one-earner families, usually made up of a male breadwinner and a female full-time homemaker (Adler, 1997). (The *Bundesrat* has ratified a law that gives same-sex couples full legal standing: beginning in 2001, gay and lesbian couples in Germany have been able to register their relationships and enjoy the same inheritance and tenant rights as heterosexual couples.) Single-parent and low-income families also have had access to subsidies, but they are much less generous than those provided in the former GDR. Furthermore, women in the former GDR were entitled to twenty-six weeks of maternity leave at full pay, while the new leave policy covers only fourteen weeks (ibid.). Similarly, in the GDR women were allowed four to six weeks of leave per year to care for sick children, while since reunification they have received only ten to twenty days – still more than most other countries (ibid.).

As a result of cuts to social services and reduced access to employment opportunities, women, particularly from the former GDR, are postponing marriage and having fewer children. Before reunification, birth and fertility rates were higher in the GDR than in the FRG (Ketelhut, 1995); after 1989 there was a sharp decline in birth rates in the east (Trzcinski, 1998). The total fertility rate of the GDR just before unification was 1.6, but by 1994 it had dropped to 0.8 in the eastern states (Adler, 1997). Over the same period the rates in the west remained relatively unchanged. At the same time, marriage rates in the east also declined, from 7.9 per 1,000 in 1989 to 3.4 per 1,000 in 1994, at that point the lowest marriage rates recorded in any nation (Adler 1997).

An In-Depth Look at Abortion Legislation before and after Reunification

A number of sources reveal that abortion has become one of the most difficult and controversial issues in German reunification (Steinberger, 1992; Rosenberg, 1996; Walker, 1996). Immediately following the Second World War, abortion was practised extensively in East Germany, but by 9 March 1950 the GDR legislature had passed a law that allowed abortion only under highly restricted medical conditions, and the 'social' grounds for abortion were eliminated (Funk, 1993). Despite lengthy discussions on the topic and considerable opposition, the restrictive legislation was passed. In reality, it simply reflected the Soviet ban on abortion. Legal abortions in East Germany had declined rapidly throughout the 1950s: researchers found only eighteen petitions for abortion for the whole of East Germany in the years between 1951 and 1955 (Harsch, 1997). Almost no petitions were found for the years from 1955 to 1964, but 113 were found for 1965 (ibid.). Some petitions were written by the women's husbands and some even by their children. The most common reasons given for the abortions in the petitions filed in the 1950s were medical. Women's employment was the most frequent grounds in the 1960s (ibid.). Most of the petitions in the 1960s were denied, and as a result, the number of illegal abortions skyrocketed. Estimates of illegal abortions were as high as 100,000 per year (ibid.). On 22 December 1971 the Politboro announced a change in abortion legislation, amounting to the legalization of abortion in the first trimester. The GDR's policy granted free and legal abortion on demand during the first twelve weeks of pregnancy (Adler, 1997). As a result, the number of abortions increased by nearly 70 per cent in one year alone (Harsch, 1997).

In the former FRG, abortion laws, regulated by paragraph 218 of the Basic Law, had been among the most restrictive in Europe. In 1970 West German women demanded the liberalizing of abortion laws and appeared to have succeeded when in 1974 a law permitting first-trimester abortions with compulsory counselling was passed. The victory was short lived: a 1975 Constitutional Court decision overturned the law, deeming it unconstitutional on the grounds that it did not guarantee the legal protection of a 'becoming life' (Funk, 1993; Rosenberg, 1996). Instead, the court proposed that abortion would be permitted if 'acceptable' reasons (indications) were given. Thus, in June 1976 first-trimester abortions could be performed if a doctor certified that a woman had justifiable reasons, if she was counselled by a state-recognized counsellor, and if the abortion was performed by a second doctor. The reasons or 'indications' for which doctors could approve abortions were danger to life and health of the mother (medical indication); danger that the child would be seriously deformed (eugenic indication); pregnancy resulting from rape or incest (criminal indication); or difficult social conditions for the mother (social indication) (Funk, 1993). Furthermore, three days must elapse between the counselling and the abortion (ibid.). To make matters more complicated, each of the individual states in the FRG had specific rules on counselling and abortions. In Bavaria, for example, there were only three non-religious counselling centres out of a total of forty. As a result, (legal) abortions were uncommon in Bavaria and in other more conservative and Catholic areas (ibid.).

Following reunification, the new government was left with the task of bridging the gap between two very different traditions on abortion law: Communist East Germany's abortion on demand and West Germany's restrictive practices that were strongly influenced in parts of the country by the Roman Catholic Church. One of the early attempts at a compromise was struck down in 1993 by the Constitutional Court on the grounds that abortion violated German Basic Law in failing to 'protect life' (*Women's International Network News*, 1995a). On that occasion, the court ruled that abortion was officially a criminal offence but would not be prosecuted if performed by a doctor, occurred in the first trimester, and the woman received counselling. Furthermore, abortion was not covered by health insurance (Adler, 1997). The court ruled that the state would provide financial assistance for abortion only in cases of mortal danger to the woman, rape, or grave deformity of the fetus (*Women's International Network News*, 1995a). But the issue did not end here. A number of opinion polls across Germany revealed that public opinion was clearly on the side of less restrictive abortion laws.

After lengthy debate, on 14 July 1995 the German federal parliament reached a compromise and passed a new abortion law. The Pregnant Women's and Families' Aid Amendment Act marked a new era in German abortion legislation; the core points reflect article 1(1) and article 2(2) of the German constitution, which protect the embryo. While the act does not explicitly sanction abortion, it includes a mixture of time limit, counselling to women, and other restrictions (indication concepts), which make having an abortion difficult (Walker, 1996). The compromise lies in the fact that the act provides no punishment for women who have abortions or doctors who perform them, and the law's usefulness lies in its lack of specificity. Abortion will continue to be legal in cases of severe fetal abnormality, post-rape pregnancies, and/or the protection of the life of the woman. Furthermore, in all cases doctors are urged to provide counselling stressing the importance of the protection of the 'unborn life.' This requirement for counselling was included to ensure that the abortion would not be taken lightly, but 'counselling' was loosely defined, allowing for considerable freedom of individual consciousness (ibid.). Under the new legislation, health insurance would cover the cost of abortions for low-income women.

Unfortunately, the debate did not end there. In 1996 the Bavarian state legislature passed two new abortion laws that jeopardized the federal compromise of 1995. One law requires women to explicitly state their grounds for seeking an abortion, essentially making the federal law's requirement for counselling more concrete. The second law prohibits doctors from earning more than 25 per cent of their income from performing abortions (Walker, 1996). However, of the nearly 1,500 gynaecologists in Bavaria, only about thirty are prepared to perform abortions, and two physicians in Bavaria account for roughly half of the state's abortions (ibid.). Presumably, many Bavarian women have to travel across state borders in search of abortions.

Owing to the high costs associated with pregnancy prevention and termination, many women in the new states have turned to sterilization as a 'solution.' Dresden, for example, experienced a 'wave of steriliza- tions,' to the point that all area hospitals were booked solid for a year in advance for the procedure (Adler, 1997). The average age of the women being sterilized was thirty-seven, and the most common reasons given were 'completed family size' and the inability to afford another child (ibid.).

A Recapitulation

Germany was divided between 1945 and 1990, and for most of this time, the two countries were remarkably different: the democratic, market-oriented west stood in sharp contrast to the east, which was classified as a 'textbook version of communist centralization' (Hobs- bawm, 1995, 504). In this wider political context, the two Germanies embraced different models of family: 'the socialist family was generally considered in the East to be as normal as the bourgeois family in the West' (Ketelhut, 1995, 128). Without a doubt, reunification would in- volve drastic changes in the everyday lives of German citizens.

The GDR was not a socialist utopia by any means. Clara Zetkin's vision of gender equality was far from achieved in the east. The GDR 'died' as it had 'lived' – a politically repressive regime that shared with 'western' systems traditional forms of gender inequality. For example, although women made up almost half of the workforce in the GDR, in the late 1980s women in top leadership positions in the educational system accounted for less than 3 per cent of the total number of execu- tives (Ketelhut, 1995). Furthermore, the gender gap in earnings for first jobs in the east was about the same as in the west (Trappe and Rosenfeld, 2000). On the other hand, it cannot be denied that in the administration of social support to mothers the GDR far surpassed its democratic western counterpart, the FRG.

In the change from a planned (socialized/socialist) economy to a market economy, a large number of social programs designed to facili- tate the combination of paid and unpaid work were lost. As a result of this and other factors, women of the former GDR were especially hard hit by German reunification. They experienced a sharp increase in both long-term and short-term unemployment and dramatic negative changes to family policies (leaves, divorce, abortion, childcare provision). To many women of the GDR, reunification meant great losses: the defeat of the socialist model of family and the perpetuation of the 'bourgeois' or patriarchal model. On the other hand, it is important to note that compared with other 'developed' nations operating within a market economy, such as the United States, the family support programs that exist in post-reunification Germany appear relatively generous. Furthermore, current leave provisions, for example, are comparable to those of other European nations (Adler, 1997). In other words, among bourgeois family models, that of post-reunification Germany's is quite moderate and generous.

Numerous comparisons show that great disparities exist among 'western' nations that adopt the bourgeois family model, particularly in levels of support for families (Freiler and Cerny, 1998). For example, western 'developed' nations, such as Britain and the United States, are said to adhere to a 'pro-family but non-interventionist model' of family policies, where responsibility for family support is taken by governments only for families in need (Gauthier, 1996). In contrast, Germany's post-reunification family policies are said to endorse a 'pro-traditional model,' where the preservation of the traditional male-breadwinner family remains a primary concern, yet the government maintains responsibility for supporting families; thus, a 'medium level' of state support for families is provided (ibid.). Today's Germany is characterized by a certain degree of traditionalism in family policies but is not attached to any pronatalist objective and remains relatively family friendly (ibid.), at least compared with many of its powerful western counterparts. In sum, reunification, at least in the eyes of many East German women, was seen and experienced as a loss of social and family supports, but compared with many other western 'developed,' non-nationalist nations, today's Germany is still has relatively 'family-friendly' social policies.

9

Post–Second World War Italy

The Political and Economic Situation in Post-War Italy

Italy's defeat in the Second World War occurred relatively early – in 1943. By 1945, the official end of the war, many parts of Italy were in ruins and plagued by slow economic development. The first steps following the war were to rebuild, restore services, and re-establish political order. This reconstruction began in 1946, when, through a referendum, Italians rejected the monarchy and became a republic. The structure of Italian politics came to reflect a parliamentary democracy with a multiparty system.

Since the end of the war, Italy has undergone profound changes in its economy, society, and politics. In the first year, the Italian Communist Party and Catholic Party emerged as dominant, and both appeared to be growing in influence. The Catholics in particular, maintained a majority for many years and held power for much of the post-war period. The Communists, in contrast, were ousted from government relatively quickly in 1947. Their declining popularity was said to have been in part related to the introduction of the American Marshall Plan in 1948 (Garraty and Gay, 1972). The Marshall Plan (the Economic Reconstruction Program), designed to rehabilitate European economies, was put in place by the Americans primarily to contain Communist expansion throughout Europe and, of course, to protect American trading markets (Deighton, 2002). It did much to 'kick start' the Italian economy in this post-war period, but was not without problems, since Italy's experience of the plan was said to have been different from that of Britain and France (Hitchcock, 2003).

Following the war, Italian Prime Minister De Gasperi sought to distance himself from the statist and interventionist economic policies of the Fascist period. Therefore, to deal with post-war inflation, Budget Minister Luigi Einaudi sought to balance national budgets not through increased production and new manufacturing capacity (as the Americans had hoped/wanted) but with sharp cuts in government expenditures (Hitchcock, 2003). Einaudi refused to accept American advice on using Marshall Plan aid and put little money towards industrial modernization. On the other hand, Italy, no less than France and Germany, enjoyed high rates of economic growth throughout the 1950s (Hitchcock, 2003; Lichtheim, 1999; Martinelli, Chiesi, and Stefanizzi, 1999).

Another significant event in this early post-war period in Italian history was the reorganization of military power and Italy's involvement in the establishment of the North Atlantic Treaty Organization (NATO). Military integration was accompanied by political and economic integration: in the early 1950s six European states (Belgium, France, Italy, Luxembourg, the Netherlands, and West Germany) federated to create the European Coal and Steel Community (ECSC), and the same six signed the Treaty of Rome in 1957, which established the European Economic Community (EEC) and the European Atomic Energy Community (EURATOM; see Keylor, 2003).

Italy's participation in the European Economic Community did much to transform its predominately agrarian economy into an industrial one, particularly in the north (Central Intelligence Agency, 1996). Despite economic revival (particularly in the north), for most of the post-war period Italy was plagued with high inflation, budget deficits, and high unemployment (Signorini, 2001). Many European countries at that time had or were approaching full employment; for example, by the early 1960s the average west European unemployment rate stood at 1.5 per cent. In contrast, throughout the 1950s Italy's unemployment rate hovered at around 8 per cent (Hobsbawm, 1995). Nonetheless, Italy did share in the economic 'golden age' of the time, especially throughout the 1950s and early 1960s, and although its economic growth was unevenly distributed, its relative position in Europe improved dramatically (Signorini, 2001). By 1975, Italy was among 'The Big Seven' (the G7), in spite of France's objections, which included Canada, the United States, Japan, France, Federal Republic of Germany, Italy, and Great Britain (Hobsbawm, 1995).

Italy was also among the European countries spending more than 60 per cent of total public outlays for welfare in the first twenty-five years following the Second World War (Hobsbawm, 1995). The Italian economy was developing rapidly, the number of Italian workers paying contributions to the programs was also expanding, and the number of beneficiaries was small (Livi-Bacci and Landes, 2001). Thus, in two generations Italy was transformed from a predominately agricultural, migrant-pool country to a prosperous economy, which itself absorbed large numbers of immigrants (Signorini, 2001).

For much of this post-war period, the Italian 'national character' was described as non-, and perhaps even anti-, national(ist) in that Italy is said to have lacked a united national identity (Cavalli and Cavazza, 2001). Italians have been described as loyal towards their 'membership groups' – family, village, and clan – and lacking in civic spirit. These qualities were believed to be part of its historical legacy: for centuries, characterized by regionalism and fragmentation into small city-states and local social systems, their group solidarity was said to be based on kinship and family, above all else (Martinelli, Chiesi, and Stefanizzi, 1999). Researchers have noted that, despite the effects of profound changes, including secularization, the family has remained the most important institution in the lives of most Italians. For example, Ginsborg (2003) wrote: 'in Italy, family is very important, both as metaphor and as reality' (xiii). This familism and localism combined with a marked distrust of government institutions and parliament (Cavalli and Cavazza, 2001) and a popular reaction to widespread corruption (Martinelli, Chiesi, and Stefanizzi, 1999) typified the Italian national character in the post-war period.

Family Policies and Women's Issues in Post–Second World War Italy

From the outset, like those of most other European nations, the Italian constitution contained sections guaranteeing the equality of women and men. For example, Article 3 on 'Equality' states that all citizens possess equal social status and are equal before the law, without distinction as to sex, race, language, religion, political opinions, and personal or social conditions (Fusaro, 2001). The constitution also declares that it is the duty of the republic to remove economic and social obstacles, because the limiting of freedom and equality of citizens prevents the full development of individuals and the participation of workers in the political, economic, and social organization of the country (ibid.). In reality, very little was actually done to ensure equality between men and women, especially before 1970, or implement state programs designed to 'protect' of the family. Article 31 (on family) of the Italian constitution stated that the republic should facilitate the formation of the family and the fulfilment of the tasks connected with it, with particular consideration for large families, and should also protect maternity, infancy, and youth by promoting institutions necessary for this purpose (ibid.).

Especially immediately following the Second World War, the Italian state interfered very little to legislate change or protection/assistance for women and mothers and for many years avoided implementing policies that even resembled 'population' policies (Gauthier, 1996). Following the Fascist experience, both citizens and state resisted involvement in anything that could be mistaken for pronatalist policies (Gauthier, 1996; Livi-Bacci and Landes, 2001). Ironically, the result was the continued implementation of policies and laws that were put in place when Fascists were in power.

Family legislation in Italy remained relatively unchanged from the 1930s to the 1960s. For example, in 1931 a royal decree prohibited the salé of contraceptives and publication of birth control 'propaganda' (Gauthier, 1996); it remained in place until the early 1970s. Similarly, a generous family allowance program was introduced in 1937, and benefit rates in the 1950s exceeded 15 per cent of the average wage of a two-parent family. By contrast, in Norway, for example, the rate was 3 per cent of the average wage (ibid.). This program remained relatively unchanged until the 1980s.

Similarly, childcare and child welfare programs under the Fascist regime and administered by the National Organization for Maternity and Infancy (ONMI), established in 1925, remained in place for about fifty years, surviving until December 1975 with only minor legislative, organizational, and ideological changes (Gandini and Edwards, 2001). In other words, for better or for worse, throughout the 1950s and 1960s the Italian state, while fearing to implement policies that could have been viewed as pronatalist, introduced few changes to existing policies and did little to promote, protect, or improve conditions for women or families.

Where the Italian state actually took a positive lead, in contrast to other countries, was the adoption of a maternity leave scheme, which provided a woman with a leave of fourteen to twenty weeks, depending on her occupation, with benefits equal to 80 per cent of her earnings (Gauthier, 1996). Interestingly enough, this plan was initiated in the

1950s, long before there was widespread need for the absences, given that women's labour force participation in Italy remained relatively low compared with that of other countries. Even more surprising was that paid maternity leave in Italy was originally introduced in 1910. It was expanded and improved only in 1950 and then again in 1971, when a uniform twenty-week leave was introduced. The new legislation also provided women with the opportunity to take an extended leave of six months during which they would receive cash benefits equalling 30 per cent of their earnings (ibid.). Over the next thirty years, it was again improved considerably (Ghedini, 2001; also see below).

Family policies in Italy changed rapidly, beginning in the 1970s. Historian Eric Hobsbawm (1995) attributed this rapid change to the development of 'a new gender consciousness,' which was manifested in 'striking ways' in Roman Catholic countries like Italy. Franca Bimbi (1993) similarly noted, at the end of the 1970s in Italy, 'the emergence of a specifically feminist approach to considerations of the relationship between women, the family and the welfare state' (138). Hobsbawm (1995) claimed that in that period traditionally faithful women revolted against unpopular doctrines of the Church. These revolts were notable in the Italian referenda in favour of divorce and the legalization of abortion, which will be discussed below.

Modern Italy (1970s–2000)

Economy and Society

Although the economic gap between the relatively prosperous north and the economically depressed south persists, Italy is now a high-ranking industrial polity (Ginsborg, 2003). Italians today are more prosperous than they have ever been (Livi-Bacci and Landes, 2001). This prosperity has also meant that Italy has shifted from labour exporter to labour importer (Signorini, 2001) and faces a tide of immigration, in particular from Africa and Albania (Martinelli, Chiesi, and Stefanizzi, 1999; Niero, 1996).

Throughout the twentieth century, as society rapidly urbanized, the size of Italy's economy increased eighteen times, its population doubled, and its per capita income increased tenfold (Livi-Bacci and Landes, 2001). Some have noted that this growth is highly unusual, since Italy has been identified as peculiar among large advanced countries because of surprising success with its unusual industrial structure (Signorini, 2001): it is said to have a first-world wage structure and a third-world industry structure. Italy is not dominated by large industries, as most other industrially advanced countries are, and almost 25 per cent of total manufacturing employment is accounted for by 'micro-industries' with fewer than ten employees (Martinelli, Chiesi, and Stefanizzi, 1999). For example, in 1996 about 65 per cent of employees in Italy worked in firms with fewer than 100 employees, in contrast to 19 per cent of German workers and 28 per cent of workers in Britain (Signorini, 2001). In other words, Italy's economic success has come via its specialization in light industries and small firms, and the family and community are believed to be the backbone of many of these local, small-scale manufacturing industries (ibid.). It is interesting to note that Italy's economic success and 'modernization' is driven by traditional social networks and institutions. Some have argued that this success is also linked to the fact that Italian parliamentary institutions have been extremely unstable – for example, between 1948 and 1973 Italy had twenty-six governments (Violante and Peyre, 2001).

The last decades of the twentieth century were especially dynamic for Italy. In the 1980s and 1990s significant forces emerged in both state and society, pushing towards strengthening democracy (Ginsborg, 2003). Furthermore, with pressures from the European Union and a change in direction from economic policy-makers, Italy came to enjoy low inflation, moderate deficits, and macroeconomic stability (Signorini, 2001). The state made attempts to decentralize and privatize parts of the welfare system in order to cope with renewed financial pressures and European economic integration. In the process, its once conservative-paternalistic, state-centred social policies that were remnants of the 1930s policies were transformed (Niero, 1996).

Since the 1970s Italians have witnessed some profound changes to social policies, particularly those connected to family life and reproductive choices. Many of the changes that took place during this period can actually be characterized as positive or progressive. Recently, Italians have enjoyed universal health care, four weeks' paid vacation for workers, relatively generous maternity leaves with full pay (plus an additional six months at half-pay), retirement benefits for women at age fifty-five and for men at age sixty-five, and pensions for housewives (Ghedini, 2001). Retirement benefits in Italy are said to be among the most generous in Europe (*Economist*, 2000; Livi-Bacci and Landes, 2001).

Women and Family Policies in 'Modern' Italy

Women, Paid Work, and Child Care

Legal equality at work was enshrined in the 1977 law on 'Gender parity of employment conditions' (Bimbi, 1993). Subsequently, Italian women, like many other European women, began entering the labour force in large numbers. Most of these working women were mothers (Mantovani, 2001). They were greatly assisted by the aforementioned changes in maternity leaves: by the early 1990s women could claim a maternity leave of two months before and three months after giving birth. A mother would also be provided with 80 per cent of her previous wage and an additional six months of optional leave. Her job would be protected for one year (Niero, 1996). Today, employed women have the right to maternal leave, on full pay for twelve weeks, plus parental leave of 40 per cent of salary until the child is one year of age (United Nations, 2000a). Between 1970 and 2000 female labour force participation increased by 70 per cent, while male rates stayed constant (Livi-Bacci and Landes, 2001). By 2000 women had come to make up approximately 40 per cent of the Italian labour force (ibid.).

From the beginning of this period, a series of actions by labour unions and women's groups resulted in the Italian parliament's passing a 1971 law that provided publicly supported childcare for infants and toddlers up to the age of three (Mantovani, 2001; Bimbi, 1993). The cost was set on a sliding scale based on the family's income and ability to pay (Mantovani, 2001). At the outset, the infant/toddler centres that were created were viewed as emergency (temporary) services, but since then they have been recognized as a necessary part of life for many Italian families.

Italy already had a publicly funded (no-cost/free) preschool system for children age three to six; established in 1968, it was almost universal (Gandini and Edwards, 2001). Recent data reveal that 94 per cent of Italian children age three to six use this system today (Mantovani, 2001). Such high rates of use have resulted in the spread of the idea that attending preschool is normal and positive for children over the age of three. The infant/toddler services introduced in the 1970s simply improved existing childcare services in Italy. Furthermore, the system that was being established at that point was quite stable and solid. The Italian childcare system for infants and toddlers and the preschool

system for children three to six years of age has benefited from continuity of caregivers (relatively low turnover rates), a result of their receiv-
ing full benefits, paid vacation, and relatively good salaries (ibid.).

By 1985 additional childcare initiatives were established, and new
services were given financial backing by new Italian laws put in place
in 1997. In fact, children have been a centre of interest in Italy throughout the 1990s, an interest manifested in the passing of Law 285 in 1997,
which provided support for initiatives in favour of improving the lives
of children from birth through adolescence. This law also renewed
government financial commitment to the infant/toddler services established in the 1970s (Ghedini, 2001). Such initiatives marked a move
away from centralized administration of care, giving local governments
greater autonomy in the planning and implementation of services
deemed necessary within their communities (ibid.). By the law 900
billion lire (about US $450 million) are allocated for three years and an
annual sum of 312 billion lire (US $156 million) is designated for three
years as of 2000. Many of the initiatives should make it easier for
women to balance paid work and family responsibilities.

It should be noted, however, that women's labour force participation
in Italy is not without problems. Italian women face barriers that are not
commonly found in other countries. For example, the organization of
time in Italy remains chaotic: school hours and school holidays do not
coincide with work hours and schedules (Livi-Bacci and Landes, 2001).
Furthermore, in the Italian labour market – unlike the North American
market, for example – there are few opportunities for women (and men,
for that matter) to find part-time employment (ibid.). Thus, despite
continued improvements in access to and availability of childcare,
women continue to face obstacles connected to balancing their paid and
unpaid work.

Falling Birth Rates

As mentioned above, despite the obvious problems that they face in the
labour force, women have entered the labour market in large numbers.
Owing to the increasing number of women seeking higher education
and employment, Italy, like many other European countries, began
experiencing demographic and population changes (Niero, 1996). In
fact, in relation to the size of the total population, the number of children born to Italians today is among the lowest in the world (Livi-Bacci

and Landes, 2001; Ghedini, 2001; Bimbi, 1993). Over the twentieth century, the population of Italy shifted from plentiful growth to the present zero growth. Between 1930 and 1960 it increased by 9 million births (Livi-Bacci and Landes, 2001). Over the next thirty years, from 1960 to 1990, the crude population increased by 6 million. By 1990 the Italian population was practically stationary, with 'the excess of deaths over births being compensated for by immigration' (139). In sum, the Italian family is shrinking. Italy's 1991 census revealed that the average family fell to 2.8 members, compared with 3.4 in 1971 (Evans, 1996). In other words, in 1991 there was approximately one grandchild for every three grandparents (ibid. 1996). Although Italy remains, in the eyes of many, a traditional society, its birth rates continue to decline.

The reduction of fertility throughout the 1980s was seen by Catholic leaders to be the result of consumerist egotism, particularly on the part of women (Saraceno, 1991). Throughout this period, female egotism was blamed for the disintegration of family and of society in general (ibid.). However, Italian tendencies are in line with what is happening in other parts of Europe: the age of first marriage for both men and women is rising, the number of single adults is increasing, marriage rates are declining, and the number of young adults living together out of wedlock is growing (Cavalli and Cavazzi, 2001). Many of these trends may also be linked to the fact that in 1995 the unemployment rate for those under the age of twenty-five reached 33 per cent in Italy – the highest in the EU after Spain (Ginsborg, 2003).

Part of the problem contributing to Italy's especially low rates has been identified as the state's reluctance to become involved in population issues, which stems from the continued mistrust and fear of Fascism and Fascist population policies (Gauthier, 1996; Livi-Bacci and Landes, 2001). Furthermore, although Italy is experiencing some of the same trends as other European countries, including an increase in cohabitation, birth to unwed couples, and a decline in gender differences regarding family rights, Italy's family structure remains somewhat distinct (Cavalli and Cavazzi, 2001). For example, the percentage of premarital and extramarital cohabitations is still relatively small (though rising) compared with that of other European countries (ibid.). Furthermore, the Italian family is still a 'long-term' family, in which the children (especially males) continue to live at home with their parents for a long time (ibid.), and divorce rates are comparatively low even after changes to the divorce law (Gauthier, 1996).

Changes in the Divorce Law

According to Article 29 of Italy's post-war constitution, the republic recognized the rights of the family as a natural association founded on marriage (Fusaro, 2001), an institution based on moral and legal equality of spouses, within the limits laid down by Italian law to safeguard the unity of the family (Fusaro, 2001). One of the 'safeguards' was the illegality of divorce. On 1 December 1970, however, after long and heated debates, the Chamber of Deputies passed the first divorce law in Italy (Langer, 1987); until that point, divorce had been illegal. This law was passed despite vigorous opposition from the Catholic hierarchy and conservatives, and even after the law was passed, Catholic leaders remained (and remain) staunch opponents, ensuring that the debate did not end there. This issue had profound implications for religious harmony in the country. It was also seen as so politically 'insoluble' that all political parties agreed to turn to a referendum to resolve the issue (Violante and Peyre, 2001).

Some have argued that because of the turbulence in the Italian political system it is often left to the Italian citizens themselves to directly resolve some of the country's most heated political debates and issues through referenda (Violante and Peyre, 2001). This was precisely what happened in the legalization of divorce debate. Even though the law legalizing divorce was passed in 1970, the issue was not resolved until 1974, when the law was confirmed by a majority of Italians (59.5 per cent), who voted in favour of it in a referendum held on 2 May. Although divorce rates remain relatively low, this was yet another significant change in the lives of Italians after the 1970s.

Changes in Laws Regarding Abortion and Contraception

A second important legal and political challenge connected to family life concerned the legalization of abortion and access to various forms of contraception. Major changes on this issue occurred in the 1970s. Although abortion in Italy was strictly illegal under all circumstances until 1978 (Keates, 1994), it was widely practised, often even under medical supervision. For example, Dr Giorgio Conciani ran a gynaecological clinic where he was said to have performed approximately ten 'illegal' abortions per day in the early 1970s, at a cost of L100 000 to L150 000 each (L100 000 at the time was less than CND $100; ibid.). Until the 1970s in Italy, abortion was treated as a crime 'against the race' (Gauthier, 1996). This was clearly a remnant of the nationalist and pronatalist ideas of the 1930s, which were maintained by the Catholic Church and Catholic political parties throughout the 1950s and 1960s. Not until 1969 was there extensive debate on lifting the ban on family planning activities and the sale of contraceptives that had been in place since a royal decree was adopted in 1931 (Livi-Bacci and Landes, 2001; Gauthier, 1996). As a result, liberal access to contraception was legally authorized in 1971 (the same year it was legalized in the United States).

It was seven years later that the abortion law was changed. By the passing of Law 194 in 1978 abortion, only in the first trimester and only when a woman's physical and psychological health was at risk, was rendered legal (Bettarini and D'Andrea, 1996). Despite those stipulations, there was a great deal of opposition, to the point where a proposal to repeal the law was seriously considered in 1981. Like the divorce legislation a decade earlier, the abortion law and the proposal to repeal it were dealt with through a referendum vote. In 1981 the proposal to repeal the law was rejected by nearly 80 per cent of Italian voters, and the law legalizing abortion was thus confirmed (Hobsbawm, 1995; Bettarini and D'Andrea, 1996; Livi-Bacci and Landes, 2001).

Since the early 1980s the number of abortions performed in Italy has been declining, from 250,000 in the early 1980s to about 150,000 in 1993 (Keates, 1994). Abortion rates peaked in 1983 at 16.9 abortions per 1,000 women of reproductive age, but dropped to 9.8 per 1,000 in 1993 (Bettarini and D'Andrea, 1996). It is interesting to note that abortion rates among Italian adolescents are considerably lower than comparable rates in other European nations (ibid.). For example, the abortion rate for Italian women ages fifteen to nineteen was 4.6 per 1,000 in 1987, while for Finnish women it was 15.7 per 1,000 and for English and Welsh women it was 20.9 per 1,000 (ibid.). Legislative restrictions requiring parental consent for the procedure to take place may in part be responsible for the difference. If they cannot obtain parental consent, women under the age of eighteen can have abortions if they obtain the authorization of a judge.

As is true in other countries, there are considerable variations in abortion rates across age groups for Italian women, but there are also significant regional differences. Although total fertility rates are relatively constant across Italy's regions, the abortion rates tend to vary considerably; the southern and island regions tend to have the highest fertility and lowest abortion rates (Bettarini and D'Andrea, 1996). There is also a correlation between the frequency of civil marriages and the rate of abortion, where both variables are also a proxy for low religiosity (ibid.). The abortion debate was rekindled in Italy in the late 1980s and again in the early 1990s, and it appears to show no signs of resolution. Abortion remains very controversial in Italy, particularly given the reactions from the Catholic hierarchy (ibid.).

There is no doubt that since the 1970s there has been a tug of war between groups seeking to 'modernize' laws and policies surrounding family and gender issues and conservative elements fighting to prevent change. As a result of this struggle, Italian family policies appear quite peculiar: ahead of their time and generous on some fronts and traditionalist and patriarchal on others. They reflect and contribute to the fact that 'the Italian family' is changing, while at the same time remaining strong and important to most Italians today (*Economist*, 2000; Ginsborg, 2003).

An Evaluation of Italy's Family Policies

Italy's family policies are no longer pronatalist and driven by nationalistic motives, but they are hardly generous when it comes to the amount and type of support granted to families in general and to young families in particular. For example, tax allowances for children are said to be extremely low: in 1991 the permitted deductions were only 50 ECU per year (United Nations, 2000a). Furthermore, child benefit allowances are distributed as family allowances to low-income families and make up a tiny portion of the national budget. In 1990 they constituted only 0.5 per cent of the GNP, compared with 2.4 per cent in 1960 (ibid.).

Some have argued that many Italians prefer minimal state involvement, since the Fascist demographic policies of the 1930s continue to loom in the Italian psyche (Livi-Bacci and Landes, 2001). As a matter of fact, many uphold the idea that it is better if the state stays away from population issues altogether (ibid.). Unfortunately, when the state 'stays away,' little is done to develop policies necessary to assist families. Consequently, the family must make up for state shortcomings in support (*Economist*, 2000; Bimbi, 1993), and it actually does fill many of the gaps (Livi-Bacci and Landes, 2001; Ginsborg, 2003). Ginsborg (2003) noted that what emerged was the 'devolving of family problems to families themselves,' resulting in 'tying individual members of families to each other as far as possible' (228), a phenomenon particularly evident in the case of old age pensions.

The role pensions play may actually come as a surprise to many living outside Italy. The country is 'greying' faster than any other European country, except Spain, because of the drop in national fertility. Italy is said to have a high net ageing rate (Niero, 1996), which has proved disadvantageous to state coffers, since Italian old age pensions are among the highest and most generous in Europe (*Economist*, 2000), but they have also had some advantages, to young Italians in particular, since ageing parents and grandparents in Italy often contribute to the support of (grand)children. In fact, it has been argued that the old age pension makes up for Italy's limited unemployment benefits (ibid.). Furthermore, the extended family is said to act like a bank: for example, it is customary for parents to help their married children to buy their first house, and 69 per cent of Italian families own their own house (ibid.; Bimbi, 1993). One study found that if in need of a loan, one Italian in three would turn to parents (only one in four would go to a bank). In contrast, in Germany, one in six would turn to parents and one in two would first go to a bank (Cavalli and Cavazza, 2001). The family is also said to act as an insurance company (*Economist*, 2000). In other words, perhaps owing to fears of a pronatalist revival and Fascist family policies, the state appears to have steered clear of assisting young families, but since it continues to generously supplement the elderly, some state support is indirectly reaching young Italians 'through the back door,' so to speak, via assistance from grandparents and parents.

Unfortunately, this assistance is not enough and has resulted in another idiosyncrasy among Italian families: 'the postponement syndrome' (Livi-Bacci and Landes, 2001). The 'postponement syndrome' refers to the putting off of the 'child launch': the steps to independence and self-reliance of young Italians are delayed and decisions to marry and have children are postponed (ibid.). Of course, this trend has been observed in a number of countries, Canada included, but it is especially common and acute in Italy. Recent Italian statistics revealed that approximately 70 per cent of unmarried men up to the age of thirty still live with their parents. In Italy in 1995, 56 per cent of all young adults, aged twenty-five to twenty-nine, lived with their parents, compared with 21 per cent in Germany and 12 per cent in the Netherlands (*Economist*, 2000). This discrepancy may be due in part to high unemployment rates among those twenty-five years of age and under and the fact that in 1995 Italy had the second highest rates in the EU: 33 per cent unemployment (Ginsborg, 2003). In 1992 the unemployment rate of men aged twenty to twenty-four was 25.6 per cent, and for women of that age it was 34.7 per cent (Martinelli, Chiesi, and Stefanizzi, 1999).

The phenomenon of adult children living with parents has become so widespread in Italy that demographers and family researchers are beginning to talk about a 'new phase' in the life cycle – an 'altogether new phenomenon,' which gives rise to an 'altogether new' family form (Scabini and Cigoli, 1997). Furthermore, while North American research demonstrates that this particular arrangement has been detrimental to the well-being of both parents and adult children, in Italy studies show that the opposite is true (ibid.). While Italian youth may rely heavily on all kinds of assistance from their parents, they do not lose their autonomy and liberty; nor do parents come to resent the arrangement. This living arrangement is said to leave young adults free, but not alone (Scabini and Cigoli, 1997). It has nonetheless contributed to declining fertility rates as young Italians postpone marriage and cohabitation (cohabitation rates are still low, but rising, compared with those of other European countries), and the rate of 'out of wedlock' births remains low.

According to Livi-Bacci and Landes (2001), a 'new model of life' has developed: the completion of education of both partners is a prerequisite for entering the labour force; full-time employment and owning a house are prerequisites for leaving the parental home; and leaving the parental home is a precondition for making decisions surrounding partnership, marriage, and childbearing. They add that each of these steps takes more time today than in the past. In the meantime, birth and marriage rates will remain low. As it stands, a number of critics have noted that there are simply not enough supports to families in general and young families in particular (ibid.).

A Recapitulation

For the most part, the Italian state in the post-war period avoided making changes to legislation surrounding family and population issues. As a matter of fact, the Italian state avoided population policy issues altogether for about thirty years. New pronatalist policies were not on the agenda, particularly given Italians' post-war resistance to intervention of this nature (Gauthier, 1996), and throughout the 1950s and 1960s very little changed. Ironically, however, many of the population and social policies related to family life that were established in the 1930s, during the Fascist period, remained in place for the next few decades. They included services for children established under Mussolini and legislation surrounding reproduction and contraception.

In the 1970s Italy's economy shifted, social services expanded, and laws regulating family and reproductive life were changed. Italians voted (in referenda) to legalize divorce and abortion, and improvements were made to already generous maternity leave and childcare programs. But economic prosperity and women's labour force participation were accompanied by declines in fertility rates that were especially sharp, even in comparison with similar decreases in several European countries. At the same time, Italian youth were experiencing 'postponement syndrome' (Livi-Bacci and Landes, 2001). While the Italian state was generous in some aspects of social welfare programs, in its struggle to avoid population issues it had not done enough to provide support to Italian youth and young Italian families (ibid.).

Some say Italy's entry into the European Union has been a 'mixed blessing.' Although membership has done much to improve the Italian economy, the EU has also placed a great deal of pressure on governments to initiate 'corrective actions' and to slash social spending (Signorini, 2001). The national budget deficit had to be cut, which resulted in cuts to social spending (Ghedini, 2001). Of course, such reduced spending will also keep pronatalist policies far off the political agenda in Italy.

Fertility rates are low and dropping, and there appears to be little expectation for change, given the direction in which Italy is moving. As for family policies, it appears that the spectres of Fascism and Fascist population policies continue to plague Italy. Ironically, though initially avoiding pronatalist policies and later responding to EU pressures to cut social spending, the Italian state now is approaching a crisis in population growth and unprecedentedly low levels of fertility. It seems neither willing nor able to do much about it.

Part III
Policies and Outcomes Compared

10

Outcomes Compared

The Impact of Political Change on Fertility Transition:
A Rudimentary Trend Analysis

An examination of each state on a case-by-case basis reveals that a nationalist leader's rise to power was accompanied by changes, or attempted changes, to family policies from relatively less to more traditional and patriarchal ones. Leaders in Fascist Italy, Nazi Germany, post-Communist Russia, and modern independent Croatia implemented, or attempted to implement, a number of pronatalist and pronuptialist state-sponsored initiatives designed to promote nationalist goals and values. The questions remain: What impact did these policy changes actually have on women and families? Were nationalist leaders 'successful' in altering the rate of family formation and fertility patterns?

Mapping out demographic patterns and trajectories in a comparative trend analysis will be useful in establishing whether dissimilar policies resulted in differing demographic outcomes. Of course, many factors other than nationalist family policies, which will not be discussed here, can and do affect both marriage and fertility rates. On the other hand, a comparative trend analysis can give us an *indication* of the impact of state-imposed family planning programs on fertility and marriage patterns.

A Caveat

Lloyd and Ross (1989) discuss a number of methods for measuring the fertility impact of family planning programs. The goal of their work is to point out strengths and weaknesses of different approaches and to make recommendations on improving the quality and value of population-based methods of measurement. They noted that population-based methods fall into two categories: those that rely on aggregate-level data from censuses or vital statistics and those that rely on individual level data from fertility and family planning surveys of women of reproductive age (Lloyd and Ross, 1989).

Technologies for analysis have become much more sophisticated as sources of data have increased, but owning to the historical nature of this study, only population-based methods that relied on aggregate data were possible because of the limited data sources, particularly for the earlier, interwar period of this analysis. The type, quality, and amount of data available improved after mid-century, but within the first half of the century there was a lack of adequate information about world populations. A 1949 United Nations report entitled *Population Census Methods* confirmed 'the inadequacy of existing population statistics' that was particularly evident in the first issue (1948) of the United Nations *Demographic Yearbook* (1949a, 1). In addition to the general lack of data for this early period, the usefulness of the statistics presented was greatly impaired by cross-national differences in definitions and methods (United Nations, 1949b). Although these shortcomings pose a significant problem, a simple, comparative trend analysis may still prove useful in identifying differing outcomes of dissimilar family policies.

Trend analysis compares an extrapolation of the pre-program fertility trend with the trend in fertility, following a program's initiation (Lloyd and Ross, 1989). Simply, trend analysis is generally designed to answer the question: Did fertility change after a program was implemented? For the purpose of this study, it seems important to establish whether aggregate fertility rates actually *rose* as a result of nationalists' efforts to boost birth rates. A *comparative* trend analysis enables us to measure change over time within one country (following a policy change), but to compare trends in countries where nationalist regimes implemented pronatalist policies with countries where governments have not. While this type of analysis cannot clearly establish causality, it can still provide an indication that there is an association between a policy change and fertility outcomes. Future research by demographers and statisticians may provide more concrete conclusions about causality.

Population Profiles

To begin the comparison, it is interesting to look at whether Hitler and Mussolini had reason to fear for the future of their respective nations because of falling birth rates and population decline. The first United Nations *Demographic Yearbook* provided a good starting point for simple cross-country comparisons. In the interwar period, the largest of the four polities was the U.S.S.R., with a population of 147,028,000 (in 1926), followed by Germany, with 69,459,825 (in 1939), Italy with 42,444,588 (in 1936), and Yugoslavia with 13,934,038 (in 1931). The different reporting dates reflect the lack of standardization of population data that was characteristic of this period (United Nation, 1949b).

The *Demographic Yearbook* revealed that the birth rate in Germany was among the lowest in Europe when Hitler came to power (crude birth rate of 14.7 in 1933). Only Austria, Sweden, and England had lower rates at the time (United Nations, 1949c). Birth rates in Italy were not low, either when Mussolini came to power, or at the height of his pronatalist drive. The crude birth rate was 32.2 in 1920 and 23.8 in 1933 (ibid.; Mitchell, 1998); although clearly sharply declining, it was significantly higher than that of Germany (and other European nations) at that time.

Figure 10.1, which plots crude birth rates, reveals that, when nationalists were in power and pronatalist policies were implemented throughout the 1930s in Italy and Germany, crude birth rates did rise somewhat. What is even more telling, however, is that they were increasing at a point when crude birth rates in other European nations such as Yugoslavia, the United Kingdom, and France were declining or remaining more or less the same (see figure 10.1). This particular observation does not, of course, prove that there is a causal relationship between the rise in crude birth rate and a nationalist rise to power, but there does seem to be a correlation. It appears that both Fascists in Italy and National Socialists in Germany did alter the trend or trajectory of aggregate birth rates throughout the second half of the 1930s. Italian and German crude birth rates rose slightly, while other countries experienced stagnation or declines (see table 10.1 and figure 10.1).

The harsh restrictions placed on the use of contraceptives in Germany in 1933, coupled with the introduction of the new Unemployment Act in the same year, which offered marriage loans to young couples, seem to have been effective in boosting birth rates somewhat.

Figure 10.1 Crude Birth Rates Compared, 1932–47

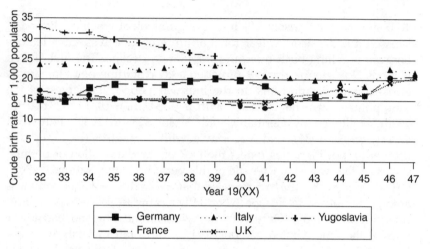

Source: United Nations (1949c)

TABLE 10.1
Crude Birth Rates Compared, 1932–47

Country	Year (19XX)															
	32	33	34	35	36	37	38	39	40	41	42	43	44	45	46	47
Germany	15	15	18	19	19	19	20	20	20	19	15	16	–	–	–	–
Italy	24	24	23.5	23	22	23	24	24	24	21	21	20	19	19	23	22
Yugoslavia	33	32	31.6	30	29	28	27	26	–	–	–	–	–	–	–	–
France	17	16	16.2	15	15	15	15	15	14	13	15	16	16	16	21	21
U.K.	16	15	15.3	15	15	15	16	15	15	14	16	17	18	16	19	21

Note: Shading indicates when nationalists were in power.
Source: United Nations (1949c)

The Unemployment Act of 1933 stipulated that 25 per cent of the loan would be cancelled on the birth of each child, so that after the birth of four children the entire loan would be repaid. By 1938 one million matrimonial loans had been granted. In 1934 new income tax and property tax laws were introduced in Germany, which greatly benefited families with a large number of children; perhaps these laws also contributed to the increase in fertility rates. Similarly, in 1938 a new decree provided a continuous allowance of 10 marks per month for the fifth child and later children under the age of sixteen (Kirkpatrick, 1938); figure 10.1 indicates that there was a slight increase in birth rates just one year later.

Unfortunately, United Nations data on crude birth rates are not available for the period preceding 1932 (see table 10.1); they would have been valuable to determine if Italy's 1931 royal decree prohibiting the sale of contraceptives resulted in an increase in birth rates. As it is, it is impossible to determine using UN data (see figure 10.2 for a presentation of another source of data). Similarly, these data make it difficult to trace whether the 1928 Fascist tax exemptions to families with seven or more children were effective. On the other hand, the 1937 introduction of a generous family allowance program may have contributed to the slight increase in crude birth rates witnessed in 1938, 1939, and 1940 (see figure 10.1 and table 10.1).

Data for revolutionary Russia under Lenin were not available from United Nations sources. The birth rates that were available corresponded with the years that Stalin was in power – a period not under investigation here. The crude birth rates for France and the United Kingdom are included in table 10.1 and figure 10.1 (in place of the Soviet Union/ Revolutionary Russia) in order to make comparisons with other European polities of the time. It should be noted, however, that at that time, in contrast to the situations of Italy and Germany, abortion in Russia was viewed as a necessary evil and was legalized in 1920. Crude birth rates were very likely to have reflected this fact.

The high but declining Yugoslav birth rates of the early decades of the twentieth century (see figure 10.1) obviously reflected de-agrarization, urbanization, and the decline of the extended family/ clan/*zadruga*, a dominant family form throughout many parts of the country. The decline was not likely to have been caused by politically motivated changes in family policies, since none had been introduced in the period. In fact, the new state did very little to help or hinder family formation and growth, other than allowing local (ethnically and religiously diverse) values and laws to remain in place and struggling with the urbanization and industrialization that were sweeping through parts of the country at the time.

In sum, figure 10.1 indicates that throughout the 1930s, when other European nations were experiencing declines in birth rates, Italy and Germany had increases. Crude birth rates in Nazi Germany seemed to have been especially positively affected. Italy began with relatively high birth rates, and under Fascist leadership, it maintained its high

Figure 10.2 Crude Birth Rates, 1920–45

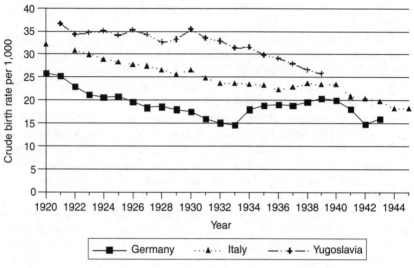

Source: Mitchell (1998)

rates with a slight increase in the late 1930s. Nazi pronatalist policies, on the other hand, seemed to have been slightly more effective, since Germany began this period with a considerably lower crude birth rate than that of Italy, but managed to boost it notably. One could say that Italy and Germany were experiencing mini baby booms, while other countries at the time experienced declines or stagnation.

Another valuable resource for comparative historical analysis is B.R. Mitchell's *International Historical Statistics: Europe, 1750–1993* (1998). Much like the United Nations figures, Mitchell's data confirm that throughout the 1930s, when nationalists in Italy and Germany were implementing pronatalist family policies, birth rates in those countries increased at a time when Yugoslav birth rates were declining steadily (see figure 10.2). Data for Russia were incomplete and therefore were excluded. Mitchell's collection is useful in that it not only includes rates from earlier in the century, but also includes historical vital statistics not found in the early United Nations *Demographic Yearbooks*, since his data are drawn from a wider collection of sources, including the United Nations *Demographic Yearbooks* and the League of Nations *Statistical Yearbooks* and national *Yearbooks*. As a result, Mitchell's (1998) data

Figure 10.3 Marriage Rate Compared, 1925–39

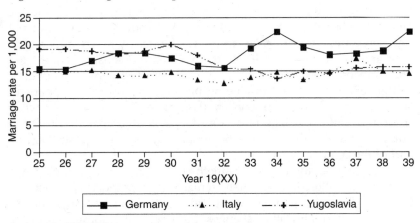

Source: Mitchell (1998)

TABLE 10.2
Marriage Rate per 1,000 Population Compared, 1925–39

Country	Year (19XX)														
	25	26	27	28	29	30	31	32	33	34	35	36	37	38	39
Germany	15.5	15.4	17.0	18.5	18.4	17.5	16.0	15.7	19.3	22.3	19.5	18.1	18.3	18.8	22.4
Italy		15.2	15.0	15.2	14.2	14.2	14.8	13.4	12.8	13.8	14.8	13.4	14.8	17.4	15.0	14.6
Yugoslavia	19.2	19.2	18.8	18.2	18.8	20.0	18.0	15.6	15.4	13.6	15.0	14.6	15.6	15.8	15.8

Note: Shading indicates a policy shift and introduction of incentives.
Source: Mitchell (1998)

provide an opportunity to assess the impact of nationalist regimes' family policies on marriage rates.

Mitchell's (1998) data also reveal that only one year after Hitler's rise to power and his immediate introduction of the matrimonial credits and loans in 1933, marriage rates peaked (see figure 10.3). In 1933, the year the loans were introduced, the marriage rate was 19.3; in the following year it jumped to 22.3 (table 10.2; Russia/U.S.S.R. data were not available). In Italy, a generous family allowance program was introduced in 1937, and, as it did in Germany under a similar program, the marriage rate immediately increased from 14.8 in 1936 to 17.4 in 1937 (table 10.2). It should be noted, however, that in both Germany and Italy the increases were short lived. In contrast, in Yugoslavia, where non-nationalists were in power, marriage rates peaked after the First World War, were high throughout the 1920s, but declined during the depression of the 1930s. Throughout this decade Yugoslavia did not experience the types of spikes in marriage rates that were apparent in Italy and Germany. Overall, although it was obviously a short-lived phenomenon, nationalist regimes in Italy and Germany attempted to and generally succeeded in altering birth and marriage rates, particularly through the use of monetary incentives. This fact is clear when crude birth and marriage rates are plotted and compared with other European nations that did not have nationalists in power in this first part of the century.

By the last decade of the twentieth century the European map had been greatly altered. While Italy remained geographically intact, the Germanies reunited and the Soviet Union and Yugoslavia broke up. As a result of these and other changes, the size of the population of the four polities was significantly different than it had been in the first half of the century. In 1998 the Russian Federation remained the largest, at 147.4 million. It was followed by Germany, at 82.1 million; Italy, at 57.4 million; and Croatia, at 4.5 million (table 10.3). While Croatia's population was considerably smaller than the others in this study, at least nine other European countries were smaller than Croatia, for example, Norway (4.4 million) and Ireland (3.7 million) (Unicef, 2002). Nonetheless, in 1994 Croatian President Tudjman openly declared his fear that 'Croatia is dying' (Foreign Broadcast Information Services, 1994). At the time, Croatia's and Russia's slightly more pronounced sex ratio imbalance and negative population growth (table 10.3) may have been part of what was fuelling nationalist fears of declining marriage and fertility rates.

By the early 1990s, when Croatia became independent, crude birth rates were continuing their free fall, from 13.1 in 1985 to 12.6 in 1987, to 11.7 in 1989, to 10.8 in 1991 (United Nations, 1999). This decline was very likely linked to ethnic tension, civil war, political unrest, and the economic consequences associated with them. Rates levelled off, at 10.5 births for three years (1992–4) once nationalist leader Franjo Tudjman began his rule over independent Croatia. They increased temporarily in 1995, 1996, and 1997, while the Tudjman government's initiatives and propaganda were in place (table 10.4; figure 10.4). This change in birth rates may seem insignificant to some, but compared with trends in other European nations, it is somewhat unusual. For example, Italy and to a somewhat lesser extent Germany experienced steady, low, and/or

TABLE 10.3
General Statistical Profiles

	Total pop. (millions), 1998*	No. births (000s), 1998*	Total fertility rate, 1998*	Mortality rate, <age 5 1998*	Females/ 100 males** 2000	Singulate mean age at marriage, 1991–8**	Pop. growth 1995– 2000**	GNP/ capita, 1998*
Croatia	4.5	47	1.6	9	107	25 (w); 28 (m)	–0.1	4,620
Germany	82.1	749	1.3	5	104	28 (w); 30 (m)	0.1	26,570
Italy	57.4	512	1.2	6	106	27 (w); 30 (m)	0	20,090
Russian Fed.	147.4	1420	1.3	25	114	23 (w); 25 (m)	–0.2	2,260

Sources: *Unicef (2002); **United Nations (2000b)

TABLE 10.4
Crude Birth Rates Compared, 1990–8

	1990	1991	1992	1993	1994	1995	1996	1997	1998
Croatia	11.6	10.8	10.5	10.5	10.5	10.7	12.0	12.1	10.5
Germany	11.4	10.4	10	9.8	9.5	9.4	9.7	9.9	9.7
Italy	9.8	9.9	10.1	9.6	9.3	9.2	9.2	9.2	9.3
Russia	13.4	12.1	10.7	9.3	9.5	9.2	8.8	8.6	8.8

Source: United Nations (1999)

Figure 10.4 Crude Birth Rates, 1990–8

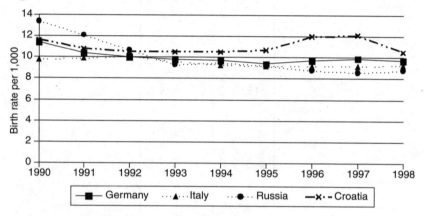

Source: United Nations (1999)

declining rates throughout the same period. Interestingly, despite its efforts, Russia experienced steady declines, very likely owing to economic factors and the state's inability to implement proposed policy changes.

Aggregate United Nations (2000b) data on total fertility rates reveal that Croatia entered the decade and its period of independence with the highest (though still low) total fertility rate of the four European nations (1.6 births per woman, compared with 1.3 in Italy, 1.3 in Germany, and 1.5 in Russia; see table 10.5). Over the decade, through its pronatalist agenda and propaganda, the state seems to have managed to maintain the total fertility rate of 1.6 births per woman. In Russia the total fertility rate dropped slightly from 1.5 to 1.3 births per woman (table 10.5). It is

TABLE 10.5
Total Fertility Rates Compared, 1990–5 and 1995–2000

	1990–5	1995–2000
Croatia	1.6	1.6
Germany	1.3	1.3
Italy	1.3	1.2
Russian Federation	1.5	1.3

Source: United Nations (2000b)

interesting to recall that this drop took place despite Yeltsin's attempts to redress the fall in the birth rate and encourage women to have children by introducing fees for abortions in 1994. That is, in 1994 there was a directive issued to remove most abortions from medical insurance coverage, making legal abortion virtually out of the reach of most women. Italy and Germany, neither of which experienced a nationalist rise to power in the period, either saw a fertility decline (Italy) or remained the same (Germany), with overall low fertility rates.

A somewhat similar pattern was seen when marriage rates were compared. Newly independent Croatia experienced slight, but steady, consecutive increases in marriage rates through the early part of the decade (figure 10.5; table 10.6). In the three other countries there were slight declines in the marriage rate over the same period. It appears that pronatalist and pronuptualist policies and attitudes were minimally successful in Croatia and not at all successful in Russia in the early 1990s. This observation is particularly clear when Croatia is compared with Italy and Germany, where pronatalist and pronuptialist policies were not implemented and both birth and marriage rates generally declined, or at best remained the same, at very low levels.

It is also interesting to note that, in spite of Russian and Croatian leaders' speeches and attempts to 'elevate' the status of motherhood and liberate women from the 'burden' of paid employment, there was little or no change to the proportion of women involved in economic activity over the last decade of the twentieth century (see table 10.7). In Croatia the proportion of employed women remained the same, while in the Russian Federation it decreased by 1 per cent. What is actually more interesting is that despite state efforts to encourage women's retreat from paid employment, the employment rates of women remained relatively constant, while those of men declined somewhat in both Croatia and the Russian Federation (table 10.7). Similarly, while

Figure 10.5 Marriage Rates Compared, 1990–3

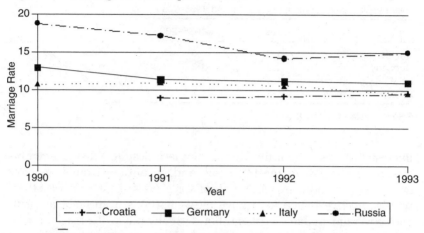

Note: Although Mitchell (2003) presents data for Germany, Italy, and Russia until 1998, comparable Croatian data are available only until 1993.
Source: Mitchell (1998)

TABLE 10.6
Marriage Rates Compared, 1990–3

	1990	1991	1992	1993
Croatia		9.0	9.2	9.6
Germany	13.0	11.4	11.2	11.0
Italy	10.8	11.0	10.6	9.6
Russia	18.8	17.2	14.2	15.0

Source: Mitchell (1998)

there were efforts in Croatia and Russia to return women to the domestic sphere, they were not reflected in the proportion of women in public office. In other words, while one would expect to see a decline in the proportion of women in elected political positions in the two polities, this did not take place. There was a slight (2 per cent) increase in the proportion of Croatian women in their lower chamber, and increases were seen in the proportion of women at both ministerial and sub-ministerial levels (table 10.8). The same was true in the Russian Federation – in fact, Russian women held a larger proportion of positions at

TABLE 10.7
Economic Activity

	Adult (15+) Economic Activity Rate (%)				Per cent of women in the labour force
	1990		1995–7		
	W	M	W	M	
Croatia	48	71	48	69	44
Germany	44*	70	47	68	43
Italy	36**	64**	35**	61**	38**
Russian Federation	60	76	59***	74	48

*Data for 1990 do not include the former German Democratic Republic.
**Data are estimated to correspond to standard age groups.
***For persons aged 15 to 72
Source: United Nations (2000a).

TABLE 10.8
Women in Public Life, 1987–99

	Per cent of parliamentary seats in single or lower chamber occupied by women			Per cent of women in decision-making positions in government			
				Ministerial level		Sub-ministerial level	
	1987	1995	1999	1994	1998	1994	1998
Croatia	–	6	8	4	12	6	20
Germany	–	26	31	16	8	5	5
Italy	13	15	11	12	13	16	9
Russian Fed.	–	13	10	0	8	3	4

Source: United Nations (2000b)

both the ministerial and sub-ministerial level in 1998 than they had in 1994. In Italy in the same period, women actually experienced a decline in their proportion of parliamentary seats, but they made some gains at the ministerial level (table 10.8). In Germany, after reunification, more women held positions in parliament than they had in the FRG before the *Wende* (although fewer than in the GDR), but women lost some ground at the ministerial level.

In sum: in the 1990s, while leaders in Croatia and Russia made attempts to convince women to become 'heroic mothers' and give up their public roles, they seemed generally unsuccessful. This was especially true in Russia, perhaps owing to the economic circumstances of the time. In neither Croatia nor Russia did women leave the labour force in droves, nor did they retire from political life. It could be said, then, that although nationalists may have attempted to re-patriarchalize gender and family relations in Croatia and Russia in the 1990s through, for example, the introduction of pronatalist policies and propaganda, they seemed somewhat less successful (especially in Russia) than their nationalist predecessors in the early part of the century in Italy and Germany. While many of the same types of pronatalist policies and propaganda programs were attempted at both the beginning and the end of the twentieth century, their overall impact seemed different. Nationalist leaders appeared to be considerably more 'successful' in the early parts of the century than nationalists at the end of the century (particularly in Russia). Furthermore, in both time periods, when 'successes' were apparent, they were short lived, lasting only two to four years.

11

Policies Analysed and Compared

Identifying and Analysing Models of Family Policies

A question that all states, new and old, face is what its responsibility is for the social and economic welfare of its citizens. Clearly, states answer this question differently at different times. It goes without saying that there are profound differences among countries, and over time within countries, in government intervention and levels of support to families. Some governments are or have been alarmist and/or interventionist when there have been actual fertility declines or perceived threats to population size and composition. Other governments have been less interventionist or have limited their intervention to specific circumstances or times – usually in cases of severe deprivation. These differing traditions have been analysed and classified by many policy analysts and researchers throughout the twentieth century.

One of the institutions that was perhaps most commonly associated with social policy analysis in the century was the Department of Social Sciences at the London School of Economics. While the department was established in December 1912, it was not until after the Second World War, under the leadership of T.H Marshall, and later Richard Titmuss, that social policy analysis became a central focus (Bulmer, Lewis, and Piachaud, 1989). Titmuss (1974) theoretically advanced the study of social policy by, in part, defining it in terms of latent rather than manifest functions or purposes. He was particularly effective in juxtaposing what he considered 'inefficiencies' of the market and state policies that promoted the market (the American classic liberal laissez-faire model, for example) with the generosity of the welfare state (as in post-war Britain). He was among the first to construct typologies of welfare provisions, both inspiring others to continue in the work of conceptually ordering the field and analysing social policy from new perspectives (Mishra, 1989). Titmuss was revered as a pioneer and called 'a social administrator, a political economist, a conservative, a socialist, a social-ist, a sociologist, a philosopher, a democrat, a leader and a visionary' (Reisman, 2004, 793). He and other pioneers also were criticized for scarcely touching on the consequences of different state policies, particularly how policies have affected women differently (Sainsbury, 1996). Furthermore, pioneers like Marshall (and his stage theory), especially those proponents of modernization theory, were criticized for assuming that the welfare state is a natural (inevitable) outcome of the democratization process (Esping-Andersen, 1987).

Since the 'Titmuss years,' dozens of scholars, including people such as Jane Lewis, Gøsta Esping-Andersen, Diane Sainsbury, and Julia O'Connor, not only have done extensive work in identifying, classifying, and explaining the ideology underlying policy creation and implementation, but also have assessed the impact of diverse policies on individuals and groups, especially women.

Social Policies and Policy Analysis in Post-Titmuss, Post-War Europe

In the post-war period, with the rise of the welfare state, numerous researchers set out to identify state variations in levels of support to citizens. Many of the typologies that emerged compared the proportion of national income devoted to social purposes, the level of benefits, the range of services, the proportion of the population covered and eligibility requirements, the types of programs introduced, the type and nature of financing, the level of commitment to full employment, and the role of private organizations, among other things. Ideal types were created and named, and states were slotted into this or that category based on their 'scoring' in the above-listed criteria in specific policy domains. Modern states were grouped, typically with the United States at one extreme and Sweden at the other (Esping-Andersen, 1990; Sainsbury, 1996; Olsen, 1998). As a result, many analyses were comparative in nature (Lewis, 1993; Olsen, 1998). Furthermore, since the 1970s analyses of welfare state policies have increasingly included the word 'crisis' (Bulmer, Lewis, and Piachaud, 1989). Throughout the 1980s and 1990s researchers wrote extensively on the 'attacks on' and the 'decline of' the welfare state. Books emerged with a more critical, often feminist, approach to social policy analysis, which was clearly reflected in their titles, for example, Williams's *Social Policy: A Critical Introduction* (1989) and Williams, Popay, and Oakley's *Welfare Research: A Critical Review* (1999). Some, like Esping-Andersen (1987), have challenged the modernist approach to understanding the welfare state by pointing to the stagnation, crises, and policy reversals apparent in modern capitalist nations. Others have contributed to the field by analysing the gender dimension of social policies, specifically focusing on how variations and policy reversals affected women differently (Bussemaker and van Kerbergen, 1999; O'Connor, Orloff, and Shaver, 1999; Sainsbury 1999a). In focusing on the gender dimension of social policies, some have looked at how changes to the welfare state have affected our understanding and experiences around the concepts of care, social care, and the commodification of care, pointing to their inevitable consequences for women (Daly and Lewis, 2000; Ungerson, 2003).

Those analysing the restructuring and retrenchment of the welfare state have closely examined how market (new/neo) liberalism (O'Connor, Orloff, and Shaver, 1999) and globalization (Mishra, 1998) have placed constraints on nation states when making or redefining social policy. They have clearly shown that neo-liberalism and globalization, opponents of the welfare state, have launched assaults on social rights (ibid.), leaving women, in particular, to pay a hefty price as their needs have been redefined by market paradigms (O'Connor, Orloff, and Shaver, 1999).

While many of these scholars were critical of this redirection of state policies, those like Francis Fukuyama (1992) were celebrating the victory of 'liberal democracy' over 'rival ideologies like hereditary monarchy, fascism, and most recently communism' (xi). Fukuyama hailed the fact that 'good news has come!' He vociferously praised liberalism, noting that 'The most remarkable development of the last quarter of the twentieth century has been the revelation of enormous weaknesses at the core of the world's seemingly strong dictatorships, whether they be of the military-authoritarian Right, or the communist-totalitarian Left ... liberal democracy remains the only coherent political aspiration that spans different regions and cultures around the globe' (xiii). Fukuyama declared that liberal principles in economics '– the "free market" – have spread, and have succeeded in producing unprecedented levels of material prosperity' (xiii). He also remarked that despite liberalism's victory, inequalities persist. He exonerated the state, especially the market, by blaming individuals or families; for example, he explained:

'lacking a home environment capable of transmitting cultural values needed to take advantage of opportunity, such youngsters [black "underclass" youth] feel the constant pull of the "street"' (293). He added that 'under these circumstances, achievement of full legal equality for blacks and the opportunities provided by the U.S. economy will not make terribly much difference to his or her life' (293–4). He celebrated what many social policy analysts feared and criticized – the spread of neo-liberal principles and the pulverizing of social rights.

Fukuyama (1992) explained that, with technological innovation, the spread of modern economic production, and liberal ideology, we will see an increasing 'homogenization of all human societies, regardless of historical origin or cultural inheritance' (xiv). In order to do this, he noted, states must 'unify nationally on the basis of a centralized state, urbanize, replace traditional forms of social organization like tribe, sect, and family with economically rational ones based on function and efficiency' (xv).

His overall claim of a liberal defeat of its rivals and his dream of a culturally homogenized globe point to his outright failure to notice that one contender, a clear opponent, has been left standing after other ideologies have supposedly been defeated: nationalism. Nationalism is an ideology that, I claim, is a conservative response to globalization, fear of the loss of 'traditional forms of social organization,' and loss of state control over ethno-national affairs. Granted, nationalists are weak and isolated opponents compared with the goliath of globalization and contemporary neo-liberalism, yet they exist and have their own social policy agendas.

Nationalist Family Policies: Neither Social Rights nor Neo-Liberal 'Freedom'

According to Esping-Andersen (1987), 'welfare policies are not just appendices to a given political-economic regime; they are integral to the regime itself' (8). A key role of nationalist state policies, as outlined in the preceding chapters, is to achieve the social control of women for the specific purposes of re-establishing a real or mythical past order and glory, and ensuring a fecund, homogeneous, ethno-national future. Of course, there are variations in the level of commitment to such an ideal. For example, I would classify Tudjman, independent Croatia's first president and self-proclaimed nationalist, as a 'true believer,' while

Yeltsin in Russia, *used* nationalism to achieve some of his desired goals. Nonetheless, similarities in (proposed) policies were apparent.

The nationalist family policies discussed in previous chapters are neither examples of 'pro-family/pronatalist' (Gauthier, 1996) variants of welfare state policies, nor in line with neo-liberal ideals of market individualism and small government (O'Connor, Orloff, and Shaver, 1999). That is, pro-family/pronatalist models place great emphasis on cash benefits to women having third and subsequent children (Gauthier, 1996). At the same time, pro-family/pronatalist models of state policies are said to typically provide relatively high levels of support for maternity leave and childcare facilities and relatively liberal abortion legislation, and the principle of voluntary parenthood prevails (ibid.). This was clearly not the case in Fascist Italy, Nazi Germany, post-Yugoslav Croatia, and post-Communist Russia.

In Germany after 1933 increasingly harsh restrictions were placed on the use of contraceptives; abortion and sterilization were 'encouraged' for 'undesirable groups' (Quine, 1996), and by 1942 abortion had become permissible solely on 'racial' grounds. For all others, supreme judicial authorities recommended capital punishment for second offenders, since abortion came to be seen as a form of treason (Bleuel, 1973). Similarly, almost immediately following Mussolini's rise to power in Italy, by 1923 there was a proposal in place to limit contraceptive use in Italy. In 1926 the severity of the punishment for abortion was increased, and a 1931 royal decree prohibited the sale of contraceptives (Quine, 1996). In post-Communist Russia, Yeltsin's government did not ban or legally restrict access to abortion, but by 1994 fees were introduced for abortions and the state had virtually stopped buying contraceptives. The 1994 directive removed most abortions from medical insurance coverage (Marsh, 1996; Sargeant, 1996), making legal abortion virtually out of the reach of most Russian women. Likewise in Croatia, abortion remained legal, but serious attempts at restricting access to it were made (B.a.B.e., 1994b), and the capital city's largest hospital prohibited doctors from performing abortions (Drakulic, 1993). While clearly pronatalist, these nationalist family policies and propaganda did not resemble comparatively conservative, pro-family models found in welfare state variants.

Nationalist family policies were equally distinct from liberal and neo-liberal directives. The neo-liberal agenda, for example, has resulted in policy-makers' desire to use women more fully in the labour market (often linked to the low-paid commodification of care) or as providers of unpaid, privatized, informal care (Daly and Lewis, 2000; Ungerson, 2003). Nationalist family policies, by contrast, have sought to remove women from the labour market and (re-)establish the legally married, male breadwinner / prolific female homemaker model as a dominant family form. From the examples presented, we have seen that the nationalist agenda has included an attempted re-patriarchalization of gender roles with the aim of raising fertility on the one hand and re-establishing state order and control on the other, for the 'good of the nation,' not for 'individual' (neo-liberal) or 'social' (welfare state) rights.

Nationalist family policies were also distinct from neo-liberal aims in their (often unfulfilled) promises to generously spend public funds to support large families. For example, in post-Communist Russia, a draft law proposed to recognize the social utility of child-rearing by a payment of a sum of no less than minimum wage for non-working parents responsible for the care of three or more children or one disabled child (Ilic, 1996). The law failed to pass second reading and was thus defeated in 1993 – not by opponents, but by the government's collapse. The law also proposed to reduce the work week to thirty-five hours for working mothers with children under the age of fourteen (ibid.). Russia's current family allowance law has been in place since 1995 and on paper appears to be quite generous: the state offers a childcare allowance for each child until the age of sixteen, supplementary childcare allowances to children of single mothers, and birth grants, given in lump sums equal to five times the minimum wage (R94.29 as of 1 May 1999, where R18.1 = US $1.00; Social Security Administration, 2002d). Overall, these state-financed initiatives appear to be quite generous on paper and are in sharp contrast to neo-liberal 'values' and the quest for 'small government.'

The (newly independent) Croatian state also offered cash benefits to families, but although the government appeared committed to providing relatively large sums of money to large families, financial restraints limited its ability to do so. For example, the Croatian Labour Act of 1996 promised generous subsidies for mothers with four or more children as well as an official title of 'mother educator' (*Narodne Novine-Sluzbeni*, 1995), but the 1996 budget could not cover the expense. Similarly, in a speech in 1994 President Tudjman promised mothers of four or more children 'the average salary earned by her social equals, so that she is able to devote herself to bringing up her children' (Foreign Broadcast Information Services, 1994). Again, the state was not financially able to commit the necessary resources to the program. What the Croatian government could actually provide fell far short of its promises: a family allowance dependent on the amount and source of income received by families, whereby single parents would receive a rate 45 per cent higher than the rest. The rate is variable and is adjusted annually according to the cost of living index (Social Security Administration, 2002a).

In sum, nationalist family policies outlined in the previous chapters of this book are neither clear-cut examples of 'pro-family/pronatalist' variants of welfare state policies, nor in line with neo-liberal ideals. Initiatives proposed or awarded for the benefit of nationalist party ideology fall under the rubric of collective ethnic rights, not universal social rights (Mishra, 1998) or individual freedom/rights (Fukuyama, 1992). This was clearly manifested in the (proposed) implementation of punitive initiatives such as a bachelor tax, the criminalization of abortion, and maximum quotas in women's employment and education, variants of which we have seen in Nazi Germany, Fascist Italy, modern independent Croatia, and post-Communist Russia.

Individual vs Social vs Nationalist Collective Rights

Fukuyama (1992) celebrated the victory of 'liberal democracy' as the victory of the doctrine of 'individual freedom and popular sovereignty' (42), or the 'rule of law that recognizes certain individual rights or freedoms *from* government control' (42; emphasis added). The key here is the notion of the 'freedom *from* government control,' where 'individuals pursue their own aims and resist cooperation in larger communities' (Fukuyama, 1995, 49). On policy matters, then, a liberal-democratic victory is one of less state involvement in the lives of citizens and, therefore, less social policy, less government expenditure on social welfare, and more 'fending for oneself' in a 'free' market. By winning these individual rights, we are clearly losing their 'rival' (to use Fukuyama's term) – social rights – since the victory of individualism involves the process of 'downgrading the social' (Mishra, 1998).

Social-democratic regimes, in contrast, *sanction* state intervention 'to modify the play of market forces in the attempt to achieve a greater measure of social equality' (Sainsbury, 1999b, 259). Thus, while social rights are granted to individuals, they are more or less universal, community, or collective provisions that imply a commitment to a minimum standard of life (Mishra, 1998). Nationalist collective rights (collective ethnic rights), as we have seen manifested in nationalist family policies, appear to be a form of social rights, with some key differences. Nationalism is an ideology that involves both a profound loyalty towards peoplehood and the primacy of the ethnic group over the interests and needs of the individual (self-sacrifice). Individuals, families, and organizations are expected to become subordinate to the state because the object of ultimate concern (Tillich, 1957) is not equality, but rather the congruence between an ethnic group's own culture and the political and economic bureaucracies that surround it (Gellner, 1994).

Nationalists often assume that there is a natural bond between members of the ethnic 'self' and a differentiation or disassociation from an ethnic 'other.' Nationalism, therefore, grants the nation a unique moral status above all other cultures, subcultures, and communities (Buchanan, 1998). Nationalist social policies, as a result, claim to be 'by us and for us' – the nation – yet are an embodiment of neither individual rights nor universal social rights. In nationalist rhetoric, the state is in place not to serve the needs of individuals within the nation, but rather to serve their totality, as a nation. Nationalist family policies are therefore not the embodiment of the notion of 'the state for the people,' but rather 'the people for the state.' They are a form of selective social/collective rights that nominally promise but often, as we have seen, cannot practically deliver ethnic communalism. But like religion, nationalism requires the intellectual sacrifice of the kind debated by Weber (1946), whereby one gives up on examining the object of ultimate concern intellectually-rationally (critically), and instead accepts on blind faith the undelivered promise of ethnic communalism, which leaves intact or even reinforces, as we have seen, various forms of inequality.

Writing on Nazi Germany, G.V. Rimlinger (1987) noted that 'social policy in National Socialist ideology became a means to enable the individual to make greater sacrifices for the good of the community' (63). Rimlinger showed that the handling of benefits in Nazi Germany was to be carried out in the spirit of party ideology, whose goal was loyalty, trust, discipline, and selflessness, for the present and future glory of the nation. On a number of levels this was true for the other cases of nationalism outlined in this book. Nationalist leaders made clear attempts to use social policy as an instrument of social control, not an extension of social rights. Many in the populations analysed seemingly accepted this form of control, since it promised (but failed) to deliver them from the economic hardship plaguing their respective nations, to re-establish order in a time of profound change and to protect them from real or perceived threats from outside the group, including the homogenizing tendencies of globalization.

In the most recent examples, nationalist social policies were conceived and/or implemented in Europe at the same time as social rights were being eroded by globalization and the spread of neo-liberal ideology and practices. For example, post-war Italy and Germany experienced the rise and decline of the welfare state. Their family policies, as outlined in chapters 8 and 9, clearly reflect this pattern. Both Germany and Italy have been identified as part of the same 'regime-cluster' corporatist welfare states (Esping-Andersen, 1990). Both have been caught up in debates between gender reconstruction (promoted by feminists) and gender reinforcement (supported by conservatives), as clearly manifested in their respective abortion debates. Their combination of conservative and 'progressive' policies have also been shaped by the policies, first of the European Commission (EC) and later by the European Union (EU). That is, while some EC funding was made available to countries to encourage training for women in male-dominated industries (Chamberlayne, 1993), and Article 119 of the Treaty of Rome mandated equal pay for equal work (O'Connor, Orloff, and Shaver, 1999), EC policies also generally placed more emphasis on market efficiency than on the guarantee of social rights (Bimbi, 1993). Similarly, after the creation of the EU, European countries made substantial commitments to 'the social (policy) agenda' and the promotion of the full participation of women in economic, scientific, social, political, and civic life (Commission of the European Communities, 2000, 2003), but an underlying goal of these commitments was 'Europe's future competitiveness and growth prospects,' which would involve 'catching up with' the United States (European Policy Centre, 2004). As a result, Italy and Germany have been under supranational pressure to cut public expenditures (Chamberlayne, 1993).

Again, what we see in the cases of Italy and Germany are states committed to corporatist welfare state policies and under supranational pressure to cut social spending. They are somewhat typical of what policy analysts are seeing emerge with the spread of neo-liberalism, although the EU is still very conscious and critical of the 'external challenges' of globalization (namely, U.S. domination; European Policy Centre, 2004). In the early 1990s Croatia and Russia, while still significantly affected by changing economic trends, to a certain extent were unwilling to accept supranational pressures towards homogenization. Nationalist family policies – typically conservative –

appear to be swimming against the neo-liberal current (mostly unsuccessfully, to be sure). Nonetheless, such policies do not share the goals either of proponents of the welfare state or of their rivals in the neo-liberal camp. Nationalist family policies are about neither 'individual freedom' nor social rights. They appear generous on some fronts, but fall short on many others. The mostly unfulfilled promises of state support to large families are accompanied by punitive measures designed to restrict access and choices in other spheres. Support to families is given in conjunction with stigmatization or barriers to women's access to more public roles. These recent attempts to implement nationalist family policies clearly have failed, mostly because of lack of funds, not lack of effort or commitment by governments. Their future prospects seem no less bleak, as Croatia clearly wants to join the EU and Russia's economic prospects have not greatly improved.

In sum, the comparison of these initiatives reveals that the 'primary policy goals' (McDaniel, 2002) of nationalist regimes vary considerably from those of non-nationalists, even under similar global constraints. While non-nationalist governments in the kingdom of Yugoslavia, revolutionary Russia, modern Italy, and post-reunification Germany generally held and promoted the primary policy goal of maintaining gender difference with some (more or less) commitment to equality, nationalist regimes in Nazi Germany, Fascist Italy, post-Yugoslavia Croatia, and post-Soviet Russia clearly set out to support the re-patriarchalization of family relations, to fulfil nationalist promises and goals. Fortunately, they have experienced little success.

12

Conclusions

Summary of Key Findings

A number of thinkers have noted that women were of particular concern to nationalist regimes because of their prescribed roles within the family (Yuval-Davis and Anthias, 1989; Kristeva, 1993; Calhoun, 1997; Dua, 1999). For example, according to Julia Kristeva (1993), with respect to nations and nationalism, 'women have the luck and the responsibility of being boundary-subjects' (Kristeva, 1993, 35). Similarly, Yuval-Davis and Anthias (1989) noted that, with the rise of nationalism, women come to be seen as biological reproducers of ethnic collectivities. My work builds upon existing research, with an aim to identify, outline, and assess the effectiveness of policies and practices that are constructed around the ideas that women physically reproduce nations through childbearing and are also culturally significant, since women more than men are viewed as the primary socializers of children.

According to Fineman (1995), 'mother' is a universally possessed symbol. Fineman noted that 'mother is a pivotal factor in defining our understanding of our own familial, sexual and social circumstance' and is significant in our construction of universal meanings (72). At the same time 'mother' is neither fixed nor containable (Fineman, 1995). In the cases presented here, it is clear that nationalists sought to exploit the malleability of the concepts of motherhood and womanhood.

My research indicates that, contrary to contemporary theories of nationalism that suggest that nationalism is a modernizing force, beneficial to *all* group members, the entry of 'the people' into politics and military life did not initially include women. 'National fraternity' and 'brothers in harmony' accurately denotes the absence of women from the early benefits of nationalism, because until recently women were excluded from national formal education, universal high culture, literacy, politics, and the promise of legal equality as citizens.

Under the nationalist regimes studied here, there have been attempts at the re-patriarchalization of gender relations, exemplified by state-directed initiatives designed to re-establish the traditional male-breadwinner family. According to nationalist ideology, women are left with the responsibility of reproducing the body and thought of the nation through biological reproduction and the dissemination of (national) identity through the socialization of children. In nationalist rhetoric, this job is believed to be far too important to be left in the hands of individual women. Within this rhetoric, it is then the role of the nationalist state to see to it that it is done 'correctly' and that women are wholly committed to the task.

This research shows that in the cases where there was a rise in nationalist sentiment and a nationalist rise to power – that is, in Fascist Italy, Nazi Germany, post-Communist Russia, and modern independent Croatia – attempts were also made to re-patriarchalize gender and family through a number of pronatalist and pronuptialist state initiatives closely connected to nationalist goals. In other words, a nationalist rise to power has been accompanied by attempts to alter gender relations and family life, such that family policies in states ruled by nationalists look different from family policies where non-nationalists are in power, even if the actual families are relatively unchanged.

The growth of nationalism and the rise to power of nationalist regimes in twentieth-century Europe have resulted in the creation and adoption of radically different family policies than would be found elsewhere or that had existed in the same polity before their ascension. Nationalist regimes studied here ceased to support family policies in place before their assumption of power and tended instead to support re-patriarchalized models of the family, through nationalist pronatalist family policies.

This research identifies a connection between nationalism and the proposed or actual implementation of pronatalist family policies. It also reveals that many of the initiatives were not always successful in altering reproductive behaviour and aggregate fertility rates. Most of the policy initiatives were outright failures, in that they did not succeed in returning women to their 'proper' place in the home, as dutiful housewives and prolific mothers. When 'successes' were achieved, in the form of increases in demographic rates of family formation and fertility, they were short lived. In most cases, not long after programs were initiated, fertility and marriage rates continued their long-term decline, and economic necessity kept many women in the labour force.

Perhaps the most important finding of this research is that one cannot assume that family policies will 'modernize' and improve with time. They do not necessarily move from being patriarchal, in the past, to being (more) egalitarian as states 'modernize' with the passage of time. Instead, while a state may appear to be 'modernizing' gender and family relations at one point, it can experience or encourage re-patriarchalization of gender relations and family life as the political and economic climate changes, particularly with the rise of nationalism. These changes are also in marked contrast to those that other European states may be experiencing, particularly under the pressure to conform to globalization and the spread of neo-liberal capitalism.

In twentieth-century Europe, in the cases I analysed, when nationalists governed, family policies did not 'modernize.' On the contrary. Therefore, while, generally speaking, nationalism has been said to be modernizing with respect to economic and general political issues (Gellner, 1983; Kohn, 1962), it does not appear to do the same for gender and family relations.

Thinkers such as Gellner (1983) and Kohn (1962) noted that nationalism was a move away from traditional forms of political organization that were unequal, irrational, and provincial. In contrast to the disconnected, decentralized form of social organization that had characterized agrarian life under the monarchies, life under nationalism was supposedly qualitatively different. According to Gellner (1983), nationalism allowed for the carving out of a new space for 'the people' in both politics and everyday life. Clearly, 'the people' did not include women. If nationalism is a truly 'modernizing' ideology, surely half a nation's population should not be forced to accept a re-patriarchization of gender relations and family life, which is exactly what was attempted when nationalist regimes took over in the countries analysed here.

Nationalism may have brought with it the ideals of 'liberty,' 'national fraternity' (McNeill, 1985), and 'brotherhood of all nationals' (Smith, 1991, 76), but my research shows that 'brotherhood' did not include 'sisterhood,' and 'national fraternity' literally included only *'frater'* and *'pater.'* We need to question whether 'movements for national liberation and independence were the main agents for political emancipation of most of the globe' (Hobsbawm, 1995, 169). Can this statement be true, when political emancipation for some resulted in attempts at the entrapment of others into rigid, traditional, and impotent social roles? Given that these nationalist regimes attempted to re-patriarchalize gender relations and families, they clearly cannot be classified as modern/ modernizing.

Kedourie (1963/1993) explained that 'nationalism looks inwardly, away from and beyond the imperfect world' (82). Understood this way, nationalism is not liberalizing and modernizing, but rather is an escape from the modern world, where clearly, the 'modern world' is increasingly characterized by globalization of markets (McDaniel, 2002), a diminishing role of the nation-state (Hobsbawm, 1995), and declining importance of ethnicity. Therefore, nationalism is better understood as a movement designed to satisfy a need to belong together in a coherent and stable community that itself may be perceived as being under threat from secularization, modernity (Kedourie, 1963/1993), and globalization. Thus, twentieth-century nationalism can be understood as a reaction and resistance to modernization and globalization.

Elie Kedourie (1963/1993) noted that the need to 'belong together' usually was satisfied by the family, the neighbourhood, or the religious community, but all three have borne the brunt of violent social and intellectual change. Nationalism is thus, in essence, a return to a patriarchal family – the national family, an expression of a wish for a community that extends throughout time, or, in the words of Allen Buchanan (1991), an 'intergenerational community.'

When writing on the origins of the welfare state in Britain, Richard Titmuss (1950) noted the role and importance that war played in its establishment. His writing on war is also very useful in this debate on nationalism; he remarked that during the Second World War people pooled resources and called on discipline, leadership, politicization, collective solidarity, consensus, and the integration of values. In my view, nationalists seek to do the same in a time of globalization or change, with and/or without violence, through state-sponsored policies and initiatives.

Nationalist family policies do not promote social rights or individual freedoms. Instead, they promote the ideas of order, authority, obedience, faith, and control at the level of nation. For nationalism to succeed, these ideas must be accepted by nationals at a personal level. This is easily done if the state is able to restore patriarchal control in the home. Critical theorist Max Horkheimer cited Saint Augustine, who seems to have captured this idea in its entirety when he wrote: 'domestic peace has a relation to civic peace – in other words, that the well-ordered concord of domestic obedience and domestic rule has a relation to the well-ordered concord of civic obedience and civic rule. And therefore it follows, further, that the father of the family ought to frame his domestic rule in accordance with the law of the city, so that the household may be in harmony with the civic order' (Saint Augustine, *The City of God*, Bk 19, chap. 16; cited in Horkheimer, 1972, 99). If nationalists succeed, the father/husband represents the law and the nation in the home. The oppression, submission, and authority learned in patriarchal family life comes to be seen as normal and acceptable in civic life. In this context it becomes much easier to understand why nations and nationalism try to control and manipulate both women, in particular, into being diligent mothers, and family in general. Families come to be seen as microcosms of the nation, hierarchically structured and authoritarian. When nationalism is understood both as a response to and fear of modernization and as an attempt to return to traditional order, the (archaic and patriarchal) treatment of women becomes lucid. Perhaps this is best understood by returning to the work of Max Weber (1978), who noted that the most elementary forms of traditional author-ity were *gerontocracy* (rule in the hands of the elders) and *patriarchalism*. If nationalism is a response to the fear of modernity, it inevitably in-volves a return to traditional authority, which in turn also calls for a return to patriarchy. Claudia Koonz (1977) clearly asserted this argu-ment when she stated that 'to counter the modernity they feared, Nazi women worked for a return to a largely mythical past in which they might win respect and feel secure' (450).

Koonz (1997) noted that nationalism is a response to insecurity, as was the case in Germany during the 1930s, where it rose from the ashes of economic crisis and defeat in the First World War. The re-patriarchalizing of gender relations and family through pronatalist poli-cies implemented by nationalist regimes attempted to place men at the head of the household and women in front of a crib. Furthermore, a man's powerlessness in a politically and economically changing society would be offset by his renewed power in the home, and her pride would be restored as she becomes a heroic childbearer, filling the most sublime profession in the nation. If her return to the home as housewife and mother is complete, the nation not only secures its future, but solves other immediate problems as well – for example, she supposedly liberates jobs that are expected to be filled by men. Therefore, the strength of nationalism lies in its ability to revive its real or mythical (and glorious) past, correct its unjust present, and secure a vibrant and fecund future glory. This is the appeal and goal of nationalism, and it plays with family order by manipulating family policies.

Pronatalist family policies are an integral part of the mythology of nationalism. Nationalism depends upon the propagation of political myths to give it credence with the public. Nationalism often embraces a 'palingenetic vision' or doctrine of genetic rebirths (the nation's biological continuity through time), which becomes an indispensable instrument of dictatorial power (Quine, 1996, 36). In other words, to help to capture the consciousness of 'the people,' nationalist regimes construct an image of the nation as the embodiment of 'a momentous national resurrection,' a particularly appealing ideation at a time of economic hardship and instability. Nationalist leaders do so by making themselves present in the lives of citizens and specifically by attempting to mould gender and family roles to fit their ethno-political needs.

The research design developed for this study (see table 1.1, p. 20) – the analysis of the same (more or less) four cases at two specific times – provided a unique opportunity to compare and assess the effects of the rise of nationalism, by controlling for other general historical forces that may be at play at a specific time. In other words, looking at two cases where nationalists were in power simultaneously with two cases where they were not can demonstrate that some of the policy changes that are implemented are not merely 'a norm' for or product of a general historical period. That is, one cannot assume that because the analysis takes place at a particular time – in the first few decades of the twentieth century, for example – all states will necessarily be committed to the same *patriarchal model* of family or particular policy type. Similarly, when looking at the last few decades of the twentieth century, one cannot assume that all policies will be 'progressive' or 'woman friendly' or equally under threat of the globalization of capital and neo-liberalism. This model demonstrates that, while at one period a state may appear to support egalitarian family policies, as time passes, it may adopt pronatalist patriarchal policies. In both periods, the cases that embraced nationalist-pronatalist policies also experienced a rise in nationalist sentiment. The model makes this correlation transparent.

It is clear that, although nationalist leaders tried, they largely failed to accomplish their desired goal of changing aggregate fertility rates. This does not mean, however, that the lives of women under the regimes did not change profoundly. While the policies may have failed to change the demographic situation, surely they altered women's lives significantly, particularly in cases where women had to turn to illegal abortions, were forced out of gratifying jobs, and faced high levels of unemployment. This research did not and could not adequately address the cost of nationalist policies to individual women. The model itself made it possible to identify macrosociological processes, but it could not deduce the level of individual suffering – a topic for future research.

This research indicates that one cannot assume that 'progress' on this matter will naturally occur. One of my main findings is that attempts at the re-patriarchalization of gender relations and families can take place after much 'progress' towards gender equality is made. This was clear in the case of Germany and its transformation from the more 'progressive' policies found in the Weimar Republic to the attempted re-patriarchalization that accompanied Hitler's rise to power soon after.

The status of women in this or any other country cannot be assumed to 'progress' over time, since it is under threat on a number of fronts. The cases analysed here are proof that no matter how 'far along' we are on the journey towards 'equality' or improved gender relations, the potential for 'regress' is not far away. Future research should expand this analysis to include a larger number of cases; a more global analysis is warranted. The Canadian case should also be closely assessed, with special attention given to understanding the potential role nationalism can play in the Canadian and Quebec sovereignty debate. Canadians in general, but Canadian women in particular, should pay close attention to the rise of nationalist sentiment in their midst. Although the national unity debate in Canada appears to be currently 'on the back-burner,' the Quebec sovereignty issue is far from resolved. Of course, many of us would like to believe that Yugoslavia 'can't happen to us,' but in fact, many Yugoslavs believed it could not happen to them.

A Final Thought

One of the *general* lessons and main findings of this particular research is that we can never assume that the 'job' of achieving gender equality is 'complete'; we see policy changes as a result of globalization, on the one hand, and a reaction to globalization – nationalism – on the other. That is, making two steps forward can be followed by three steps back, depending on the political and economic circumstances of the time. While one government may champion the rights of women and families, its successor, particularly if it has a nationalist orientation, may attempt to fling women backward by decades or more. Recent history and the bulk of this work teach us that 'progress' today may not result in progress tomorrow. Women in the Weimar Republic enjoyed more rights than many of their contemporaries in other parts of Europe, only to lose them with the rise of nationalism. Women in Croatia, prior to the nationalist victory and their subsequent secession, were not the 'most' privileged or 'equal' in Europe, but they did enjoy a number of rights that were under threat when Tudjman ruled newly independent Croatia. Women in North America should not consider themselves 'safe' from the re-patriarchalizing tendencies of nationalism.

References

Abbott, Pamela, and Claire Wallace. 1992. *The Family and the New Right*. London: Pluto Press.

Abel, Theodore. 1938. *Why Hitler Came into Power*. New York: Prentice Hall.

Adams, Alice E. 1994. *Reproducing the Womb: Images of Childbirth in Science, Feminist Theory, and Literature*. Ithaca, NY: Cornell University Press.

Adler, Marina A. 1997. 'Social Change and Declines in Marriage and Fertility in Eastern Germany.' *Journal of Marriage and Family* 59 (1), 37–50.

Afshar, Haleh. 1989. 'Women and Reproduction in Iran.' In Nira Yuval-Davis and Floya Anthias (eds), *Women-Nation-State*, 110–25. New York: St Martin's Press.

Albrecht-Carrié, René. 1966. *Italy: From Napoleon to Mussolini*. New York: Columbia University Press.

Anderson, Benedict. 1983/1991. *Imagined Communities*. London: New Left Books.

Anthias, Floya, and Nira Yuval-Davis. 1992. *Racialized Boundaries: Race, Nation, Gender, Colour and Class, and the Anti-Racist Struggle*. London: Routledge.

Aron, Raymond. 1965. *Democracy and Totalitarianism*. London: Weidenfeld and Nicolson.

Åslund, Aslund, and Martha Brill Olcott (eds), 1999. *Russia after Communism*. Washington, DC: Carnegie Endowment for International Peace.

Attwood, Lynne. 1996. 'The Post-Soviet Woman in the Move to the Market.' In Rosalind Marsh (ed.), *Women in Russia and Ukraine*, 255–66. Cambridge: Cambridge University Press.

Atwood, Margaret. 1985. *The Handmaid's Tale*. Toronto: McClelland & Stewart.

Ayçoberry, Pierre. 1999. *The Social History of the Third Reich, 1933–1945*. New York: New Press.

B.a.B.e. (Be active, Be emancipated). 1994a. 'Organization's Goals and Mission.' Zagreb: B.a.B.e.

– 1994b. 'Petition For Legal and Safe Abortion in Croatia.' Zagreb: B.a.B.e.

– 1995. 'Status of Women in Croatia.' Zagreb: B.a.B.e.

Baban, Adriana, and Henry P. David. 1994. *Voices of Romanian Women: Perceptions of Sexuality, Reproductive Behaviour, and Partner Relations During the Ceausescu Era*. Washington and Bucharest: Centre for Development and Population Activities.

Babić, Goran. 1992. *Bespuća Franje Tuđmana (Tracklessness of Franjo Tudjman)*. Zemun: Grafopublik.

Bahro, Rudolf. 1978. *The Alternative in Eastern Europe*. London: New Left Books.

Baker, Maureen. 1994. 'Family and Population Policy in Quebec: Implications for Women.' *Canadian Journal of Women and Law* 7 (1), 116–32.

– 1995. *Canadian Family Policies: Cross-National Comparisons*. Toronto: University of Toronto Press.

– 1998. 'Women, Family Policies and the Moral Right.' *Canadian Review of Social Policy* 40 (Winter), 47–64.

Barth, Fredrik. 1969a. *Ethnic Boundaries*. Oslo: Norwegian University Press.

– 1969b. *Ethnic Groups and Boundaries: The Social Organization of Cultural Difference*. London: George Allen & Unwin

Bauman, Zygmunt. 1992. 'Soil, Blood and Identity.' *Sociological Review* 40(4), 675–701.

Baynes, Norman H. (ed). 1942. *The Speeches of Adolf Hitler: April 1922 – August 1939*. Vol. 1. London: Oxford University Press.

Bell-Fialkoff, Andrew. 1993. 'A Brief History Of Ethnic Cleansing.' *Foreign Affairs* 72 (3), 110–21.

Belyakova, A.M., Z.S. Beliayeva, N.N. Sheptulina, and V.N. Tolkunova (eds). 1978. *Soviet Legislation on Women's Rights: Collection of Normative Acts*. Moscow: Progress.

Bettarini, Silvana Salvini, and Silvana Schifini D'Andrea. 1996. 'Induced Abortion in Italy: Levels, Trends and Characteristics.' *Family Planning Perspectives* 28 (6), 267–71, 277 (on line).

BIJUS. 2002. 'Loi fondamentale pour la République fédérale d'Allemagne, Mai 1949.' <www.jura.uni-sb.de/BIJUS/grundgesetz/gesetz.htm>.

Bilandzic, Dusan, et al. 1991. *La Croatie entre la Guerre et l'independence*. Zagreb: OKC.

Bimbi, Franca. 1993. 'Gender, "Gift Relationship" and Welfare State Cultures in Italy.' In Jane Lewis (ed.), *Women and Social Policies in Europe: Work, Family and the State*, 138–69. Aldershot, UK: Edward Elgar.

Birnbaum, Lucia Chiavola. 1986. *Liberazione Della Donna: Feminism in Italy*. Middletown, CT: Wesleyan University Press.

Blagojevic, Marina. 1994. 'War and Everyday Life: Deconstruction of Self/ Sacrifice.' *Sociologija* 36 (4), 469–82.

Blanchet, Didier, and Olivia Ekert-Jaffé. 1994. 'The Demographic Impact of Family Benefits: Evidence from Micro-Model and from Macro-Data.' In John Ermisch and Naohiro Ogawa (eds), *The Family, the Market and the State in Aging Societies*, 79–104. Oxford: Claredon Press.

Bleuel, Hans Peter. 1973. *Sex and Society in Nazi Germany.* New York: J.P. Lippincott.

Bock, Gisela, and Pat Thane. 1991. *Maternity and Gender Policies: Women and the Rise of the European Welfare States, 1880s-1950s.* London: Routledge.

Bodrova, Valentina. 1995. 'The Russian Family in Flux.' *Transition: Events and Issues in the Former Soviet Union and East-Central and Southeastern Europe* 1 (16), 10–12.

Böhm, Tatiana. 1993. 'The Women Question as a Democratic Question: In Search of Civil Society.' In Nanette Funk and Magda Mueller (eds), *Gender Politics and Post-Communism*, 151–9. New York: Routledge.

Boh, Katja, and Nevenka Černigoj Sadar. 1992. *Childhood as a Social Phenomenon: National Report Yugoslavia.* Vienna: Eurosocial.

Bonacich, Edna. 1980, 1991. 'Class Approaches to Ethnicity and Race.' In Norman R. Yetman (ed),. *Majority and Minority: The Dynamics of Race and Ethnicity in America*, 59–76. 5th ed. Wellesley, MA: Allyn and Bacon.

Borocz, Jozsef, and Katherine Verdery. 1994. 'Gender and Nation: Introduction.' *East European Politics and Society* 8 (2), 233–4.

Bortolotti, Franca Pieroni. 1978. *Femminismo e partiti politici in Italia, 1919–1926.* Rome: Editori Riuniti.

Bradshaw, York, and Michael Wallace. 1991. 'Informing Generality and Explaining Uniqueness: The Place of Case Studies in Comparative Research.' In Charles Ragin (ed.), *Issues and Alternatives in Comparative Social Research*, 154–71. Leiden, The Netherlands: E.J. Brill.

Breuilly, John. 1994. *Nationalism and the State.* 2nd ed. Chicago: University of Chicago Press.

Bridenthal, Renate. 1977. 'Something Old, Something New: Women between the Two World Wars.' In Renate Bridenthal and Claudia Koonz (eds), *Becoming Visible: Women in European History*, 422–4. Boston: Houghton Mifflin.

Bridenthal, Renate, Atina Grossman, and Marion Kaplan. 1984. *When Biology Became Destiny.* New York: Monthly Review Press.

Bridenthal, Renate, and Claudia Koonz (eds). 1977. *Becoming Visible: Women in European History.* Boston: Houghton Mifflin.

Brooker, Paul. 1995. *Twentieth-Century Dictators: The Ideological One-Party States.* London: Macmillan.

Brubaker, Rogers. 1996. *Nationalism Reframed.* Cambridge: Cambridge University Press.

Brym, Robert J. 1995. 'Voters Quietly Reveal Greater Communist Leanings.' *Transition* 1 (6), 32–49.

Brzezinski, Zbigniew K. 1961. *The Permanent Purge.* New York: Washington Square Press.

Buchanan, Allen. 1991. *Secession: The Morality of Political Divorce from Fort Sumter to Lithuania and Quebec.* Boulder, CO: Westview.

– 1998. 'What's So Special about Nations?' In J. Couture, K. Nielsen, and M. Seymour (eds), *Rethinking Nationalism*, 283–309. Calgary: University of Calgary Press.

Bulic-Mrkobrod, Mare. 1996. Untitled article. *Globus*, 5 January, 14.

Bulmer, Martin, Jane Lewis, and David Piachaud. 1989. 'Social Policy: Subject or Object?' In Martin Bulmer, Jane Lewis, and David Piachaud (eds), *The Goals of Social Policy.* London: Unwin Hyman.

Burlatsky, Feodor. 1998. 'Who or What Broke up the Soviet Union?' In Metta Spencer (ed.), *Separatism: Democracy and Disintegration*, 139–60. New York: Rowman & Littlefield.

Burstyn, Varda, and Dorothy Smith. 1985. *Women, Class, Family and the State.* Toronto: Garamond Press.

Bussemaker, Jet, and Kees van Kerbergen. 17999. 'Contemporary Social-Capitalist Welfare States and Gender Ideology.' In Diane Sainsbury (ed.), *Gender and Welfare States Regimes*, 15–46. Oxford: Oxford University Press.

Caiazza, Amy. 2002. *Mothers and Soldiers.* New York: Routledge.

Calhoun, Craig. 1993. 'Nationalism and Ethnicity.' *Annual Review of Sociology* 19, 211–39.

– 1997. *Nationalism.* Minneapolis: University of Minnesota Press.

Catterall, Tony. 1992. 'A Germany Divided: Reconciling Abortion Laws Splits Ruling Coalition, Opens Old Wounds.' *Montreal Gazette*, 22 June 1992, E5.

Cavalli, Alessandro, and Fabio Luca Cavazza. 2001. 'Reflections on Political Culture and the Italian National Character.' *Daedalus* 130 (3), 119–37.

Cederna, Camilla (ed.), 1989. *Caro Duce: Lettere di donne Italiane a Mussolini (Dear Duce: Letters from Italian Women to Mussolini).* Milan: Rizzoli Libri.

Central Intelligence Agency (CIA). 1996. *The World Fact Book: 1996–7.* Washington, D.C.: Brassey's.

Chamberlayne, Prue. 1993. 'Women and the State: Changes in Roles and Rights in France, West Germany, Italy and Britain, 1970–1990.' In Jane Lewis (ed.), *Women and Social Policies in Europe: Work, Family and the State*, 170–93. Aldershot, UK: Edward Elgar.

Chanteur, Janine. 1992. *From War to Peace.* Boulder, CO: Westview Press.

Charles, Nickie, and Helen Hintjens, eds. 1998. *Gender, Ethnicity and Political Ideologies*. London: Routledge.

Chloros, A.G. 1970. *Yugoslav Civil Law: History, Family, Property*. London, Oxford University Press.

Chodorow, Nancy. 1978. *The Reproduction of Mothering: Psychanalysis and the Sociology of Gender*. Berkeley: University of California Press.

Chow, Esther Ngan-Ling, and Catherine White Berheide, eds. 1994. *Women, the Family and Policy: A Global Perspective*. Albany: State University of New York.

Clements, Barbara Evans. 1997. *Bolshevik Women*. Cambridge: Cambridge University Press.

Cobban, Alfred. 1969. *The Nation State and National Self-Determination*. New York: Thomas Y. Crowell.

Cohen, Carl (ed.). 1972. *Communism, Fascism, and Democracy: The Theoretical Foundations*. 2nd ed. New York: Random House.

Coleman, Janet. 1990. *Against the State*. London: BBC Books.

Commission of the European Communities. 2000. 'Communication from the Commission to the Council, the European Parliament, the Economic and Social Committee and the Committee of the Regions: Social Policy Agenda.' Brussels, 28.6.2000 COM (2000) 379 final.

– 2003. 'Communication from the Commission to the Council, the European Parliament, the Economic and Social Committee and the Committee of the Regions: Mid-Term Review of the Social Policy Agenda.' Brussels, 2.6.2003 COM (2003) 312 final.

Commission on Security and Cooperation in Europe (CSCE). 1993. *Human Rights and Democratization In Croatia*. Washington, D.C.: CSCE.

Constitution of the Republic of Croatia. 1991. *The Constitution of the Republic of Croatia*. Zagreb: Sabor Republike Hvatske.

Couture, Jocelyne, Kai Nielsen, and Michel Seymour (eds). 1998. *Rethinking Nationalism*. Calgary: University of Calgary Press.

Croatian Democratic Union. 1990. 'Croatian Democratic Union (Hrvastka Demokratska Zajednica – HDZ): Election Proclamation to the Entire Croat Nation.' *East European Reporter* 4 (2), 86–7.

Curlin, Peggy. 1995. 'Talking about a Revolution.' *Freedom Review* 26 (5), 17–19.

Dahbour, Omar. 1998. 'The Nation-State as a Political Community.' In J. Couture, K. Nielsen, and M. Seymour (eds), *Rethinking Nationalism*, 311–43. Calgary: University of Calgary Press.

Dahrendorf, Ralf. 1969. *Society and Democracy in Germany*. Garden City, NY: Anchor Books.

Daly, Mary, and Jane Lewis. 2000. 'The Concept of Social Care and the Analysis of Contemporary Welfare States.' *British Journal of Sociology* 51(2), 281–98.

Davis, Horace. 1967. *Nationalism and Socialism: Marxist and Labor Theories of Nationalism to 1917.* New York: Monthly Review Press.

Davis, Kingsley. 1959. *Human Society.* New York: Macmillan.

De Beauvoir, Simone. 1952. *The Second Sex.* New York: Knopf.

DeConcini, Dennis, and Steny H. Hoyer. 1993. *Human Rights and Democratization in Croatia.* Washington, DC: CSCE.

DeGrand, Alexander. 2000. *Italian Fascism: Its Origins and Development.* 3rd ed. Lincoln: University of Nebraska Press.

DeGrazia, Victoria. 1992. *How Fascism Ruled Women: Italy, 1922–1945.* Berkeley: University of California Press.

Deighton, Anne. 2002. 'The Remaking of Europe.' In Michael Howard and W.M. Roger Louis (eds), *The Oxford History of the Twentieth Century*, 190–201. Oxford: Oxford University Press.

Demeny, Paul. 1986. *'Pronatalist Policies in Low-Fertility Countries: Patterns, Performance and Prospects.'* Working Paper 129. Center for Policy Studies, Population Council, New York.

Denitch, Bogdan. 1976. *The Legitimation of a Revolution: The Yugoslav Case.* New Haven, CT: Yale University Press.

– 1994. *Ethnic Nationalism: The Tragic Death of Yugoslavia.* Minneapolis: University of Minnesota Press.

Dennis, Mike. 1999. 'The East German Family: Change and Continuity.' In Chris Flockton and Eve Kolinsky (eds), *Recasting East Germany: Social Transformation after the GDR*, 83–100. London: Frank Cass.

Detragiache, Denise. 1980. 'Un aspect de la politique démographique de l'Italie fasciste: La répression de l'avortement.' *Mélange de l'Ecole Française de Rome: Moyen Age–Temps Modernes* 92 (2), 691–735.

Deutscher, Isaac. 1949/1976. *Stalin: A Political Biography.* Harmondsworth, UK: Penguin.

Dickinson, James, and Bob Russell (eds). 1986. *Family, Economy and State: The Social Reproduction Process under Capitalism.* New York: St Martin's Press.

Djordjevic, Dimitrije (ed.). 1980. *The Creation of Yugoslavia, 1914–1918.* Santa Barbara, CA: Clio Books.

Dölling, Irene. 1993. '"But the Pictures Stay the Same ..." The Image of Women in the Journal *Für Dich* before and after the "Turning Point."' In Nanette Funk and Magda Mueller (eds), *Gender Politics and Post-Communism*, 168–79. New York: Routledge.

Drakuli , Slavenka. 1993. 'Women and the New Democracy in the Former Yugoslavia.' In Nanette Funk and Magda Mueller (eds), *Gender Politics and Post-Communism*, 123–30. New York: Routledge.

Drobizheva, L. 1993. 'Perestroika and the Ethnic Consciousness of Russians.'

In Gail Lapidus, Victor Zlavslavsky, with Philip Goldman (eds), *From Union to Commonwealth*, 98–113. Cambridge: Cambridge University Press.

Dua, Enakshi. 1999. 'Beyond Diversity: Exploring the Ways in which the Discourse of Race Has Shaped the Institution of the Nuclear Family.' In E. Dua (ed.), *Scratching the Surface: Canadian Anti-Racist Feminist Thought*, 237–60. Toronto: Women's Press.

Duhaček, Daša 1993. 'Women's Time in the Former Yugoslavia.' In Nanette Funk and Magda Mueller (eds), *Gender Politics and Post-Communism*, 131–7. New York: Routledge.

Durham, Martin. 1998. *Women and Fascism*. London: Routledge.

Durkheim, Emile. 1893. *De la division du travail social*. Paris: Alcan.

East, Roger. 1992. *Revolutions in Eastern Europe*. London: Pinter.

Eatwell, Roger. 1996. *Fascism: A History*. London: Vintage.

Edmondson, Linda. 1996. 'Equality and Difference in Women's History: Where Does Russia Fit?' In Rosalind Marsh (ed.), *Women in Russia and Ukraine*, 94–108. Cambridge: Cambridge University Press.

Economist. 2000. 'Mamma Mia.' *Economist* 355 (8164), 46.

Eichler, Margrit. 1991. *Nonsexist Research Methods: A Practical Guide*. New York: Routledge.

– 1997. *Family Shifts: Families, Policies and Gender Equality*. Oxford: Oxford University Press.

Eisenstein, Zillah. 1996. 'Sexual Equality in Post-Communism.' In Barbara Wejnert, Metta Spencer, with Slobodan Drakulic (eds), *Women in Post-Communism*, 103–10. Greenwich, CT: JAI Press.

Ekert, Olivia. 1986. 'Effets et limites des aides financières aux familles: Une expérience et un modèle.' *Population* 41 (2), 327–48.

Emmert, Thomas A. 1999. '*Ženski Pokret*: The Feminist Movement in Serbia in the 1920s.' In Sabrina P. Ramet (ed.), *Gender Politics in the Western Balkans*, 32–49. University Park: Pennsylvania State University Press.

Engel, Barbara. 1977. 'Women as Revolutionaries: The Case of Russian Populists.' In Renate Bridenthal and Claudia Koonz (eds), *Becoming Visible: Women in European History*, 346–69. Boston: Houghton Mifflin.

Enloe, Cynthia. 1990. *Bananas, Beaches and Bases: Making Feminist Sense of International Politics*. Berkeley: University of California Press.

– 1993. *The Morning After*. Berkeley: University of California Press.

Enzensberger, Hans Magnus. 1993. *Civil Wars: From L.A. to Bosnia*. New York: New Press.

Erlich, Vera S. 1966. *Family in Transition: A Study of 300 Yugoslav Villages*. Princeton, NJ: Princeton University Press.

Ermisch, John. 1990. *Fewer Babies, Longer Lives: Policy Implications of Current Demographic Trends*. York, UK: Joseph Rowntree Foundation.

– 1991. *Lone Parenthood: An Economic Analysis*. Cambridge: Cambridge University Press.

Esping-Andersen, Gøsta. 1987. 'The Comparison of Policy Regimes: An Introduction.' In Martin Rein, Gøsta Esping-Andersen, and Lee Rainwater (eds), *Stagnation and Renewal in Social Policy: The Rise and Fall of Policy Regimes*, 3–12. London: M.E. Sharpe.

– 1990. *The Three Worlds of Welfare Capitalism*. Cambridge: Polity Press.

European Policy Centre. 2004. 'Lisbon Revisited: Finding a New Path to European Growth.' EPC Working Paper 08, Accenture.

Evans, Lucinda. 1996. 'Italy's Fertility Rate Falls as Women Reject Childbearing.' *British Journal of Medicine* 312 (7030), 530.

Evans, Richard. 1976. *The Feminist Movement in Germany, 1894–1933*. London: Sage.

Evans, Richard, and W.R. Lee (eds). 1981. *The German Family*. London: Croom Helm.

Fisher, H.A.L. 1935. *A History of Europe*. London: Collins.

Ferree, Myra Marx. 1993. 'The Rise and Fall of "Mommy Politics": Feminism and Unification in (East) Germany.' *Feminist Studies* 19 (1), 89–116.

– 1996. 'Institution, Identity, and the Political Participation of Women in the New *Bundesländer*.' In Barbara Wejnert, Metta Spencer, with Slobodan Drakulic (eds), *Women in Post-Communism*, 19–34. Greenwich, CT: JAI Press.

Filtzer, Donald. 1996. 'Industrial Working Conditions and the Political Economy of Female Labour during Perestroika.' In Rosalind Marsh (ed.), *Women in Russia and Ukraine*, 214–27. Cambridge: Cambridge University Press.

Fineman, Martha Albertson. 1995. *The Neutered Mother, the Sexual Family and Other Twentieth Century Tragedies*. New York: Routledge.

Fitzgerald, Walter. 1946. *The New Europe: An Introduction to Its Political Geography*. London: Methuen.

Flora, Peter. 1983. *State, Economy and Society in Western Europe, 1815–1975*. Volume 1. *The Growth of Mass Democracies and Welfare States*. Frankfurt: Campus Verlag.

Foreign Broadcast Information Service. 1994. 'President Tudjman's State of the Nation Address.' *Daily Reports*. 27 December. FBIS-EEU-(94-248), 52–72.

Fourier, Charles. 1971. *Utopian Vision of Charles Fourier: Selected Texts on Work, Love, and Passionate Attraction*. Trans., ed., and intro. Jonathan Beecher and Richard Bienvenu. Boston: Beacon Press.

Frasca, Rosella Isidori. 1983. *... E il duce le volle sportive*. Bologna: Patron Editore.

Freiler, Christa, and Judy Cerny. 1998. *Benefiting Canada's Children: Perspectives on Gender and Social Responsibility*. Ottawa: Status of Women Canada.

Frevert, Ute. 1989. *Women in German History*. New York: Oxford.

Friedlander, Walter, and Earl Dewey Myers. 1940. *Child Welfare in Germany before and after Naziism*. Chicago: University of Chicago Press.

Fukuyama, Francis. 1992. *The End of History and the Last Man*. New York: Free Press.

– 1995. *Trust: The Social Virtues and the Creation of Prosperity*. London: Penguin.

Funk, Nanette. 1993. 'Abortion and German Unification.' In Nanette Funk and Magda Mueller (eds), *Gender Politics and Post-Communism*, 194–200. New York: Routledge.

Funk, Nanette, and Magda Mueller (eds). 1993. *Gender Politics and Post-Communism*. New York: Routledge.

Fusaro, Carlo (ed.). 2001. 'Italy – Constitution.' *International Courts Network*. <www.uni-wuerzburg.de/law/it00000_.html>.

Gailus, Manfred. 2002. 'Overwhelmed by Their Own Fascination with the "Ideas of 1933": Berlin's Protestant Social Milieu in the Third Reich.' *German History*, 20 (4) 462–93.

Gallucci, Carole C. 1995. 'Alba De Cespedes's *There's No Turning Back*: Challenging the New Woman's Future.' In Robin Pickering-Lazzi (ed.), *Mothers of Invention: Women, Italian Fascism, and Culture*, 200–19. Minneapolis: University of Minnesota Press.

Gams, Andrija. 1966. *Bračno i Porodično Imovinsko Pravo*. Belgrade: Izdavačko-štamparsko preduzeče 'Obod.'

Gandini, Lella, and Carolyn Pope Edwards. 2001. Introduction in Lella Gandini and Carolyn Pope Edwards (eds), *Bambini: The Italian Approach to Infant/Toddler Care*, 1–11. New York: Teachers' College Press.

Garraty, John, and Peter Gay (eds). 1972. *The Columbia History of the World*. New York: Harper & Row.

Gauthier, Anne Hélène. 1996. *The State and the Family: Comparative Analysis of Family Policies in Industrialized Countries*. Oxford: Clarendon Press.

Gellner, Ernest. 1983. *Nations and Nationalism*. Ithaca, NY: Cornell University Press.

– 1994. *Encounters with Nationalism*. Oxford: Blackwell.

Ghedini, Patrizia. 2001. 'Change in Italian National Policy for Children 0–3 Years Old and Their Families: Advocacy and Responsibility.' In Lella Gandini and Carolyn Pope Edwards (eds), *Bambini: The Italian Approach to Infant/Toddler Care*, 38–48. New York: Teachers College Press.

Giddens, Anthony. 1991. *Modernity and Self-Identity*. Stanford: Stanford University Press.

Gigli, Susan. 1995. 'Towards Increased Participation in the Political Process.' *Transition: Event and Issues in the Former Soviet Union and East-Central and Southeastern Europe* 1 (16), 18–21.

Gilbert, Felix. 1984. *The End of the European Era, 1890 to the Present*. 3rd ed. New York: Norton.

Ginsborg, Paul. 2003. *Italy and Its Discontents, 1980–2001*. London: Penguin.

Giolitti, Giovanni. 1904/1990. 'Giolitti Assesses His First Year in Office.' In Arthur Marwick and Wendy Simpson (eds), *Documents 1: 1900–1929*, 23–5. Buckingham, UK: Open University Press.

Goble, Paul. 1995. 'Three Faces of Nationalism in the Former Soviet Union.' In Kupchan, Charles A. (ed.), 122–35. *Nationalism and Nationalities in the New Europe*. Ithaca, NY: Cornell University Press.

Gorbachev, Mikhail. 1987. *Perestroika*. New York: Harper & Row.

Gorenburg, Dmitry. 2001. 'Nationalism for the Mass: Popular Support for Nationalism in Russia's Ethnic Republics.' *Europe-Asia Studies* 53 (1), 73–104.

Goscilo, Helena. 1996. *Dehexing Sex: Russian Womanhood during and after Glasnost*. Ann Arbor: University of Michigan Press.

Goyer, Doreen S., and Eliane Domschke. 1983. *The Handbook of National Population Censuses: Latin America and the Caribbean, North America, and Oceania*. New York: Greenwood Press.

Goyer, Doreen S., and Gera E. Draaijer. 1992. *The Handbook of National Population Censuses: Europe*. New York: Greenwood Press.

Grant, Linda. 1993. 'Horror of Rape.' *Calgary Herald*, 8 August, A11.

Graziosi, Mariolina. 1995. 'Gender Struggle and Gender Identity.' In Robin Oickering-Lazzi (ed.), *Mothers of Invention: Women, Italian Fascism and Culture*, 26–51. Minneapolis: University of Minnesota Press.

Greenfeld, Liah. 1992. *Nationalism: Five Roads to Modernity*. Cambridge: Harvard University Press.

Hall, John. 1993. 'Nationalisms: Classified and Explained.' *Daedalus* 122 (3), 1–28.

Halpern, Joel M. 1969. 'Yugoslavia: Modernization in an Ethnically Diverse State.' In Wayne S. Vucinich (ed.), *Contemporary Yugoslavia*, 316–50. Berkeley: University of California Press.

Halpern, Joel M., and Barbara Kerewsky Halpern. 1972. *A Serbian Village in Historical Perspective*. New York: Holt, Rinehart and Winston.

Hampele, Anne. 1993. 'The Organized Women's Movement in the Collapse of the GDR: The Independent Women's Association (UFV).' In Nanette Funk and Magda Mueller (eds), *Gender Politics and Post-Communism*, 180–93. New York: Routledge.

Harris, Ruth. 1993. 'The "Child of the Barbarian": Rape, Race and Nationalism in France during the First World War.' *Past and Present* 141, 170–206.

Harsch, Donna. 1997. 'The State and Abortion in East Germany, 1950–1972.' *American Historical Review* 102 (1), 53–84.

Hasso, Frances S. 1998. 'The "Women's Front": Nationalism, Feminism, and Modernity in Palestine.' *Gender and Society* 12 (4), 441–65.

Hayes, Carlton. 1960. *Nationalism: A Religion.* New York: Macmillan.

Heitlinger, Alena.1979. *Women and State Socialism: Sex Inequality in the Soviet Union and Czechoslovakia.* Montreal: McGill-Queen's University Press.

Henry, Clarissa, and Marc Hillel. 1977. *Children of the SS.* London: Corgi.

Hirschfeld, Magnus. 1946. *The Sexual History of the World War.* New York: Cadillac.

Hitchcock, William. 2003. *The Struggle for Europe: The Turbulent History of a Divided Continent, 1945 to the Present.* New York: Anchor.

Hitler, Adolf. 1925/1943. *Mein Kampf.* Boston: Houghton Mifflin.

Hobsbawm, E.J. 1990. *Industry and Empire.* London: Penguin.

– 1992. *Nations and Nationalism since 1780: Programme, Myth, Reality.* 2nd ed. Cambridge: Cambridge University Press.

– 1995. *Age of Extremes: The Short Twentieth Century.* London: Abacus.

Hodson, Randy, Dusko Sekulic, and Garth Massey. 1994. 'National Tolerance in the Former Yugoslavia.' *American Journal of Sociology* 99 (6), 1534–58.

Horkheimer, Max. 1972. *Critical Theory: Selected Essays.* New York: Seabury Press.

Horkheimer, Max, and Theodor W. Adorno. 1972. *Aspects of Sociology.* John Viertel (trans.). Boston: Beacon Press.

Horowitz, Donald. 1985. *Ethnic Groups in Conflict.* Berkeley: University of California Press.

Hosking, Geoffrey. 1985. *The First Socialist Society: A History of the Soviet Union from Within.* Cambridge: Harvard University Press.

– 1998. *Russia: People and Empire, 1552–1917.* London: Fontana Press.

Human Rights Watch / Helsinki. 1995. *Civil and Political Rights in Croatia.* New York: Human Rights Watch.

Hyer, Janet. 1996. 'Managing the Female Organism: Doctors and the Medicalization of Women's Paid Work in Soviet Russia during the 1920s.' In Rosalind Marsh (ed.), *Women in Russia and Ukraine,* 111–20. Cambridge: Cambridge University Press.

Ignatieff, Michael. 1993. *Blood and Belonging: Journeys into the New Nationalism.* Toronto: Penguin.

Ilic, Melanie. 1996. '"Generals without Armies, Commanders without Troops": Gorbachev's "Protection" of Female Workers.' In Rosalind Marsh (ed.). *Women in Russia and Ukraine,* 228–40. Cambridge: Cambridge University Press.

Ipsen, Carl. 1996. *Dictating Demography.* Cambridge: Cambridge University Press.

Issraelyan, Yevgenia. 1995. 'Women's Activism in Russia: Losses and Gains, 1989–1993.' *Canadian Woman Studies* (Winter). 16 (1), 75–79.

– 1996. 'Russian Women: Challenges of the Modern World.' In Barbara Wejnert, Metta Spencer, with Slobodan Drakulic (eds), *Women in Post-Communism*, 157–68. Greenwich, CT: JAI Press.

Istituto Centrale di Statistice. 1968. *Sommario di statistiche storiche dell'Italia 1861–1965*. Naples: Istituto Poligrafico.

– 1986. *Sommario di statistiche storiche, 1926–1985*. Tivoli: Grafiche Chicca.

Ivekovic, Rada. 1995a. 'Women, Democracy, and Nationalism after 1989: The Yugoslav Case.' *Canadian Woman Studies* 16 (1), 10–13.

– 1995b. 'The New Democracy – With Women or Without Them.' In S. Ramet and Ljubiša S. Adamovich (eds), *Beyond Yugoslavia: Politics, Economics, and Culture in a Shattered Community*. Boulder, CO: Westview Press.

Jackson, Peter, and Jan Penrose (eds). 1993. *Constructions of Race, Place and Nation*. London: UCL Press.

Jallinoja, Riitta. 1989. 'Women between Family and Employment.' In Katja Boh, Maren Bak, Cristine Clason, Maja Pankratova, Jens Qvortrup, Giovanni B. Sgritta, and Kari Waerness (eds), *Changing Patterns of European Family Life: A Comparative Analysis of 14 European Countries*, 95–122. London: Routledge.

Jancar, Barbara Wolfe. 1978. *Women under Communism*. Baltimore: Johns Hopkins University Press.

Jancar-Webster, Barbara. 1990. *Women and Revolution in Yugoslavia, 1941–1945*. Denver, CO: Arden Press.

Janoski, Thomas. 1991. 'Synthetic Strategies in Comparative Sociological Research: Methods and Problems of Internal and External Analysis.' In Charles Ragin (ed.), *Issues and Alternatives in Comparative Social Research*, 59–81. Leiden, The Netherlands: E.J. Brill.

Jelavich, Barbara. 1997. *History of the Balkans*. Vol. 2. Cambridge: Cambridge University Press.

Jelavich, Charles. 1990. *South Slav Nationalism: Textbooks and Yugoslav Union before 1914*. Columbus: Ohio State University Press.

Jetter, Alexis, Annelise Orleck, and Diana Taylor (eds). 1997. *The Politics of Motherhood: Activist Voices from Left to Right*. Hanover, NH: University Press of New England.

Kay, Rebecca. 1997. 'Images of an Ideal Woman: Perceptions of Russian Womanhood through the Media, Education and Women's Own Eyes.' In Mary Buckley (ed.), *Post-Soviet Women: From the Baltic to Central Asia*, 77–98. Cambridge: Cambridge University Press.

Keates, Timothy. 1994. 'Debate over Abortion Law in Italy.' *Lancet* 344 (892), 532.

Kedourie, Elie. 1963/1993. *Nationalism*. 4th ed. Malden, MA: Blackwell.

Kennan, George.1961. *Russia and the West under Lenin and Stalin*. Boston: Little, Brown.

Ketelhut, Barbara. 1995. 'The Family in the German Democratic Republic from a Western Point of View.' In Barbara Lobodzinski (ed.), *Family, Women and Employment in Central-Eastern Europe*, 123–30. Westport, CT: Greenwood Press.

Keylor, William R. 2003. *A World of Nations: The International Order since 1945*. New York: Oxford University Press.

Khrushchev, Nikita. 1956/1957. 'The Stalin Era.' In Hans Kohn. *Basic History of Modern Russia*, 180–4. New York: Van Nostrand Reinhold.

– 1956/1972. 'The Cult of Personality.' In Robert Daniels (ed.), *The Stalin Revolution: Foundations of Soviet Totalitarianism*, 145–56. Lexington, MA: D.C. Heath.

Kirkpatrick, Clifford. 1938. *Nazi Germany: Its Women and Family Life*. Indianapolis: Bobbs-Merrill.

Koblitz, Ann Hibner. 1995. 'Women under *Peristroika* and *Doi Moi*: A Comparison of Marketization in Russian and Vietnam.' In *Canadian Woman Studies* 16 (1), 54–9.

Kochan, Lionel, and John Keep. 1997. *The Making of Modern Russia*. London: Penguin.

Kohn, Hans. 1945. *The Idea of Nationalism*. New York: Macmillan.

– 1957. *Basic History of Modern Russia*. New York: Van Nostrand Reinhold.

– 1962. *The Age of Nationalism*. New York: Harper & Row.

Kolinsky, Eva. 1999. 'Women, Work and Family in the New Länder: Conflicts and Experiences.' In Chris Flockton and Eve Kolinsky (eds), *Recasting East Germany: Social Transformation after the GDR*, 101–25. London: Frank Cass.

Kollontai, Alexandra. 1971. *The Autobiography of a Sexually Emancipated Communist Woman*. New York: Herder and Herder.

Koonz, Claudia. 1977. 'Mothers in the Fatherland: Women in Nazi Germany.' In Renate Bridenthal and Claudia Koonz (eds), *Becoming Visible: Women in European History*, 445–73. Boston: Houghton Mifflin.

– 1981. *Mothers in the Fatherland*. New York: St Martin's Press.

Kotkin, Stephen. 2001. *Armageddon Averted: The Soviet Collapse, 1970–2000*. New York: Oxford University Press.

Kristeva, Julia. 1993. *Nations without Nationalism*. New York: Columbia University Press.

Kupchan, Charles A. (ed.). 1995. *Nationalism and Nationalities in the New Europe*. Ithaca, NY: Cornell University Press.

Laslett, Barbara, and Johanna Brenner. 1989. 'Gender and Social Reproduction: Historical Perspectives.' *Annual Review of Sociology* 15, 381–404.

Langer, William L. 1987. *An Encyclopedia of World History*. London: Harrap/ Galley Press.

Lapidus, Gail.1993. 'From Democratization to Disintegration: The Impact of Perestroika on the National Question.' In Gail Lapidus, Victor Zaslavsky, with Philip Goldman (eds), *From Union to Commonwealth*. 45–70. Cambridge: Cambridge University Press.

Laqueur, Walter (ed.). 1978. *Fascism: A Reader's Guide*. Berkeley: University of California Press.

Lenin, V.I. 1917/1972. 'State and Revolution.' In Carl Cohen (ed.), *Communism, Fascism and Democracy*, 137–64. 2nd ed. New York: Random House.

– 1970. *Lenin on War and Peace*. Peking: Foreign Languages Press.

– 1972. *Opportunism and the Collapse of the Second International*. Moscow: Progress.

– 1977. *Collected Works*. 4th ed. Vols 1–32. Moscow: Progress.

Lenman, Bruce P., and Katherine Boyd (eds). 1994. *Dictionary of World History*. Edinburgh: Chambers.

Levine, Andrew. 1998. 'Just Nationalism.' In J. Couture, K. Nielsen, and M. Seymour (eds), *Rethinking Nationalism*, 345–64. Calgary: University of Calgary Press.

Lewis, Jane (ed.). 1993. *Women and Social Policies in Europe: Work, Family and the State*. Aldershot, UK: Edward Elgar.

Lichtheim, George. 1999. *Europe in the 20th Century*. London: Weidenfeld & Nicolson.

Linz, Juan. 1978. 'Some Notes towards a Comparative Study of Fascism in Sociological Historical Perspective.' In Walter Laqueur (ed.), *Fascism: A Reader's Guide*, 3–121. Berkeley: University of California Press.

Lipset, Seymour. 1959/1983. *Political Man: The Social Bases of Politics*. London: Heinemann.

Lipset, Seymour, and Stein Rokkan. 1967. *Party Systems and Voter Alignments*. New York: Free Press.

Lissyutkina, Larissa. 1993. 'Soviet Women at the Crossroads of Perestroika.' In N. Funk and M. Mueller (eds), *Gender Politics in Post-Communism*, 274–86. New York: Routledge.

Livi-Bacci, Massimo, and David Landes. 2001. 'Too Few Children and Too Much Family.' *Daedalus* 130 (3), 139–55.

Lloyd, Cynthia B., and John A. Ross. 1989. 'Methods for Measuring the Fertility Impact of Family Planning Programs: The Expereince of the Last Decade.' Working Paper No. 7. Population Council, New York.

Luker, Kristin. 1984. *Abortion and the Politics of Motherhood*. Berkeley: University of California Press.

Lund, Caroline. 1970. Introduction. In Leon Trotsky, *Women and the Family*, 7–18. New York: Pathfinder Press.

Macciocchi, Maria Antonietta. 1976. *La Donna 'Nera': 'Consenso' femminile e fascismo*. Milan: Giangiacomo Feltrinelli Editore.

MacKinnon, Catharine. 1993. 'Turning Rape into Pornography: Postmodern Genocide.' *Ms*. 4 (1), 24–30.

MacMillan, Margaret. 2001. *Paris 1919*. New York: Random House.

Makarenko, A.S. 1937/1967. *The Collective Family: A Handbook for Russian Parents*. New York: Doubleday.

Makus, Ingrid. 1996. *Women, Politics and Reproduction: The Liberal Legacy*. Toronto: University of Toronto Press.

Malysheva, Marina. 1995. 'Gender Identity in Russia: A Comparison of Post–World War II and Post-Communist Experiences.' *Canadian Woman Studies* 16 (1), 22–7.

Mamonova, Tatyana. 1989. *Russian Women's Studies: Essays on Sexism in Soviet Culture*. Oxford: Pergamon Press.

– (ed.). 1984. *Women and Russia: Feminist Writings from the Soviet Union*. Boston: Beacon Press.

Mann, Michael. 1992. 'The Emergence of Modern European Nationalism.' In John Hall and I.C. Jarvie (eds), *Transition to Modernity*, 137–66. Cambridge: Cambridge University Press.

Mantovani, Susanna. 2001. 'Infant-Toddler Centres in Italy Today: Tradition and Innovation.' In Lella Gandini and Carolyn Pope Edwards (eds), *Bambini: The Italian Approach to Infant/Toddler Care*, 23–37. New York: Teachers College Press.

Markowitz, Fran. 1995. 'Striving for Femininity: (Post) Soviet Un-Feminism.' *Canadian Woman Studies* 16 (1), 38–42.

Marsh, Rosalind. 1996. Introduction. 'Women's Studies and Women's Issues in Russia, Ukraine and the Post-Soviet States.' In Rosalind Marsh (ed.), *Women in Russia and Ukraine*, 1–28. Cambridge: Cambridge University Press.

– 1998. 'Women in Contemporary Russia and the Former Soviet Union.' In Rick Wilford and Robert L. Miller (eds), *Women, Ethnicity and Nationalism*, 87–119. London: Routledge.

Martinelli, Alberto, Antonio M. Chiesi, and Sonia Stefanizzi. 1999. *Recent Social Trends in Italy, 1960–1995*. Montreal: McGill-Queen's University Press.

Martinez, Andrea. 1995. 'International Symposium: Women and the Media – Access to Expression and Decision-Making.' UNESCO. Toronto, 28 February–3 March.

Marx, Karl, 1848/1933. 'Manifesto of the Communist Party.' In V. Adoratsky (ed.), *Karl Marx: Selected Works*. Volume 1, 189–241. New York: International.

Marx, Karl, and F. Engels. 1844/1974. *Karl Marx and F. Engels: Collected Works*. Vol. 3. *Economic and Philosophical Manuscripts of 1844 – Third Manuscript*. New York: International.

McDaniel, Susan. 2002. 'Women's Changing Relations to the State and Citizenship: Caring and Intergenerational Relations in Globalizing Western Democracies.' *Canadian Review of Sociology and Anthropology* 39 (2), 125–50.

McKinsey, Kitty. 1992. 'Croatia Seeks Ways to Boost Birthrate,' *Montreal Gazette*, 22 June, B1.

– 1993. 'The Bestiality of War.' *Calgary Herald*, 24 January, B3.

McLaren, Angus. 1990. *Our Own Master Race: Eugenics in Canada, 1885–1945*. Toronto, McClelland & Stewart.

McNeill, William. 1985. *Polyethnicity and National Unity in World History*. Toronto: University of Toronto Press.

McRoberts, Kenneth. 1989. *Quebec: Social Change and Political Protest*, 3rd ed. Toronto: McClelland & Stewart.

Meldini, Piero. 1975. *Sposa e madre esemplare*. Florence: Guaraldi Editore.

Merkl, Peter. 1975. *Political Violence under the Swastika: 581 Early Nazis*. Princeton, NJ: Princeton University Press.

Meshcherkina, Elena. 2000. 'New Russian Men: Masculinity Regained?' In Sarah Ashwin (ed.), *Gender, State and Society in Soviet and Post-Soviet Russia*. London: Routledge, 105–17.

Michaels, Paula. 2001. 'Motherhood, Patriotism and Ethnicity: Soviet Kazakhastan and the 1936 Abortion Ban.' *Feminist Studies* 27 (2), 307–33.

Milič, Andjelka. 1993. 'Women and Nationalism in Former Yugoslavia.' In Nanette Funk and Magda Mueller (eds), *Gender Politics and Post-Communism*, 109–22. New York: Routledge.

– 1995. 'Women and Work in Former Yugoslavia and Their Present Situation.' In Barbara Łobodzi ska (ed.), *Family, Women, and Employment in Central-Eastern Europe*, 237–44. Westport, CT: Greenwood Press.

Mill, John Stuart. 1910/1991. *Utilitarianism: On Liberty, Considerations on Representative Government*. Rutland, VT: Everyman's Library.

Mishra, Ramesh. 1989. 'The Academic Tradition in Social Policy: The Titmuss Years.' In Martin Bulmer, Jane Lewis, and David Piachaud (eds), *The Goals of Social Policy*, 64–83. London: Unwin Hyman.

– 1998. 'Beyond the Nation State: Social Policy in an Age of Globalization.' *Social Policy and Administration* 32 (5), 481–500.

Mitchell, B.R. 1975. *European Historical Statistics, 1750–1970*. London: Macmillan.

– 1992. *International Historical Statistics: Europe, 1750–1988*. 3rd ed. New York: Stockton Press.

– 1998. *International Historical Statistics: Europe, 1750–1993*. 4th ed. London: Macmillan Reference.

– 2003. *International Historical Statistics: Europe, 1750–2000*. 5th ed. London: Palgrave Macmillan.

Mitterauer, Michael. 1996. 'Family Contexts: The Balkans in European Comparison.' *History of the Family* 1 (4), 387–407.

Mladenovič, Marko. 1974. *Razvod braka i uzroci za ragvod braka*. Belgrade: Izdavačko Preduzeće 'Rad.'

Mladjenovic, Lepa. 1993. 'Serbian Women Unite against the War.' *Madre* (Summer), 6–7.

Moore, Barrington. 1954. *Terror and Progress: USSR*. Cambridge: Harvard University Press.

– 1966. *Social Origins of Dictatorship and Democracy*. Boston: Beacon Press.

Moorehead, Alan. 1958. *The Russian Revolution*. London: Readers Union.

Morokvašić, Miriana. 1998. 'Natonalism, Sexism and Yugoslav War.' In N. Charles and Helen Hintjens (eds), *Gender, Ethnicity and Political Ideologies*, 65–90. London: Routledge.

Morvant, Penny. 1995. 'Bearing the "Double Burden" in Russia.' *Transition* 1 (6), 4–10.

Mosse, George L., Rondo E. Cameron, Henry Bertram Hill, and Micheal B. Petrovich (eds), 1957. *Europe in Review*. Chicago: Rand McNally.

Mussolini, Benito. 1928/1998. *My Rise and Fall*. New York: Da Capo Press.

– 1933. *The Political and Social Doctrine of Fascism*. Authorized trans. Jane Soames. London: Hogarth Press.

– 1964a. 'Discorso dell'Ascensione.' In *Opera omnia di Benito Mussolini*. Vol. 22, 360–90. Florence: La Fenice.

– 1964b. 'Il numero come forza.' In *Opera omnia di Benito Mussolini*. Vol. 23, 209–17. Florence: La Fenice.

– 1964c. 'Macchina e Donna.' In *Opera omnia di Benito Mussolini*. Vol. 26, 310–11. Florence: La Fenice.

– 1964d. 'La Razza Bianca Muore.' In *Opera omnia di Benito Mussolini*. Vol. 26, 312–15. Florence: La Fenice.

– 1964e. 'Matrimoni Giovani.' In *Opera omnia di Benito Mussolini*. Vol. 26, 332. Florence: La Fenice.

Narodne Novine-Sluzbeni List Republike Hrvatske (official newspaper of the Republic of Croatia). 1995. [*Year*] 157 (38), *Godiste*, 8 June, 1185.

Ng, Roxana. 1991. 'Sexism, Racism and Canadian Nationalism.' In Jesse Vorst et al. (eds). *Race, Class, Gender: Bonds and Barriers*. 2nd ed. Toronto: Garamond Press.

Nickel, Hildegard Maria. 1993. 'Women in the German Democratic Republic and the New Federal States: Looking Backward and Forward (Five Theses).' In Nanette Funk and Magda Mueller (eds), *Gender Politics and Post-Communism*, 138–50. New York: Routledge.

– 1995. 'The Dual Transformation in Germany and Its Ambivalent Consequences.' *Canadian Woman Studies* 16 (1), 64–9.

– 1998. 'With a Head Start on Equality from the GDR into the Trap of Modernization in the Federal Republic: German Women after the "*Wende*."' In Aysan Sever (ed.), *Frontiers in Women's Studies: Canadian and German Perspectives*, 25–56. Toronto: Canadian Scholars Press.

Niero, Mauro. 1996. 'Italy: Right Turn for the Welfare State.' In Vic George and Peter Taylor-Gooby (eds), *European of Welfare Policy*, 117–35. Basingstoke, UK: Macmillan.

Noether, Emiliana. 1982. 'Italian Women and Fascism: A Reevaluation.' *Italian Quarterly* 23 (90), 69–80.

Nolte, Ernst. 1969. *Three Faces of Fascism*. New York.

Nootens, Genevieve. 1998. 'Liberal Restrictions on Public Arguements.' In J. Couture, K. Nielsen, and M. Seymour (eds), *Rethinking Nationalism*, 237–60. Calgary: University of Calgary Press.

Northrop, Douglas. 2001. 'Nationalizing Backwardness: Gender, Empire and Uzbek Identity.' In Ronald Grigor Suny and Terry Martin (eds), *A State of Nations: Empire and Nation-building in the Age of Lenin and Stalin*, 191–220. Oxford: Oxford University Press.

Novelli, Cecilia Dau. 1994. *Famiglia e modernizzazione tra le due guerre*. Rome: Edizioni Studium.

O'Connor, Julia S., Ann Shola Orloff, and Sheila Shaver. 1999. *States, Markets, Families: Gender, Liberalism and Social Policy in Australia, Canada, Great Britain and the United States*. Cambridge: Cambridge University Press.

Olsen, Gregg M. 1998. 'Locating the Canadian Welfare State: Family Policy and Health Care in Canada, Sweden and the United States.' In Julia S. O'Connor and Gregg M. Olsen (eds), *Power Resources Theory and the Welfare State: A Critical Approach*, 183–206. Toronto: University of Toronto Press.

O'Rourke, Shane. 1996. 'Women in a Warrior Society: Don Cossack Women, 1860–1914.' In Rosalind Marsh (ed.), *Women in Russia and Ukraine*, 45–54. Cambridge: Cambridge University Press.

Overy, R.J. 1994. *The Inter-War Crisis, 1919–1939*. London: Longman.

Owen, Robert. 1837/1972. 'An Address from the Association of All Classes of All Nations to the Government and People of All Nations.' In Carl Cohen (ed.), *Communism, Fascism and Democracy*, 22–32. 2nd ed. New York: Random House.

Pain, Emil. 2000. 'The Russian Question: From Internationalism to Nomenklatura Nationalism?' *Russian Social Science Review* 41(6), 48–56.

Palmer, Alan. 1992. *Dictionary of Twentieth Century History, 1900–1991*. London: Penguin.

Parfitt, Tom. 2003. 'Russia Moves to Curb Abortion Rates.' *Lancet* 362 (9388), 968.

Parkin, Frank. 1982. *Max Weber*. London: Routledge.

Parsons, Talcott. 1975. 'Some Theoretical Considerations on the Nature and Trends of Change of Ethnicity.' In Nathan Glazer and Daniel Moynihan (eds), *Ethnicity: Theory and Experience*, 56–71. Cambridge: Harvard University Press.

Patton, Carl V., and David S. Sawicki. 1993. *Basic Methods of Policy Analysis and Planning*. 2nd ed. Englewood Cliffs, NJ: Prentice Hall.

Pavlovi , Tatjana. 1999. 'Women in Croatia: Feminists, Nationalists, and Homosexuals.' In S. Ramet (ed.), *Gender Politics in the Western Balkans: Women and Society in Yugoslavia and the Yugoslav Successor States*, 131–52. University Park: Pennsylvania State University Press.

Petrovic, Ruzica. 1996. 'Family Research and Theory in Yugoslavia.' *Marriage and Family Review* 22 (3–4), 259–87.

Pickering-Lazzi, Robin (ed.). 1995. *Mothers of Invention: Women, Italian Fascism and Culture*. Minneapolis: University of Minnesota Press.

Powell, Carla. 1999. 'Brits Should Be More Like Italians.' *New Statesman* 128 (4439), 14.

Pugh, Martin. 1997. 'The Rise of European Feminism.' In Martin Pugh (ed.), *A Companion to Modern European History, 1871–1945*, 155–73. Oxford: Blackwell.

Quataert, Jean H. 1979. *Reluctant Feminists in German Social Democracy, 1885–1917*. Princeton, NJ: Princeton University Press.

Quine, Maria Sophia. 1996. *Population Politics in Twentieth Century Europe*. London: Routledge.

Ragin, Charles. 1987. *The Comparative Method: Moving Beyond Qualitative and Quantitative Strategies*. Berkeley: University of California Press.

Ramet, Sabrina. 1999a. *Balkan Babel: The Disintegration of Yugoslavia from the Death of Tito to the War for Kosovo*. 3rd ed. Boulder, CO: Westview Press.

– (ed.). 1999b. *Gender Politics in the Western Balkans: Women and Society in Yugoslavia and the Yugoslav Successor States*. University Park: Pennsylvania State University Press.

Ramet, Sabrina, and Ljubiša S. Adamovich (eds). (1995). *Beyond Yugoslavia: Politics, Economics, and Culture in a Shattered Community*. Boulder, CO: Westview Press.

Rankin-Williams, Amy. 2001. 'Post-Soviet Contraceptive Practices and Abortion Rates in St. Petersburg, Russia.' *Health Care for Women International* 22, 699–710.

Re, Lucia. 1995. 'Fascist Theories of Women.' In Robin Pickering-Lazzi (ed.), *Mothers of Invention: Women, Italian Fascism and Culture*, 76–99. Minneapolis: University of Minnesota Press.

Reeves, Joy B. 1995. 'Women, Work and Family in Former Yugoslavia.' In Barbara obodzi ska (ed.), *Family, Women, and Employemnt in Central-Eastern Europe*, 245–58. Westport, CT: Greenwood Press.

Reisman, David. 2004. 'Richard Titmuss: Welfare as Good Conduct.' *European Journal of Political Economy* 20, 771–94.

Rener, Tanja, and Mirjana Ule. 1998. 'Back to the Future: Nationalism and Gender in Post-Socialist Societies.' In R. Wilford and Robert L. Miller (eds), *Women, Ethnicity and Nationalism: The Politics of Transition*, 120–32. London: Routledge.

Reynolds, David. 2000. *One World Divisible: A Global History since 1945*. New York: W.W. Norton.

Riasanovsky, Nicholas V. 1984. *The History of Russia*. 4th ed. New York: Oxford University Press.

Richardson, Beth. 1995. 'Women in Russia: The More Things Change the More Things Stay the Same.' *Canadian Woman Studies* 16 (1), 48–53.

Rimlinger, G.V. 1987. 'Social Policy under German Fascism.' In Martin Rein, Gøsta Esping-Andersen, and Lee Rainwater (eds), *Stagnation and Renewal in Social Policy: The Rise and Fall of Policy Regimes*, 59–77. London: M.E. Sharpe.

Riordan, James. 1996. 'Sexual Minorities: The Status of Gays and Lesbians in Russian–Soviet-Russian Society.' In Rosalind Marsh (ed.), *Women in Russia and Ukraine*, 156–72. Cambridge: Cambridge University Press.

Roksandic, Drago. 1992. 'The Unbearable Weight of Croatia's Being.' *East European Reporter* 5 (3), 50.

Rose, Ramona. 1973. *Position and Treatment of Women in Nazi Germany: As Viewed from English Language Press, 1933–1945*. Vancouver: Tantalus Research.

Rosenberg, Dorothy J. 1996. 'A Land of Brothers United? Xenophobia and the Reassertion of Patriarchy in the New Germany.' In Barbara Wejnert and Metta Spencer with Slobodan Drakulic (eds), *Women in Post-Communism*, 35–62. Greenwich, CT: JAI Press.

Rosenthal, Bernice Glatzer. 1977. 'Love on the Tractor: Women in the Russian Revolution and After.' In Renate Bridenthal and Claudia Koonz (eds), *Becoming Visible: Women in European History*, 370–99. Boston: Houghton Mifflin.

Sachße, Christoph. 1993. 'Social Mothers: The Bourgeois Women's Movement and German Welfare-State Formation, 1890–1929.' In Seth Koven and Sonya Michel (eds), *Mothers of the New World: Maternalist Politics and the Origins of Welfare States*, 136–58. New York: Routledge.

Sainsbury, Diane. 1996. *Gender Equality and Welfare States.* Cambridge: Cambridge University Press.

– 1999a. 'Gender and Social-Democratic Welfare States.' In Diane Sainsbury (ed.), *Gender and Welfare State Regimes*, 75–114. Oxford: Oxford University Press.

– 1999b. 'Gender, Policy Regimes and Politics.' In Diane Sainsbury (ed.), *Gender and Welfare State Regimes*, 245–73. Oxford: Oxford University Press.

Sanborn, Joshua. 2001. 'Family, Fraternity and Nation-building in Russia.' In Ronald Grigor Suny and Terry Martin (eds), *A State of Nations: Empire and Nation-building in the Age of Lenin and Stalin*, 93–110. Oxford: Oxford University Press.

Saporiti, Angelo. 1989. 'Historical Changes in Family Reproduction.' In Katja Boh, Maren Bak, Cristine Clason, Maja Pankratova, Jens Qvortrup, Giovanni B. Sgritta, and Kari Waerness (eds), *Changing Patterns of European Family Life: A Comparative Analysis of 14 European Countries*, 191–216. London: Routledge.

Saraceno, Chiara. 1991. 'Redefining Maternity and Paternity: Gender, Pronatalism and Social Policies in Fascist Italy.' In Gisela Bock and Pat Thane (eds), *Maternity and Gender Policies*, 196–212. London: Routledge.

Sargeant, Elena. 1996. 'The "Women Question" and Problems of Maternity.' In Rosalind Marsh (ed.), *Women in Russia and Ukraine*, 269–85. Cambridge: Cambridge University Press.

Scabini, Eugenia, and Vittorio Cigoli. 1997. 'Young Adult Families: An Evolutionary Slowdown or a Breakdown in the Generation Transition.' *Journal of Family Issues* 18 (6), 608–26.

Schaeffer, Robert. 1990. *Warpaths: The Politics of Partition.* New York: Hill and Wang.

Schenk, Christina. 1993. 'Lesbians and Their Emancipation in the Former German Democratic Republic: Past and Future.' In Nanette Funk and Magda Mueller (eds), *Gender Politics and Post-Communism*, 160–8. New York: Routledge.

Scott, Joan W., Cora Kaplan, and Debra Keates. 1997. *Transitions, Environments, Translations: Feminisms in International Politics.* New York: Routledge.

Seager, Joni. 1997. *The State of Women in the World.* London: Penguin.

Seton-Watson, Hugh. 1965. *From Lenin to Khrushchev: The History of World Communism.* New York: Frederick A. Praeger.

Shirer, William L. 1960. *The Rise and Fall of the Third Reich.* New York: Simon and Schuster.

Shoup, Paul. 1968. *Communism and the Yugoslav National Question.* New York: Columbia University Press.

Signorini, Luigi Federico. 2001. 'Italy's Economy: An Introduction.' *Daedalus* 130 (2), 67–92.

Simić, Andrei. 1999. 'Machismo and Cryptomatriarchy: The Traditonal Yugoslav Family.' In Sabrina P. Ramet (ed.), *Gender Politics in the Western Balkans*, 11–29. University Park: Pennsyvania State University Press.

Singleton, Fred. 1994. *A History of the Yugoslav Peoples*. Cambridge: Cambridge University Press.

Skocpol, Theda. 1979/1995. *State and Social Revolution*. Cambridge: Cambridge University Press.

Smith, Anthony. 1991. *National Identity*. London: Penguin.

– 1994. 'The Problem of National Identity: Ancient, Medieval and Modern.' *Ethnic and Racial Studies* 17 (3), 375–99.

Social Security Administration. 2002a. *Social Security Programs throughout the World, 1999: Croatia*. <www.ssa.gov/statistics/ssptw/1999/English/croatia.htm>.

– 2002b. *Social Security Programs throughout the World, 1999: Germany*. <www.ssa.gov/statistics/ssptw/1999/English/germany.htm>.

– 2002c. *Social Security Programs throughout the World, 1999: Italy*. <www.ssa.gov/statistics/ssptw/1999/English/italy.htm>.

– 2002d. *Social Security Programs throughout the World, 1999: Russia*. <www.ssa.gov/statistics/ssptw/1999/English/russiafed>.

Solzhenitsyn, Aleksandr. 1991. *Rebuilding Russia: Reflections and Tentative Proposals*. New York: Farrar, Straus and Giroux.

Spencer, Metta. 1996. 'Post-Social Patriarchy.' In Barbara Wejnert and Metta Spencer, with Slobodan Drakulic (eds), *Women in Post-Communism*, 267–86. Greenwich, CT: JAI Press.

Statistischen Zentralkommission. 1920. *Statistisches Handbuch für die Republik Österreich*. Vienna: Österreichisches Staatsdruckerei.

Steinberger, Helmut. 1992. 'Germany Reunified: International and Constitutional Problems.' *Brigham Young University Law Review* 1992 (1), 23–40.

Stevens, Jacqueline. 1999. *Reproducing The State*. Princeton, NJ: Princeton University Press.

Stoehr, Irene. 1991. 'Housework and Motherhood: Debates and Policies in the Women's Movement in Imperial Germany and the Weimar Republic.' In Gisela Bock and Pat Thane (eds), *Maternity and Gender Policies: Women and the Rise of the European Welfare States, 1880s–1950s*, 213–32. London: Routledge.

Suny, Ronald. 1993. 'State, Civil Society, and Ethnic Cultural Consolidation in the USSR: Roots of the National Question.' In Gail Lapidus, Victor

Zaslavsky, with Philip Goldman (eds), *From Union to Commonwealth*, 22–44. Cambridge: Cambridge University Press.

Tannenbaum, Edward R. 1972. *The Fascist Experience: Italian Society and Culture, 1922–1945*. New York: Basic Books.

Tanner, Marcus. 1997. *Croatia: A Nation Forged in War*. New Haven, CT: Yale University Press.

Tartakovskaya, Irina. 2000. 'The Press and Representation of Gender Roles.' In Sarah Ashwin (ed.), *Gender, State and Society in Soviet and Post-Soviet Russia*, 118–36. London: Routledge.

Tax, Meredith. 1993. 'The Five Croatian "Witches": A Casebook on "Trial by Public Opinion" as a Form of Censorship and Intimidation.' Paper prepared for the International PEN Women Writers' Committee.

Thomas, Katherine. 1943. *Women in Nazi Germany*. London: Victor Gollancz.

Thönnessen, Werner. 1976. *The Emancipation of Women: The Rise and Decline of the Women's Movement in German Social Democracy, 1863–1933*. Glasgow: Pluto Press.

Thurer, Shari L. 1994. *The Myths of Motherhood: How Culture Reinvents the Good Mother*. Boston: Houghton Mifflin.

Thurlow, Richard. 1997. 'European Fascism.' In Martin Pugh (ed.), *A Companion to Modern European History, 1871–1945*, 194–210. Oxford: Blackwell.

Tidl, Georg. 1984. *Die Frau im National-Sozialismus*. Vienna: Europaverlag.

Tillich, Paul. 1957. *Dynamics of Faith*. New York: Harper Torchbooks.

Tilly, Charles. 1978. *From Mobilization to Revolution*. Reading, MA: Addison-Wesley.

– 1993. *European Revolutions, 1492–1992*. Oxford: Blackwell.

Tilly, Charles, Louise Tilly, and Richard Tilly. 1975. *The Rebellious Century, 1830–1930*. Cambridge: Harvard University Press.

Tillyard, Stella. 2000. 'Italy's Shrinking Families.' *Wilson Quarterly* 24 (4), 120.

Tindemans, Leo (chairman). 1996. *Unfinished Peace: Report of the International Commission on the Balkans*. Washington, DC: Carnegie Endowment for International Peace.

Titkow, Anna. 1993. 'Political Change in Poland: Cause, Modifier, or Barrier to Gender Equality?' In Nanette Funk and Magda Mueller, *Gender Politics and Post-Communism*, 253–6. New York: Routledge.

Titmuss, Richard M. 1950. *Problems of Social Policy*. London: H.M. Stationery Office.

– 1974. *Social Policy*. London: George Allen and Unwin.

Tolz, Vera. 1998. 'Forging the Nation: National Identity and Nation Building in Post-Communist Russia.' *Europe-Asia Studies* 50 (6), 993–1022.

Tomanovic, Smiljka. 1994. 'Socialization of the Child under Conditions of a Changed Everyday Life of the Family.' *Sociologija* 36 (4) 483–93.

Tönnies, Ferdinand. 1940. *Fundamental Concepts of Sociology (Gemeinschaft und Gesellschaft)*. Trans. Charles P. Loomis. New York: American Book.

Townson, Duncan. 1995. *Dictionary of Modern History, 1789–1945*. London: Penguin.

Trappe, Heike, and Rachel A. Rosenfeld. 2000. 'How Do Children Matter? A Comparison of Gender Earnings Inequality for Young Adults in the Former East Germany and Former West Germany.' *Journal of Marriage and Family* 62 (2), 489–508.

Treaty of Versailles. 1919. 'Part viii: Reparations.' <http://www.yale.edu/lawweb/avalon/imt/part viii.htm>

Trifunovska, Snezana, ed. 1994. *Yugoslavia through Documents, from Its Creation to Its Dissolution*. Dodrecht: Martinus Hijhoff.

Tröger, Annemarie. 1984. 'The Creation of a Female Assembly-Line Proletariat.' In Renate Bridenthal, Atina Grossman, and Marion Kaplan (eds), *When Biology Became Destiny*, 237–70. New York: Monthly Review Press.

Trotsky, Leon. 1970. *Women and the Family*. New York: Pathfinder Press.

Trzcinski, Eileen. 1998. 'Gender and German Unification.' *Affilia* 13 (1), 69–102.

Tudjman, Franjo. 1981. *Nationalism in Contemporary Europe*. New York: Columbia University Press.

Turchi, Boone A. 1975. *The Demand for Children: The Economics of Fertility in the United States*. Cambridge: Ballinger.

Ugrešić, Dubravka. 1998. *The Culture of Lies*. London: Phoenix House.

Ungerson, Clare. 2003. 'Commodified Care Work in European Labour Markets.' *European Studies* 5(4), 377–96.

Unicef. 2002. 'The Progess of Nations: Statistical Tables.' http://www.unicef.org/pon00/statistics.htm.

United Nations. 1949a. *Population Census Methods*. New York: United Nations.

– 1949b. *Fertility Data in Population Censuses*. New York: United Nations.

– 1949c. *Demographic Yearbook, 1948*. New York: United Nations.

– 1979. 'Convention on the Elimination of all Forms of Discrimination Against Women.' United Nations Division for the Advancement of Women, Department of Economic and Social Affairs, New York.

– 1989a. *Compendium of Statistics and Indicators on the Situation of Women*. New York: United Nations.

– 1989b. *Trends in Population Policy*. New York: United Nations.

– 1991a. *The World's Women, 1970–1990: Trends and Statistics*. New York: United Nations.

– 1991b. *Compendium of Social Statistics and Indicators, 1988*. New York: United Nations.

- 1995. *The World's Women, 1995: Trends and Statistics*. New York: United Nations.
- 1997. *1995 Demographic Yearbook*. Forty-Seventh Issue. New York: United Nations.
- 1999. *1999 Demographic Yearbook: Natality Statistics*. New York: United Nations.
- 2000a. *Fertility and Family Surveys in Countries of the ECE Region: Standard Country Report: Italy*. By Paolo De Sandre, Fausta Ongaro, Rosella Rettaroli, and Silvana Salvini. New York: United Nations.
- 2000b. *The World's Women, 2000: Trends and Statistics*. New York: United Nations.
- 2002. 'Maternity Leave Benefits, as of 1998.' <http://www.un.ord/depts/unsd/ww2000/table5c.htm>.
United Nations Economic and Social Council (Economic Commission for Europe). 1994. 'Regional Platform for Action: Women in a Changing World. Call for Action: An ECE Perspective. Preambular Declaration.' Vienna, 17–21 October.
Upshall, Michael (ed.). 1994. *The Hutchinson Guide to the World*. 2nd ed. Oxford: Helicon.
Van Benthem van den Bergh, Godfred. 1993. 'Myth and Process: Two Meanings of the Concept of Nation.' Working Paper Series No. 145. Institute of Social Studies. The Hague.
Vanden Heuvel, Katerina. 1993. 'Right-to-Lifers Hit Russia.' *Nation* 257 (14), 489–92.
Verdery, Katherine. 1993. 'Whither "Nation" and "Nationalism?"' *Daedalus* 122 (3), 37–46.
- 1994. 'From Parent-State to Family Patriarchs: Gender and Nation in Contemporary Eastern Europe.' *East European Politics and Society* 8 (2) 225–55.
Violante, Luciano, and Henri Peyre. 2001. 'Italian Parliamentary Institutions: An Evolutionary Overview.' *Daedalus* 130 (3), 47–71.
Völgyes, Iván. 1989. *Politics in Eastern Europe*. Pacific Grove, CA: Brooks/Cole.
Vucinich, Wayne S. 1969. *Contemporary Yugoslavia: Twenty Years of Socialist Experiment*. Berkeley: University of California Press.
Walby, Sylvia. 1996. 'Woman and Nation.' In Gopal Balakrishnan (ed.), *Mapping the Nation*. London: Verso.
Walker, Ruth. 1996. 'Bavarian Abortion Law Tears as Fragile Consensus.' *Christian Science Monitor* 88 (175), 76.
Waters, Elizabeth. 1993. 'Finding a Voice: The Emergence of a Women's Movement.' In N. Funk and M. Mueller (eds), *Gender Politics in Post-Communism*. New York: Routledge.

Weber, Max. 1946. 'Science as a Vocation.' In H.H. Gerth and C. Wright Mills (eds), *From Max Weber: Essays in Sociology*, 129–56. New York: Oxford University Press.

– 1978. *Economy and Society.* Ed. Guenther Roth and Claus Wittich. Berkeley: University of California Press.

Weedon, Chris. 1995. 'Women in East Germany' *Canadian Dimensions* 29 (2), 47–50.

Weiner, Myron (ed.). 1966. *Modernization: The Dynamics of Growth*. New York: Basic Books.

West, Lois A. (ed). 1997. *Feminist Nationalism*. New York: Routledge.

West, Rebecca. 1941. *Black Lamb and Grey Falcon: A Journey through Yugoslavia*. New York: Viking Press.

Wilford, Rick, and Robert L. Miller (eds). 1998. *Women, Ethnicity and Nationalism: The Politics of Transition*. London: Routledge.

Williams, Christopher. 1996. 'Abortion and Women's Health in Russia and the Soviet Successor States.' In Rosalind Marsh (ed.), *Women in Russia and Ukraine*, 131–55. Cambridge: Cambridge University Press.

Williams, Fiona. 1989. *Social Policy: A Critical Introduction.* Cambridge: Polity Press.

Williams, Fiona, Jennie Popay, and Ann Oakley (eds). 1999. *Welfare Research: A Critical Review*. London: UCL Press.

Wilson, Fiona, and Bodil Folke Frederiksen (eds). 1995. *Ethnicity, Gender, and Subversion of Nationalism*. London: Frank Cass

Wolchik, Sharon and Alfred Meyer (eds.). 1985. *Women, State and Party in Eastern Europe*. Durham, NC: Duke University Press.

Wollstonecraft, Mary. 1792/1988. *A Vindication of the Rights of Woman*. New York: Norton.

Women's International Network News. 1995a. 'Country Reports on Human Rights Practices for 1994: Germany.' *Women's International Network News* 21 (2), 25.

– 1995b. 'Germany: Poverty Has a Female Face: From Official Discussion in German Government.' *Women's International Network News* 21 (1), 65.

– 1996. 'Italy Has the Most Extensive Provisions.' *Women's International Network News* 22 (3), 78.

Yeltsin, Boris. 1989. *Against the Grain*. London: Jonathan Cape.

Yetman, Norman R. (ed.). 1991. *Majority and Minority: The Dynamics of Race and Ethnicity in America*. 5th ed. Wellesley, MA: Allyn and Bacon.

Yovanovitch, Dragolioub. 1929/1990. 'From the Economic and Social Effects of the War in Serbia.' In Arthur Marwick and Wendy Simpson (eds), *Documents 1: 1900–1929*, 86–7. Buckingham, UK: Open University Press.

Yuval-Davis, Nira. 1997. *Gender and Nation.* London: Sage.

Yuval-Davis, Nira, and Floya Anthias (eds). 1989. *Woman-Nation-State.* New York: St Martin's Press.

'Zaginflatch: Foglio Di Informazione Di Zagabria – Aborto.' 1995. *Germinal.* September-December. Trieste. 6.

Zajovic, Stasa. 1995. 'Abuse of Women on a Nationalist and Militarist Basis.' In Laurence Hovde et al. (trans.), *Women for Peace*, 176–80. Belgrade: Women in Black.

Zametica, John. 1992. *The Yugoslav Conflict.* London: Brassey's.

Zaslavsky, Victor. 1993. 'The Evolution of Separatism in Soviet Society under Gorbachev.' In Gail W. Lapidus et al. (eds). *From Union to Commonwealth*, 71–97. Cambridge: Cambridge University Press.

Zetkin, Clara. 1984. *Clara Zetkin: Selected Writings.* New York: International.

Zimmerman, Shirley, Anatolyi I. Antonov, Marlene Johnson, and Vladimir A. Borisov. 1994. 'Social Policy and Families.' In James W. Moaddock, M. Janice Hogan, A.I. Antonov, and M.S. Matskovsky (eds). *Families before and after Perestroika: Russian and U.S. Perspectives*, 186–234. New York: Guilford Press.

Index

Studies in Comparative Political Economy and Public Policy